AMERICAN ETHNIC
AND CULTURAL STUDIES

John C. Walter and Johnnella E. Butler

Series Editors

AMERICAN ETHNIC AND CULTURAL STUDIES

The American Ethnic and Cultural Studies series presents critical interdisciplinary, cross-disciplinary, and comparative studies of cultural formations and expressions of racialized peoples of North America. Focusing on African Americans, American Indians, Asian Americans, Chicanos/as, and Latinos/as, and on comparative works among these groups and racialized Euro-Americans, the series also explores new and changing configurations of race and ethnicity as shaped by gender, class, and religion in global and domestic contexts. Informed by research in the humanities, arts, and social sciences; transnational and diasporic studies; film studies; legal studies; public policy, environmental, urban, and rural studies, books in the series will aim to stimulate innovative approaches in scholarship and pedagogy.

Color-line to Borderlands:
The Matrix of American Ethnic Studies
Edited by Johnnella E. Butler

Being Buddhist in a Christian World:
Gender and Community in a Korean American Temple
Sharon A. Suh

Being Buddhist in a Christian World

GENDER AND COMMUNITY
IN A KOREAN AMERICAN TEMPLE

Sharon A. Suh

UNIVERSITY OF WASHINGTON PRESS
Seattle and London

Copyright © 2004 by the University of Washington Press
Designed by Pamela Canell
Printed in the United States of America
13 12 11 10 09 08 07 06 05 04   5 4 3 2 1

All rights reserved. No part of this publication may be reproduced or transmitted in any form or by any means, electronic or mechanical, including photocopy, recording, or any information storage or retrieval system, without permission in writing from the publisher.

University of Washington Press
PO Box 50096, Seattle, WA 98145
www.washington.edu/uwpress

Library of Congress Cataloging-in-Publication Data
Suh, Sharon A.
   Being Buddhist in a Christian world : gender and community in a Korean American temple / Sharon A. Suh.
       p. cm.
   Includes bibliographical references (p.) and index.
   ISBN 0-295-98378-7 (cloth : alk. paper)—ISBN 0-295-98379-5 (pbk. : alk. paper)
   1. Sa Chal (Temple : Koreatown, Los Angeles, Calif.)   2. Buddhism—California—Los Angeles.   3. Korean Americans—United States—Religious life.   4. Buddhism—Social aspects—California—Los Angeles.
   5. Buddhism—Korea.   6. Christianity and other religions—Buddhism.
   I. Title.
BQ6377.L672S84   2004   294.3'089'95709494—DC22   2003065751

The paper used in this publication is acid-free and recycled from 10 percent post-consumer and at least 50 percent pre-consumer waste. It meets the minimum requirements of American National Standard for Information Sciences—Permanence of Paper for Printed Library Materials, ANSI Z39.48-1984.♾

A portion of chapter 6 appears in *Revealing the Sacred in Asian and Pacific America*, ed. Jane Iwamura and Paul Spickard (Routledge, 2003), under the title "To Be Buddhist Is to Be Korean."

CONTENTS

Acknowledgments   vii

1 / Introduction   3

2 / Finding and Knowing One's Mind   16

3 / Sa Chal Context, Programs, and Demographics   33

4 / Buddhist Practice and Self-Transformation   57

5 / Buddhism—An Anchor in an Uncertain World and a Source of Independence   96

6 / Finding Male Selves: Men's Religious Practices   133

7 / Being Buddhist in a Christian World   165

8 / Epilogue   204

Notes   211

Bibliography   225

Index   237

ACKNOWLEDGMENTS

Since I have always thought of this book as a collaborative effort, there are many people to thank for its creation and completion. First and foremost, I would like to express my gratitude to the members of Sa Chal temple who welcomed me to their place of worship and shared their life stories with me. Without their kindness and openness, this book would not exist. It was through my relationships with the men and women of Sa Chal that I began to look at the study of religion in a new way. Rather than focusing on translations of centuries old texts to understand the Buddhist tradition, through my visits to Sa Chal and conversations with temple members I learned what Buddhism means to people in their own terms. In other words, I began to attend to questions of faith and, in so doing, learned how lay Buddhists seek and find orientation in their lives, especially during difficult times.

Three particular individuals have made this study of everyday Buddhism possible—Do Ahn Kim, Don Shin, and Jennifer Lee. Without Do Ahn Kim's support, enthusiasm, and generosity, I would not have met the individuals at Sa Chal whose stories I tell in this book. It was from my interactions with Do Ahn Kim that the idea of writing a book about the temple came into being. When I first arrived at Sa Chal, I was warmly welcomed with a cup of tea, a string of Buddhist prayer beads, a tour of the temple, and an introduction to the resident monks.

Do Ahn Kim and Don Shin also provided one of the most memorable experiences of my life—traveling to North Korea to observe the temple's noodle factory and famine relief efforts. This was an extraordinary oppor-

ACKNOWLEDGMENTS

tunity and one that I will always be grateful for. I would also like to thank Jennifer Lee, who, along with Don, treated me like family and taught me invaluable lessons about selflessness and friendship. Jennifer offered and continues to act as my second mom by looking after my health, checking my pulse, and making sure that my personal relationships are going well. Throughout my two years of research in Los Angeles, I spent many an afternoon with Don, Jennifer, and various friends from the temple eating my favorite Korean noodle dishes and tofu casseroles. Jennifer and Don always made sure that I had a "proper Korean lunch" and took it upon themselves to drive us to local restaurants in Los Angeles's Koreatown where I could taste the house specialties.

During graduate school, I was fortunate to study with a number of wonderful teachers who challenged me to constantly rethink and reassess my work. Charles Hallisey played a tremendous role in my development from a master's student to a doctoral student in the Study of Religion program. He often posed the most difficult questions that would take me quite a while to figure out, oftentimes many weeks. Yet it was those challenging questions that helped me develop in my work. I also would like to thank Diana Eck for helping me shape and reshape my work to provide a more accurate reflection of what it was that I sought in the first place. Thanks also to Mary Waters for offering sound scholarly advice and direction.

I wish to extend my thanks to the people at the University of Washington Press who have worked with me to bring this book to fruition—Michael Duckworth, executive editor; Pamela Canell, designer; and Leila Charbonneau, for her succinct and clear copyediting. Special thanks also to Paul Spickard and David Yoo, who served as readers for the University of Washington Press, and to Pat Berger for her assitance in preparing the index. I would also like to thank Susanne Mrozik, who, as a scholarly bodhisattva since the days of my master's program, has continued to offer support and guidance. A graduate fellowship from Harvard University and a Summer Faculty Fellowship from Seattle University made the preparation of this book possible.

I have been extremely fortunate to have a father who has encouraged me since I was a young child to have a vision and stick with it. He has always had tremendous respect for my desire to pursue an advanced degree in the study of religion and has often helped me contextualize my studies in a larger picture. At the same time, he has always supported my decisions to do things my own way and encouraged my independence. I hope that I will be able to offer him and my own children the same support.

I have learned so much from Alex, Emily, and Olivia and have come to know what Shusaku Endo calls the irreplaceable bonds between individuals. Alex has always encouraged me since my graduate school days to forge my own path—a path that took me from Cambridge, Massachusetts, to Los Angeles and now to Seattle. From my daughters, I continually experience joy and have learned how to be present in the moment, how to improvise, and how to "try, try again."

BEING BUDDHIST

IN A CHRISTIAN WORLD

1

Introduction

The long historical presence of Korean Americans in the United States began with the first wave, or exodus, from Korea in 1903 to the Hawaiian Islands for work on the sugar plantations. Ever since the early stages of Korean immigration to America, Christianity has had a tremendous impact on the lives of immigrants both as a missionary presence in Korea and then as a source of social, economic, and political support following settlement. The Immigration Act of 1965 brought further waves of Korean immigrants, and they settled in urban centers such as Los Angeles, Detroit, Chicago, and New York, creating the many Koreatowns of the United States.

The centrality of religion in the lives of Korean Americans cannot be overstated. An estimated 70 to 80 percent of all Korean Americans claim affiliation with Korean Christian churches, yet 40 percent of that population is said to have converted to Christianity following immigration.[1] By 1990, of the 49 percent of Koreans living in Korea who reported themselves to be religious, 54 percent reported that they were Christians.[2] Nationwide studies indicate a total of at least 2,800 Korean Christian churches serving the immigrant community.[3] This total represents one ethnic Korean church for approximately every four hundred Koreans living in the United States.

While these statistics indicate that indeed Korean Americans are highly religious, they tend to perpetuate the myth and stereotype that *all* Korean Americans are Christian. Yet the reality is that not all Korean Americans convert to Christianity after immigration. In fact, a substantial number of Buddhists choose to continue worshipping at the eighty-nine temples serving the Korean American community in the larger United States. At the same time, it is very difficult to arrive at the total number of Buddhists in the Korean American community, because many Buddhists purposely avoid drawing attention to their religious identity within the ethnic community out of concern over social and business relationships with co-ethnic Christians.[4]

To date, scant attention has been paid to the Korean American Buddhist communities worshiping in the United States. Most works about Korean American religions focus on the Christian tradition; recent works that offer any information on Korean American Buddhism compare Buddhist institutions with Christian churches and deal primarily with issues of acculturation on a large sociological scale.[5] It is by looking at the Korean American Buddhist community in detail that one can gain a more accurate perspective of Korean American religiosity, which is by no means monolithic. A study of Korean American Buddhism reveals quite fascinating results in the areas of gender relationships, ethnicity, and identity that differ greatly from Korean American Christianity.

This book, the first in-depth study of Korean American Buddhism in the United States, draws on my two years of ethnographic research conducted at Sa Chal temple in Koreatown, Los Angeles. Sa Chal is one of the country's largest ethnic Korean Buddhist temples, established in 1974.[6] I examine the relationships between immigration, fragmentation of the self, and the reconstruction (religious, ethnic, and gender) of identity in the context of an urban Buddhist temple. The central component is the process of relocation that Buddhist men and women experience both spatially and psychologically as they adjust to living in the United States and attempt to lay down bicultural roots.

It has been said that immigration is a theologizing experience and that religion provides one of the strongest narratives and frameworks of meaning to help migrants make sense of their shifting worlds.[7] Throughout the following chapters, I show how Korean American members of Sa Chal temple interpret and apply religious discourses to specific life conditions to reconcile troubling life events, increase self-esteem, and develop an inward-gazing subjectivity. The experiences shared and retold by members of Sa Chal in *Being Buddhist in a Christian World* reveal a critical point that cannot be overlooked: religion is a highly gendered phenomenon that results in distinctly male and female forms of worship and constructions of identity.

Asserting a Buddhist identity enables many women to resist the idea of being defined by conventions of Confucian culture and also recreate a positive sense of self following a loss of meaning and identity upon arrival in the United States.[8] For men, however, a rational male Buddhist identity is often expressed in opposition to what Korean American men view as a dependent and emotional female Buddhist identity. According to these men, women are more inclined to pray to the Buddha to fulfill wishes and are more comfortable bowing down to the Buddha and offering devotional forms of worship. By viewing themselves as the more intellectual and superior Buddhists who understand the philosophical tenets of the tradition, men at Sa Chal construct an identity that attempts to reinforce conventional Confucian views of men as scholars, financial supports, and heads of households. In so doing, men perceive their worship at Sa Chal as less devotional and more intellectual; hence they are less inclined to attend weekly services and pray. They claim that they meditate rather than bow down to the Buddha. In both cases, however, the assertion of a Buddhist identity through worship and interpretation of teachings is directly related to a desire to construct a positive sense of self. Attending to religion's contribution to highly personal and idiosyncratic needs demonstrates how religious teachings and practices continue to thrive and maintain their relevance for individuals through time.

Buddhist discourses on selfhood have often denied the existence of a permanent sense of the ego or "I." The self that ordinary individuals perceive is but one in a series of selves that are constantly reborn; hence there is no permanent self. While this lack of enduring self is one of the first ideas discussed in introductory studies of Buddhism in the West, the discourse on selflessness was historically aimed at the most highly trained of monastic Buddhist scholars interested in questions of ontology and was not a concern of the ordinary lay Buddhist. Most everyday Buddhists do not conceive of themselves as lacking an inherent sense of self. That is, a religious discourse on selflessness does not translate into a lack of subjectivity and self-interest for ordinary Buddhists. Because the scholastic virtuoso monastic has dominated most studies of Buddhism, we have assumed that the approach must reflect the perceptions of the self among

INTRODUCTION

Buddhists. My own interaction with everyday Buddhists, however, indicates otherwise.

Rather than discovering a community of selfless individuals motivated solely by religious goals of higher rebirths and enlightenment, I discovered housewives, husbands, mom and pop shop owners, parents, and sons and daughters whose lives were deeply concerned with the development of a positive sense of self. As the women and men at Sa Chal temple put it, Buddhism helps to "find and know one's mind" by offering teachings that help center and create a coherent sense of self in the midst of life's vicissitudes.

"To find one's mind" and "to know one's mind" are the phrases participants used to define the most important aspects of Buddhist teachings and main reasons for religious practice. This discourse about finding and knowing one's mind is an interpretation of general Buddhist teachings and addresses common concerns aimed at liberating oneself from problems like marital distress and discrimination. Rather than being concerned with liberation of the self from the cycle of rebirth and the attainment of the salvational goal of nirvana, ordinary Buddhists are primarily concerned with liberation from everyday suffering.

The discourse of liberation, "to know one's mind," means to realize that it is an unawakened and ignorant mind that has become subject to personal obstacles and suffering. To "find one's mind" means to liberate the suffering mind and find one's true Buddhist mind, which can transcend suffering. "Finding and knowing one's mind" thus refers to the belief held by members of this temple that the self can be transformed and the act of doing so can lead to remarkable changes in one's life. This book examines the process of transformation and the efficacy of Buddhist doctrines and worship in making life more manageable in the present. It therefore argues that Buddhism is practical in orientation because it addresses everyday concerns and that discourses of liberation are also articulated through everyday concerns.

The Korean American Buddhist community of Los Angeles offers a fascinating view of the efficacy of religion in coping with struggles for self-confidence experienced by many immigrant groups. Instead of orienting their religious practices and beliefs toward soteriological goals obtainable in the distant future, Buddhist teachings provide the cohesive agent to help people re-center fragmented selves. One of the powers of religious teachings resides in the ability to operate "on the ground" to resolve relationship conflicts, gender hierarchies, changes in economic and social status, and other forms of personal dislocation exacerbated by the experience of living outside of one's homeland.

As primarily first-generation immigrants, many of the fifty men and women interviewed in this study have experienced a tremendous threat to their sense of security by moving from a country of monoethnicity, relative economic comfort, and an easy fluency in Korean cultural norms to a position of marginality in the United States. Most of the one hundred or so active first-generation Korean Americans at Sa Chal have yet to learn to speak English fluently and indicate that they have experienced a downward shift in social, economic, and political status.[9] They also admit to having an added burden of being a religious minority (Buddhist) among a majority of Christians within their own ethnic group. In spite of these experiences of multiple dislocation that could lead to a crisis of identity, Buddhists at Sa Chal turn to religion as a source of empowerment and flourishing. In the daily lives of men and women, religion offers security, comfort, and resistance to influences that detract from high self-esteem, and it plays a crucial role in centering the self in everyday action. Through praying, bowing, meditation, and applying Buddhist teachings to life events, men and women seek to reorganize their lives and realign their values to find inner peace in their new country. As such, their worship, devotional practices, and beliefs are not aimed at selflessness but rather self-fulfillment.

We have little material documenting gender relations within Asian American religious institutions, for there has been a tendency to view women's experiences as isomorphic with male experiences, based on their shared race and ethnicities.[10] While a few studies of Korean American women and gender relations in the Christian church have emerged recently, scholars have all but ignored the subject of Korean American laymen and women in Buddhist communities. Recent studies of Korean Christian churches in America by Young In Song and Ai Ra Kim indicate that while women comprise the majority of Korean American Christian congregations throughout the country, they do not hold positions of leadership in the church.[11]

In Korean American Christian churches, it is the men who act as elders and deacons while women remain in the pews and in the kitchens preparing food. The predominance of male public leadership roles in the church has been attributed to the desire among Korean American men to seek high status positions within the church—something they do not have access to in the larger context of American culture. Song attributes the concentration of male lay leadership roles to the anxiety produced by moving from a position of high Confucian male status to its inversion in America. Hence, according to these studies Korean American men appear to turn to the religious institution to reaffirm their male hierarchical status.

While the structure of Korean churches in the United States provides for such male leadership roles, this is not the case at Sa Chal. The organizational structure of the Buddhist temple incorporates few lay leadership roles, and this is a point of contention for some men. Most positions of male leadership in the temple are reserved for the male monastics—the abbot and three resident monks. Thus, given that neither men nor women have access to public leadership roles, it would seem that relations in the temple would be more gender equitable than in the church. Nonetheless, it is still the women in the temple who actively prepare the weekly luncheon following the 11:00 A.M. service and serve the food to all participants. The main differences in gender relationships in a Korean Christian church and a Buddhist temple are that no formal lay leadership roles are held exclusively by male members in the temple and that there is little theological or doctrinal justification for the subordination of women to men that has been found in the studies of the Korean Christian churches.

THE CONTEXT OF THE STUDY: HOW THIS ALL BEGAN

To illustrate the interpretation and application of Buddhist teachings to daily life in an urban temple, I draw upon interview data, individual narratives, and observations during my two years of interaction with members of Sa Chal from June 1997 to June 1999. I distinctly recall sitting in the office of a Koreatown nonprofit organization where I had served as the executive director in Los Angeles in the summer of 1997 and receiving a phone call from a gentleman who would later become one of my dearest friends and a teacher at the temple—David Jeon. Mr. Jeon had just read an article about my position at the museum in one of the local Korean-language newspaper and learned about my educational background in Buddhist studies.

On a typically hot June day in Los Angeles, I was invited to meet Mr. Jeon and the abbot of Sa Chal temple at a nearby Korean restaurant. This was followed by a visit to the temple—the place I would spend nearly every weekend for the next two years. I was compelled to visit the temple out of curiosity and was intrigued by what the abbot and Mr. Jeon told me: much was written about Korean American Christianity but scant attention was paid to the Korean American Buddhist communities in the United States. Following my visit to the temple, I accepted an invitation by the abbot to teach a Buddhist youth group class at Sa Chal and eventually served as a lecturer at the temple's Buddhist College for adult education. It was these two positions that gave me a unique opportunity to meet the men and women whose stories I share in this book.

My research methodology includes an analysis of data collected through observation and on-site participation, along with extensive field notes, surveys, in-depth open-ended interviews, and oral histories. What proved most useful for meeting participants was an informal snowballing method of interviewing; I met potential interview participants through men and women I had come to know on a personal basis. The series of conversations we had, more formally known as select open-ended interviews and short oral histories, consisted of specific questions with regard to their lives in America, their views on gender relations and norms, and their perceptions of religion.[12] Excerpts from these fifty interviews are presented in this study.

I regard the testimonials, personal narratives, and interview data as ethnographic religious biographies wherein religious motivations are revealed and subjectivities enacted. Oral historians David Dunaway and Willa Baum have argued that the technique of oral history enables scholars to focus on the person "to tell tales of everyday life," including all of its idiosyncrasies and vicissitudes.[13] Oral history collections are particularly relevant for studies of gender and identity, for they draw attention to those individuals largely left out of historical records. Although I do not attempt to create full in-depth oral histories of all the interview participants, I do rely on techniques of interviewing relevant to the collection of such histories.[14] During my interviews, I often placed control of the dialogue in the hands of the participant, thus enabling access to that person's ideas, expe-

INTRODUCTION

riences, and memories.¹⁵ Fundamental to this approach is the use of multiple interviews to allow for feedback to information previously elicited, attention to the importance of self-reflexivity, and exact reproduction of the participant's personal expression and narrative qualities.

In presenting this experience-near form of fieldwork, I allow the individual voices of men and women to emerge through detailed ethnographic portraits to present a study of persons in context. As a result, this layering of voices throughout the text will provide some areas of similarity which serve to highlight and exemplify the main points of this study.

REFLEXIVITY AND SITUATIONAL ACCURACY

While my research consists of ethnographic field methods and multiple interviews with temple worshippers, my aim has not been to present a seamless ethnography of a Korean Buddhist temple. Rather, I present a study of how individuals make meaning in their lives and struggle to find a coherent sense of self within the context of religion. As such, I am in agreement with the words of anthropologist Ruth Benedict, who argued against a wide-angled view of culture that obscures the idiosyncratic, for "there is a very real hurt done our understanding of culture when we systematically ignore the individual."¹⁶ One aspect of the Korean Buddhist community that has struck me is the remarkable way in which many participants were extremely open about their private lives. In fact, most of the Korean Buddhists I have met have been quite forthcoming with information about their lives, largely because of the level of closeness I was able to establish with them. I have had an opportunity to visit people in their offices and their homes as we sat on the floor around traditional Korean lacquer tables sipping tea.

Although I use pseudonyms in order to protect certain aspects of individual lives, most Buddhists to whom I gave consent forms and explained the confidentiality of our conversations did not seem to mind their names being mentioned. In fact, most of them laughed about the idea of confidentiality and led me to believe it would be fine to use their names. For some, perhaps the public recognition was seen as a positive means of edifying the self. For others, an already established bond between us made mutual trust a given.

In dealing with the religious lives of Buddhist men and women, I aim for a situational accuracy in presenting humans flourishing in the social setting of a primarily first-generation Korean American Buddhist temple. Thus some of the comments, analyses, and questions raised may appear critical, though the only objective was to bring attention to the very issues that entwine and complicate my participant's lives. Choosing not to mention the problems experienced by members of this community out of a desire to protect the temple and its participants risks the disservice of oversimplification. I have never considered myself an outsider coolly observing how others make meaning in their lives, for I too am implicated in this process of constructing selves.

The many individuals who have shared their experiences and views with me have expressed a desire to assist in this endeavor, all along wondering if their comments and stories would in fact "help in some small way." Without their generous contribution of time, the details of their lives, and their commitment to spreading the dharma, this project would never have gotten off the ground. In this study I deliberately chose to locate myself and be located by others as researcher, participant, volunteer, teacher, and student to point out where and how I fit into the larger social setting of the temple. Through religious worship and idioms, people use the tools at hand to craft and reconstitute selves that are always in flux in both the Buddhist and the postmodern sense. At times, I too have been approached for the opportunity to air grievances, test out English skills, and perhaps enlist help with second-generation offspring—all along I have been honored that people would consider me capable and worthy of such an important task.

One of the interesting aspects of doing this type of qualitative research lies in the situational effectiveness of both myself and research partners as we negotiate and present the best possible versions of ourselves to one another. Thus, although interviews that I have conducted have been done as informally as possible, the very fact of an interview situation creates a certain amount of constraint and artifice that I have sometimes found difficult to overcome.

This emerged particularly in my interviews with male participants at Sa Chal. Since we did not share the same gender, many men in my research project were somewhat more reserved in our discussions. In a few cases, the interviews had a slow start because the respondent was not sure how to react to me. Some, like Mr. Lee, wondered, "Why do you want to talk to *me*? Talk to my wife. I don't have anything interesting to say." This sort of beginning led to a much more limited interview style, for men like Mr. Lee were less willing to impart any personal information or would often dismiss my questions without answering them.

Most Korean men that I have interviewed and discussed life experiences with still retained much of the Confucian ideology of men as the intellectual/political actors in the family and women as the emotional supports who maintain the household. I do not fit the mold of Korean women that most men envision and as a result some men have been standoffish while others have been genuinely forthcoming and desirous of helping me with my project. Confronted with the same ambiguous individual, women were much more inclined to respond by casting me in the role of a quasi daughter in our conversations, perhaps in some cases as an ideal substitute daughter who made an effort to speak Korean well, despite being born in the United States, and was interested in Buddhism.

My interest in Buddhism has always been a source of puzzlement for Sa Chal members who assume that a second-generation Korean American would be much more inclined to go to Christian churches and be interested in studying them. While I sometimes thought that some might view me with suspicion since most Buddhists have had feelings of alienation from the larger Korean Christian population, all of my participants have been both accepting and even encouraging with my research, urging me to attend more events so that I could "tell the mainstream American public about Korean Buddhism." Others, like the temple's abbot, have worked to assign me the role of a teacher of Buddhism, and this has enabled me to travel to places like North Korea and allowed me access to meetings and events perhaps not available to other women or men at the temple. Thus I have been extremely privileged as a researcher but I do not think that this has been threatening to anyone at the temple, since I have also been in the position of learner, student, and daughter.

ORGANIZATION OF THE BOOK

Each chapter in this book illuminates the different ways men and women participate in Sa Chal worship and the range of interpretations of Buddhist teachings held by both genders. The chapters focusing on interview participants' responses are organized to highlight the specific ways reli-

INTRODUCTION

gious practices and doctrines are utilized to enact self-transformation. Chapters four and five focus on women's beliefs and practices while chapter six is dedicated specifically to men's practices. Chapter seven is devoted to an analysis of both men's and women's responses to a shared experience between the genders—religious minority status within the Korean American community.

Chapter two begins with a discussion of selfhood in Buddhism and examines the idiom "finding and knowing one's mind" as it relates to Buddhist teachings of Buddha Nature and self-awakening. This chapter then moves into an examination of selfhood and subjectivity as they relate to the lives of the Korean Americans studied in this work. In so doing, I examine conceptions of selfhood in anthropological, Buddhist, feminist, and psychological studies of the self.

Chapter three, "Sa Chal Context, Programs, and Demographics," provides a brief history of Korean immigration to the United States and the historical development of the temple where I conducted my research. This chapter also describes the mission, programs, survey results, and demographic information of the temple to provide the sociohistorical context of Sa Chal. I describe daily rituals and interactions at the temple to illustrate the patterns of religious life in a contemporary Korean American Buddhist community. I also include a description of the context in which my interviews took place and the circumstances leading to this study.

Chapter four, "Buddhist Practice and Self-Transformation," examines the relationship between religious practice, psychological healing, and the development of self-esteem for Korean Buddhist women through a detailed study of their personal lives. In this chapter, I discuss how Buddhist idioms and teachings of self-knowledge, Buddha Nature, and karma shape women's struggles to combat depression and relationship discord. Part one of this chapter focuses on one particular Korean American woman who has turned to religion to combat depression. Part two reveals how women's religious faith can offer a means of coping with a life that has "gone awry." Part three examines the dual religious practices of women at Sa Chal to illustrate how women creatively interpret religion to address their personal needs. In these sections, emphasis is placed on showing how women reinterpret suffering and pain through religious language and worship to become agents of change and self-transformation.

INTRODUCTION

In Chapter five, I show how religion acts as a strategy for adapting to a new culture by serving as a haven in the new land for those Korean women who have yet to adjust to postimmigration life and as a source of inspiration for those who have sought to live in America as independent women. I examine how religious idioms of "finding and knowing one's mind" and temple participation enable women to ease the anxiety and sense of alienation they feel while living in America. Through their religious practices, women seek psychological comfort and security in a community that indexes the homeland they left behind. Section two shows how Buddhist ideologies of self-knowledge and self-reliance are employed by women to develop assertiveness and independence as they seek to fulfill their American dreams. Key to their success is the interpretation of religious language to justify those actions that run counter to traditional Confucian models of proper female comportment.

Chapter six, "Finding Male Selves: Men's Religious Practices," examines male participation and practices at Sa Chal to illustrate how the male members of this temple interpret similar Buddhist idioms through a distinctly male subjectivity with remarkably different results. In so doing, this chapter demonstrates how Sa Chal functions as gendered space and the efforts men undertake to create meaningful roles for themselves in the temple—roles they consider separate from and superior to women's religious practices.

Chapter seven, "Being Buddhist in a Christian World," examines the Buddhist response to the increasing Christianization of the Korean American community and illustrates how Buddhists respond to their religious minority status by drawing sharp character distinctions between the members of both traditions. I draw specific attention to how Buddhist women's and men's interpretations of and responses to their religious minority status vary and how they seek to maintain self-integrity in the face of perceived and actual marginality. I illustrate how Buddhists cite "finding and knowing one's mind" in order to make claims for themselves as more open-minded, self-reliant, more intelligent, more liberal, and, by extension, "more American" than their Christian counterparts.

Despite the apparent success of the Korean American churches in providing for the social, economic, and political needs of the ethnic community, Buddhists seek to elevate their self-esteem by recourse to a set of

INTRODUCTION

psychological standards developed through Buddhist worship and practice that they deem superior to those of Christians. I examine, in particular, the tensions revolving around what it means to be American for this Buddhist community, which, on the one hand, symbolizes the positive values of self-reliance and independence and, on the other, the erosion of the traditional Korean values that hold families together.

2

Finding and Knowing One's Mind

On Sunday afternoons at Sa Chal in an empty dharma hall or the library after a vegetarian luncheon, I often discussed with temple members what they considered the most important aspects of Buddhist teachings and the most compelling reasons for their worship. While each shared the details of how Buddhist teachings resonated with his or her own life experiences, I was surprised to note common references in each response to the idioms "to find one's mind" and "to know one's mind."[1] The striking similarities between men's and women's answers can be found in the following statements drawn directly from some of our conversations:

"Buddhism helps me find my own mind."

"In Buddhism, you have to know yourself to cleanse the mind and your troubles."

"You have to know yourself and you have to look within your own mind."

"The Buddhist method is about knowing things on your own."

"I want to study [and know] my mind, so that is why I come to temple regularly."

"In Buddhism, you are the subject, therefore you have to come to a realization of yourself [i.e., know yourself] and figure out your own well-being through the teachings."

While Sa Chal members made little mention of the textual references underlying their interpretations of Buddhism, their comments do reflect Buddhist doctrines concerning the Buddha Nature (the teaching that all sentient beings are inherently enlightened) and refer to related ideas about self-awakening and self-knowledge. This potential to become a Buddha takes on a particularly nuanced meaning in Korean Buddhism through the commentaries of Chinul, the famed twelfth-century Korean Son scholar monk. Chinul believed that individuals must have faith not only in their own potential to become Buddhas but also in the fact that they already *are* Buddhas. In other words, the individual awakens to his or her own enlightenment through self-realization wherein one "realize[s] directly the nature of our own True Mind." In his treatise *Direct Explanation of True Mind*, Chinul defines the perception of the nature of one's True Mind as follows: "that everyone is originally Buddha; that all people intrinsically possess the perfect Buddha nature; and that the marvelous essence of *nirvana* is perfectly complete in everyone. Hence, there is no need to search anywhere else, because since the beginning, those have been complete in oneself."[2]

The process of realizing one's True Mind serves as the doctrinal basis for the lay interpretation of the main goals of Buddhism as "finding and knowing one's mind." This religion-based phrase also has immediate relevance to everyday issues of self-esteem, for it reflects an underlying trust among practitioners in their own ability to get at the root of problems and solve them. This confidence comes from the belief that one is already a Buddha and that one can and must awaken that faith within oneself. In many ways, ordinary Buddhists associate Buddha Nature and relate the processes of self-realization with the ability to cope with problems that emerge in their daily lives. Individuals can overcome troubles through a process of "finding and knowing one's mind," which is based on self-reliance and self-realization.

"Finding and knowing one's mind" also refers to a process of finding oneself and finding one's bearings, especially during situations of stress and change. Thus the efficacy of Buddhist doctrines and worship derives from having practical applications in making daily life more manageable rather than just guiding an individual to a better rebirth or enlightenment in the future.

SUBJECTIVITY AND SELF-ESTEEM

When I began my fieldwork, I became very interested in how Buddhists at Sa Chal viewed themselves and articulated their identities particularly after immigrating to a new country. Throughout my research, I discovered that women and men talked about themselves, their experiences, and their religious practices in ways that revealed a concern and focus on cultivating subjectivity and self-esteem. In this book I refer to subjectivity as an individual's self-consciousness of himself or herself as the primary actor, subject, and agent of his or her actions. That is, an individual experiences and occupies a subject position and views himself or herself as an autonomous being acting in self-interest.[3]

Subjectivity and self-esteem are discovered, constructed, and asserted in relation with others, for "[j]ust as people grow up in particular bodies, people grow up in particular places and their selves and subjectivities develop accordingly."[4] That is, an individual's consciousness of an autonomous self acting in self-interest leads to the development of self-esteem and worth in the context of others who may enhance or detract from that experience. Therefore, one of the aims of this book is to view persons within their communities while paying special attention to the individual in social relationships. The relational view of the self posited in this study reflects how the participants identify themselves—as individuals, spouses, parents, family members, friends, Buddhists, and Koreans.

For Buddhists at Sa Chal, the goal of "finding and knowing one's mind" is the key ingredient in the development of self-esteem and subjectivity, which in turn leads, as some members put it, to "the ability to take matters into one's own hands." The positive characteristics of self-reliance and independence emerge from the often complicated circumstances of their lives, the contexts from which they must find and know the causes and the antidotes to their suffering. Therefore, Buddhists claim that they can make changes in their lives on their own by viewing obstacles to their success and happiness as not only self-generated and the results of their own karma, but ultimately self-resolvable. In viewing problems as transformable through their own efforts, individuals can develop a positive sense of self— a self who has understood the injunction to find and know one's mind. The process thus has a particular value in a study of subjectivity, for it suggests that self-knowledge and self-reliance are developed *for and by oneself.*

This particular interpretation of Buddhist teachings and worship rests on a process of mental transformation characterized by several conditions. First, the person must take a good look at the conditions of her/his life in order to locate his or her true confident self held to exist despite experiences of personal suffering. The person then reflects upon the conditions leading up to the perceived problems and learns to address them appropriately and as they truly are—impermanent and subject to change. In other words, because the conditions creating states of suffering like stress, depression, and loneliness are impermanent, they carry the potential for change. Finally, change comes when the individual intuits that he or she is the person who has created those conditions based on his or her own karma and not some outside force. To find and know oneself means, then, to see things as they truly are—subject to change, a condition that has the potential to alleviate suffering and increase self-esteem.

Throughout my discussions with Buddhists, I discovered a certain degree of flexibility in interpreting religious teachings to apply to the development of confidence and self-esteem. The association of Buddhism with "finding and knowing one's mind" encourages individuals to develop and tout self-reliance as one of the cardinal virtues of Buddhism. Buddhist practice and belief encourages one to develop independence and self-knowledge, which in turn helps to transform sources of personal suffering from influences outside the self to oneself. In transforming the agent of suffering from an external source to an internal one (usually associated with one's own karma), men and women learn to accept responsibility for past troubles. More important, this acceptance of individual responsibility allows the person to control or change what had previously been a source of suffering. That individuals are empowered to enact change results in the acquisition of greater self-esteem.

Yet, at the same time, problematic events such as the inability to prohibit one's child from converting from Buddhism to Christianity—a common phenomenon among second-generation Korean Americans—may be rationalized by recourse to the same Buddhist injunction of finding and knowing one's mind. For a Buddhist presumably understands that individuals must be self-reliant and, at the same time, are propelled through life by the actions of their individual karma. As one of the many parents of increasingly Christianized children explains, "One cannot change the fate (nor religious identity) of one's child. Instead, the child must be left to decide for him or herself what religion he or she wishes to profess." To force another person to bend to one's will is then seen as a most un-Buddhist act. As a religious doctrine that discourages intrusion, "finding and knowing one's mind" mitigates an individual's sense of helplessness in not being able to control the actions and lives of others. Given the various ways in which religious teachings are applied to real-life situations, religion can appear to be a rather improvisational project.

Buddhist teachings of independence and self-reliance encourage men and women to develop a sense of agency and subjectivity where decisions are made and conflicts resolved by oneself alone. Yet, because the laws of karma also dictate an individual's actions, a tension remains between the desire to be a self-reliant agent of change and the rhetoric that advocates nonintrusion in the affairs of others outside of one's control. In this regard, Buddhist values of finding and knowing one's mind are dually interpreted to encourage the power to control oneself and certain forces outside the self, and the ability to recognize that there are limits to what a person can do. This crucial distinction is where finding and knowing one's mind comes into play. In this way, the self is absolved of responsibility for the actions of others and at the same time empowered to cope with the challenges that beset the development of self-esteem.

WOMEN'S RELIGIOUS PARTICIPATION AND RESPONSES

On any given Sunday from 11:00 to 12:30 P.M., Sa Chal's main worship hall is filled with eighty to one hundred members; of that group, only 15 to 20 percent are male. While it is commonly said that women are the true bearers and preservers of religious traditions, this book questions what that gender imbalance signifies for a religious community and its individuals in transition. When I originally asked temple participants if their husbands attended Sa Chal services, women gave responses such as:

"Men just don't attend temple."
"Men play golf on the weekends."
"It is women's responsibility to go to temple."
"Men do not have time to attend."
"Why should men go to temple?"

Based on these responses, it appeared at first that Korean American women attended temple for reasons consistent with Korean Confucian ideologies of female gender roles—that is, women are the caretakers of others, the cultural transmitters of the family, and responsible for the family's religious values. However, when I began to compare what people *said* about women's roles with what women actually *did* at the temple, a very different picture began to emerge.

Just like male members, Sa Chal women took on active roles as public speakers during services, spoke out in response to the abbot's dharma talks, and moved freely about the temple engaged in open conversation during the daily services. Women shifted from the main dharma hall to the kitchen to the various Buddhist altars in the temple to worship privately or chat with friends. The older women even have a private room equipped with a bed designed specifically for their use. At any given time on Sunday, one enters the room to find a group of women gossiping, trading clothing, admiring one another's jewelry, and resting. There is no equivalent space for men in the temple.

While sitting with women at Sa Chal and engaging them in in-depth interviews, I discovered that while religion provides a bond between family members and while women agreed that they should pray for the welfare of the family, these were not their primary motivations for religious practice. Instead the main goals of their religious practice were self-transformation and the development of individual agency that they interpreted through the Buddhist doctrines of karma, the universal Buddha Nature, and potential enlightenment in all beings. Women often claimed that finding and knowing one's mind was the most essential aspect of the Buddha's teachings—not teaching children about religion or praying for one's husband's business as many men seemed to believe.

These women maintain that religious practice can lead to enlightenment for the individual only through "finding and knowing one's mind," described as self-knowledge and self-actualization. By cultivating self-knowledge, women can get at the root of all problems—ignorance and negative karma. The latter was not understood on an abstract philosophical level but on the level of everyday experience. Rather than reacting to their experience of multiple dislocations as fated victims, many Buddhist women take responsibility for their circumstances by citing themselves as both the culprits and the conquerors of their troubles. In so doing, they experience a process of self-transformation characterized by increased self-esteem, a reinterpretation of past suffering, and the courage to forge ahead in a new culture.

In conducting this study, I found that existing scholarly works on Korean American women and religion did not resonate with what I discovered at Sa Chal, for such works posit an automatic association of Christian theology with Confucianism. This association can often result in the religiously sanctioned submission of women to men, which can be potentially harmful to women's self-esteem since religion is so heavily bound up with Confucian patriarchy.[5] I have found that at Sa Chal, because there is no reference made to the theological subordination of women to men, religion (Buddhism) can enable women to challenge tradition (Confucian culture), which continues to play a predominant role in shaping social interaction among Korean immigrants. This lack of theological justification for the subordination of women to men does not necessarily result in an obviously gender-equitable situation at Sa Chal. Yet it does allow women to employ the Buddhist language of self-knowledge and karma to make changes in lived experiences that are often constrained by culturally defined gender codes.

For some women, a Buddhist identity characterized as independent and driven by self-knowledge is both juxtaposed against and chosen over Confucian roles for women as housewives dedicated to their husbands. In the pursuit of self-valuation, Korean Buddhist women often pose religious models of an ideal Buddhist self not defined by gender characteristics to counter culturally determined Confucian gender ideologies that proscribe ideal female behavior (often experienced as oppressive). In this way, Buddhist women associate and claim a religious identity for themselves that they deem more authoritative than a Confucian-based female identity.

Yet, while women appear to challenge traditional gender codes derived from Confucianism, there are personal stakes as well as gains to be made. By agreeing that perhaps women's minds are emotionally stronger than men's and by stating that men have less time to spend worshipping at the temple, many women uphold Confucian gender hierarchies while simultaneously creating a space for themselves that men are not privy to. Rather than lamenting the lack of male participation in the temple, women publicly resign themselves to the Confucian belief that religion is women's work, yet they can also reap the benefits in maintaining that cultural system in ways that enhance the development of agency and self-esteem. The fact that these women do not always internalize these hierarchies became readily apparent when I began to attend to their activities and expressions outside of the public domains of the worship hall in the more private spaces of informal conversations and interviews, where criticisms could be leveled without the risk of being overhead. In this way, Buddhist women at Sa Chal prove to be quite similar to their Korean Christian counterparts who also engaged in the tacit forms of resistance to male dominance, as documented by Jung Ha Kim.[6]

MEN'S RELIGIOUS PRACTICES AND RESPONSES

Throughout my interviews with twenty-five male members at Sa Chal, I discovered that unlike the women, men tended to cite status inversion more than loneliness and relationship problems as the primary reason for the personal stress and dislocation that impinged on their lives. These men also felt that after immigrating to America, they were no longer in dominant economic and social positions. This perspective tended to emerge in their complaints that the temple did not offer enough programs to keep men occupied and that Christian churches offered more opportunities for business ventures and social networking in the Korean American community. Yet these men choose to avoid going to the Korean Christian churches, which they believe infringe on their privacy and detract from their independence because churches tend to require regular attendance. At the same time, men do not actively participate in the general worship services at the temple nor bow down in full prostration in front of the Buddha like the women do. In fact, it was only during special dharma talks offered by guest speakers that the numbers of men in attendance would increase to nearly equal that of the women.

When I inquired about this change, the men replied that they were more interested in a Buddhism that appealed to the intellect (e.g., scholarly discussions) and political issues, such as North–South Korea reunification. They explained their preferences by distinguishing these activities from the more "emotional" forms of religion that they attributed to women at the temple. For example, on one particular Sunday afternoon, a professor of early Son Buddhist philosophy visiting from China gave a lecture on Korean Son Buddhism during the general worship service. At this service male attendance accounted for at least 50 percent of the congregation. The very next week, male attendance decreased to 15 percent, for there were no guest speakers scheduled to present the dharma talk.

Some of the male participants in this study attributed the larger presence of women at Sa Chal services to the fact that women had fewer opportunities than men to let off steam by drinking and playing golf with friends. Instead, women were said to go to temple to pray to the Buddha to overcome personal hardships and stress. These comments suggest that Korean American men at the temple view women's religion as more emotionally based whereas men's religious practices are seen as more intellectual and rational. Furthermore, many of the men cited Confucian gender ideology as the source for this division between the public and private or intellectual and emotional spaces—differences they believed were embodied in distinct male and female forms of practice. This may be one reason why many temple participants claim that men are often too embarrassed to bow down to the Buddha in the presence of women.

Mr. Yim, a first-generation immigrant I met at Sa Chal, believes that temple participation is more popular with women because it provides a culturally acceptable space for them to work through emotional problems. However, he also believes that Sa Chal fails to appeal to men's needs for psychological comfort in a way that addresses their desire for intellectual and high-status identities. Furthermore, he maintains that since Buddhism is about finding and knowing one's mind, an individual can freely worship when and wherever he wants—in the car, waiting in line, or in the office without need of a mediating influence like a temple or a monk. By citing the notion of karma, Buddha Nature, and self-realization, this Korean American Buddhist man decides for himself how he should practice. For Mr. Hong, waking up, reading the Diamond Sutra, and bowing at home suffices for religious practice. While he attends temple on a weekly basis, he does not attend the general worship service. Rather, he sits in one of the temple offices and volunteers his time as an accountant. Like many men, Mr. Yim and Mr. Hong do not feel the need or desire to take part in the more communal forms of religion. By associating women with emotionalism and communalism, the men invoke Confucian ideologies that see men as rationalists, breadwinners, and public figures who don't have the time or need to worship at the temple. In their minds, that task falls to the women.

While investigating the motivations for active participation and the religious meanings held at Sa Chal, I found it necessary to move beyond a structural study of the religious organization as an institution. Instead I needed to focus on the individuals who made up its membership. During my extensive conversations with members, I learned about the experiences of women and men not only in the temple but also in their homes, their workplaces, and their social networks to determine how Korean Americans experience and negotiate their hyphenated identities and the impact of religion on that process. Throughout my participation in the daily life of Sa Chal members, I sought to discover how Sa Chal enables Korean American women and men to adjust to the larger context of American culture and Buddhism's capacity to provide a framework for the development of subjectivity. I was drawn in particular to the following questions: What role do religious practices play in restructuring gendered identities and self-perception following experiences of dislocation like immigration? Does the experience of dislocation lead individuals to participate more in religious life? How and why are religious doctrines deployed and interpreted to make sense of life transitions?

DISCOURSES OF THE SELF

Buddhism and recent studies in anthropology share a similar concern with viewing the self as nonunitary and problematic when perceived otherwise. According to classical Buddhist discourse, the perception of a unitary, permanent self can lead to suffering and ignorance as the person attaches himself or herself to what is continually in flux. For anthropologists critiquing the Western notion of the bounded essentialized self, the self can best be understood as relational and improvisational. Since the advent of postmodernism, the idea that we live in a world of increasing fragmentation comes as no surprise. Looking at the continually redeveloping self reveals how individuals may deploy religious meanings to make sense of, construct, and at times resist everyday events. In so doing, they engage in a reconstruction of self and identity.

FINDING AND KNOWING ONE'S MIND

One of the most compelling anthropological arguments against a reified self can be found in Dorinne Kondo's ethnography, *Crafting Selves: Power, Gender and Discourses of Identity in a Japanese Workplace*. Kondo contends that selfhood and identities are perpetually recreated and, as such, performative. Everyday practices are approached as arenas for the formulation, enactment, and constraint of subjectivities and identities. For Kondo, selfhood and identity are not "fixed, bounded entities" characterized by an essential interior referent which is then set in distinction to an external social world that is "spatially and ontologically distinct from the self"; they shift according to time and place.[7]

Viewing the self as crafted can illuminate the potentials, constraints, and meanings of resistance and the assertion of religious identities within the social setting of Sa Chal. Through religious activities individuals can reconstruct identities that have become fractured in a new culture, for selves are always discursively constructed in situ. In other words, if selves are constantly recast in different social contexts, power relations between individuals that exist in one context can be resisted in another. In those sites where power and authority are formulated and acted on to discipline ideal selves, there is always room for resistance where behavior exceeds expectations. Buddhists consider free choice and self-knowledge as the most important aspects of the Buddha's teachings. While the discourse of power in the temple leaves the monks at the top of the hierarchy, there are times when lay people can set aside such deferential treatment.

For example, on one occasion, I asked a woman I had seen cooking special meals for the monks during the weekdays and preparing lanterns for the Buddha's birthday if she supported the abbot's famine relief project in North Korea. Much to my surprise, this usually polite woman began to shout, "North Korea famine relief? You're crazy if you think I'll give those ... Reds a dime!" Illustrating her fierce opposition to the abbot's program, she proceeded to hurl a long list of profanities in English. What a sight it was to observe this sixty-year-old grandmother dressed in the gray *bopbok* (lay robes) shouting every single derogatory word she could think of at the mention of the abbot's program. Naively, I had presumed that since this woman came to the temple dressed in her lay robes and volunteered each week she would naturally support such optional programs at the temple. It soon become clear, however, that the abbot's influence only goes so far. While it often remains unchallenged in the public sphere, members feel perfectly free to critique the monks and their behavior in private.

When, on a separate occasion, I asked a choir member whom I had observed serving food and volunteering around Sa Chal whether this temple was similar to Chogye temples in Korea, she quickly replied, "Well, yes, I suppose it is." She then quickly looked around the empty dining hall to see if anyone was close enough to hear her and continued in a soft voice, "Well, you know, things are a *little* different here. They [monks] always seem so interested in the budget. Here, they even print up the cost of things in the weekly pamphlets! They never do that in Korea. When I come to this temple, the monks often just sit there half asleep!" As we continued our conversation, I realized that women in the temple did not actually internalize the hierarchical relationships established between the monks and the laity. Many criticized the monks for caring more about financial matters than personal interaction with the laity; at the same time, propriety dictates that a laywoman should not openly criticize a monk, ideologically her superior, particularly in a public setting. The same situation applied to the male members of Sa Chal, although the men tended to be less secretive about their complaints leveled against the temple's monastic authorities. While they did not criticize the monks in their presence, the men often argued that the monks were not well enough educated to properly teach the laity and that monks were more concerned with raising their own status in the Korean American community than with providing for the needs of their temple members. Many regular male members also chose to avoid coming to the temple when they disagreed with the policies of the monastic authorities.

In the context of a contemporary urban religious setting, there are plenty of opportunities for the laity to challenge the authority of the monks, a situation the abbot himself readily admits. During one of our interviews, he acknowledged: "Well, I know that some people don't agree with our sending support over to North Korea, but you know, they are just caught up in the idea of Communism. Besides, it is up to each person to decide for him or herself what they want to do." The abbot's comments were followed with a wry smile as he concluded that such members were blinded by ignorance and unable to see that Buddhist compassion extends beyond Communist history.

Attention to the everyday practices of lay worshippers reveals the strategies individuals employ to make meaning in their lives when things fall apart, and the motivations to maintain certain forms of propriety that may appear antithetical to a project dedicated to self-edification. Individuals do not always resist or challenge various forms of authority around them like the abbot, gender ideologies, or American culture per se, but they find opportunities where excesses of compliance and agreement spill forth and find expression. This insight is particularly important for the study of women at Sa Chal who may not wish to explicitly contradict and resist gender hierarchies, but rather wish to find ways of making those experiences more endurable.[8]

The view of the self as created in situ links up with the critique of the depersonalized self by a proponent of an experience-near methodology, anthropologist Unni Wikan. In her ethnography of Balinese culture, Wikan argues that individuals experience "double-anchored" selves (with public faces and private concerns) and that an individual's struggle to think well of herself always occurs in a world of lived predicaments and not in the world of theory, text, or cultural abstraction.[9] Refusing to rely on cultural abstractions to *read* how individuals experience their worlds enables us to take into account the particular circumstances of individuals, for lives are neither abstractions nor embodiments of culture. In other words, culture does not necessarily dictate actions. Rather, individuals facing actual predicaments employ cultural templates to manage real-life events.

Participants at Sa Chal often take an ideal view of the self (in this case, a self-reliant Korean American Buddhist self) and then attempt to embody or match that ideal vision. The participants in my own study can be said to abstract from and define the ideals of Buddhism as "finding and knowing one's mind," which they believe leads to self-reliance, and then they strive to embody those qualities. In so doing, they are engaged in a process of developing subjectivity and a positive sense of self. By viewing individuals in everyday life, we can see religious meanings are applied to everyday concerns. Thus the full value and function of religious behavior and identity formation cannot be ascertained without examining the compelling reasons that drive men and women to seek out religion in the first place. The failure to do so runs the risk of taking the public self as a true representation of a private internal self. A totalized view of religion eliminates the context from which to judge the validity of theories about the experiences of others. That is, the primacy of cultural and theoretical abstractions over lived experience hinders our ability to interpret the "insider's" perspective.

Public symbols and rituals are significant precisely because they speak to internal struggles. In many ways, the significance of religion in the life of the individual takes place in the realm of private meaning. Public and textual discourses like karma and Buddha Nature are thus deployed to make sense of the individual's private concerns. But how best does one attend to the deployment of cultural (and religious) meanings in private matters of utmost concern? It is in response to this question that an experience-near methodology that draws upon the individual's personal matters proves most useful to a study of the lives of Korean American Buddhists in Los Angeles.

THE PROBLEMATICS OF TELLING ONE'S STORY

Engaging people in a dialogue about their lives can be quite complicated, for there is a tendency to accept narrative as reflecting experience, an emphasis that obscures the role silence may play in self-expression and the ability to see where human endeavors to construct coherent selves fail.[10] A critique of narrative as reflecting experience plays an important role in an analysis of religion "on the ground," for we are forced to recognize that the individual's idealized accounts of the self (which we derive from interviews, life stories, and oral histories) provide only a partial account of the high points in life and not the low ones. In interpreting religious behavior, rituals, and self-narrations, we also must address multiple concerns often subsumed or kept below the surface.

Nonetheless, the very act of telling one's story and illustrating one's life according to a narrative schema can offer crucial insights into self-construction. By analyzing the language, models, emotions, and expressions that individuals bring to bear in describing their lives, we gain critical access to what that person deems relevant to his or her narrative. Viewing narrative as a restrospective organizing event in the "endless desire to think well of oneself" can help alleviate some of the misunderstandings that a

FINDING AND KNOWING ONE'S MIND

use of narrative as an unproblematic reflection of self-experience might bring about.[11] What is critically important here is that in telling their stories, Korean American Buddhists retrospectively come to a positive assertion of the self that silence cannot convey: by sharing a story they enact an ideal view of themselves through the performative method of speech.

Such a process enables us to see the value of the individual's creative actions to offset the dislocation of the self. That is, focusing on the fragmented nature of experience leads to the crucial question: How do individuals creatively respond to religion as they combat the fragmentation of everyday life?

BUDDHISM AND SELFHOOD

Scholars in the field of Buddhist studies such as Steven Collins and Melford Spiro have also problematized the notions of selfhood and identity within the tradition itself. In their studies of selflessness, both authors have shown that the Buddhist language of no-self as the definition of the *true* self often has the opposite effect of positing a self-identity in distinction to others. Collins draws attention to the dissonance between the self and representations of the self and argues that Buddhist teachings of no-self were consciously used in early Theravada literature to distinguish monks from their Brahmanic counterparts by inverting the Brahmanic equation of *atman* with Brahman.[12] In other words, the concept of no-self was both a philosophical discourse *and* a rhetorical device.

For the religious virtuoso, the language of no-self functions as a tool in the quest for enlightenment by indicating *how* a monk should view the self; both usages point to the performative nature of selflessness.

In a similar manner, anthropologist Melford Spiro argues against viewing Buddhists through the lens of selflessness lest we risk perpetuating Clifford Geertz's distinction between an individuated Western self and the unbounded non-Western self in which "others are included within the boundaries of the self"; this distinction is determined by the fact that "[m]ost of these studies assume that the cultural conceptions of the person are isomorphic with the actor's conceptions of the self, and . . . also assume that they are isomorphic with the actors' mental representations of their self, and with their self itself."[13] Yet, selves can be elusive and hide their intentions; thus subjectivities cannot be fully understood through an analysis of cultural symbols such as images, institutions, or behaviors alone. In other words, the actual internalization of nonself simply does not exist.

Rather than theorizing away the self-centered subject, I am more interested in showing how religion enables people to come to terms with factors that impinge on self-esteem and to resist the negative consequences that may be incurred from changes like immigration, the coming of age of one's children, illness, and relationship troubles. In examining how Korean men and women use the language of religion both to take responsibility for events that "go wrong" and, at the same time, to absolve themselves from responsibility for other events through the doctrine of karma, we can understand in detail how individuals cope with change. Individuals are drawn to religious models in their endeavors to find significance or meaning in their lives and to assert their identities. As such, a study of religious behavior can "explain how people translate the generalities of their orientations to the world into the specific resolutions of life's most difficult moments."[14]

In drawing together discourses of the self and identity, I approach the individual in action to understand how religion is lived and experienced in everyday life. My usage of the term "self" assumes that a person's quest for self-value and subjectivity is an improvisational project that compels a person to act with, through, and sometimes in resistance to others in different times and places. This improvisational view of the self entails seeing identity as fluid and multiply oriented, yet it also includes viewing the individual as possessing a coherent sense of self and purpose as he or she goes about composing a life of significance.[15] The person is thus approached as "embedded" and created in relationships that reveal the salience of religion in everyday life.

An embedded agency constructed in dialogue with others also refers to what feminist scholar Morwenna Griffiths calls a "web of identity." In proposing a theory of self based on interrelatedness, Griffiths argues:

> Self-identity is to be understood as a kind of web, the construction of which is partly under guidance from the self, though not in its control. Thus it is marked by competing constraints and influences which overlap and fuse. The theory is one that affirms that the creation of identity is a collective affair

FINDING AND KNOWING ONE'S MIND

in which each person has a valuable contribution to make. It is thus highly individualistic, in the sense that it values the individual, and does not hold that some are dispensable, or more dispensable, than others. Each individual creates her own identity, although she is constrained by circumstance in doing so.[16]

While religion is a form of coping and resistance, it can also be seen as a way of being in and acting on the world in the context of others. In developing subjectivity, Korean American Buddhists' lives are thus constrained and move in relational webs.

3
Sa Chal Context, Programs, and Demographics

Korean immigrants first arrived in the United States in the territory of Hawaii in 1903, the initial stage of the Korean exodus from the homeland.[1] Compelled to emigrate because of heavy taxation, corruption, and massive droughts that plagued Korea at the end of the nineteenth century, this group of 101 immigrants went to work on the sugar plantations. A ready labor pool to replace Japanese and Chinese migrant workers feared of inciting insurrections, Koreans were an attractive source of cheap workers for plantation owners.[2] Generally known as the beginning of the first wave of Korean immigration (1903–41), the period between 1903 and 1905 brought in a total of 7,226 immigrants consisting of 6,048 males, 637 females, and 541 children; of this original group, 40 percent are reported to have been Korean Christians strongly influenced by the presence of Christian missionaries in Korea.[3] For these original immigrants, Christianity symbolized both Western modernity and an escape from political and economic struggle.[4]

The first pool of immigrants from Korea consisted of government officials, ex-soldiers, scholars, students, Christian evangelists, a few Buddhist monks, political refugees, farmers, peasants, and servants.[5] Following this influx, approximately one thousand picture brides arrived between 1910 and 1924 to help correct the highly imbalanced gender ratio of the previous group. The arrival of young picture brides led to the birth of the first group of second-generation Korean Americans and "thus transformed the Koreans from sojourners to permanent settlers."[6] The final influx of Koreans during the first wave of immigration consisted of nine hundred students, intellectuals, and political exiles, a group which later formed the largest contingent of anti-Japanese occupation sentiment in the United States.[7] From 1924 until the end of World War II, immigration from Korea came to a standstill because of the Immigration Act of 1924, which set a maximum of 150,000 immigrations allowed into the United States per annum and deemed all aliens ineligible for citizenship barred from entry.

The second wave of immigration from Korea took place from 1946 to 1964 as a result of the War Brides Act of 1946 and the McCarran and Walter Act of 1952 that opened immigration to "alien wives and children of U.S. servicemen on a non-quota basis."[8] Between 1945 and the beginning of the Korean War in 1950, only about one hundred immigrants arrived from Korea. However, as a direct result of the Korean War, the second wave of immigration included 6,423 war brides, 5,348 orphans, and approximately 2,300 workers and students.[9]

The third wave of Korean immigration began with the passage of the Immigration Act of 1965, which dismantled the earlier national origins quota in favor of setting an annual limit of 120,000 immigrants from the Western Hemisphere and 170,000 from the Eastern Hemisphere. The period after 1965 witnessed the largest influx of Korean immigrants to the United States, primarily in the urban centers of Los Angeles, New York, and Chicago. A newly established preference system favored those immigrants who were in professional fields such as medicine and nursing and set in motion an immigration policy that deemed family members (parents, children, and spouses) exempt from this quota. As a result of this landmark immigration legislation, in the period between 1965 and 1979 over 264,000 immigrants from Korea arrived in the United States.[10] Between 1980 and 1996 about 484,338 Koreans entered the United States and there were approximately 42,362 return migrants.[11] At present, over 90 percent of the population of Korean Americans are post-1965 immigrants.[12]

The majority of first-generation Korean immigrants interviewed in this study arrived after the Immigration Act of 1965 removed "national origins" as the basis of immigration, and they make up the majority of Sa Chal's membership. The 1990 U.S. Census reported that there were 798,849 Koreans living in the United States. Of that population, 32.5 percent reside in California with about 200,000 in Los Angeles, approximately 25 percent of

SA CHAL CONTEXT, PROGRAMS, AND DEMOGRAPHICS

the total Korean population in the United States.[13] The 2000 Census reports 1,228,427 Koreans living in the United States.

HISTORICAL CONTEXT OF SA CHAL'S DEVELOPMENT IN THE UNITED STATES

While Korean Christian churches sprang up immediately after the initial wave of immigration to Hawaii in 1903 and played a central role in the adjustment of Korean immigrants to the United States, the first Buddhist temple was not established until 1972.[14] The first Korean monk to visit the United States was Seo Kyongbo Sunim, who arrived in New York to offer dharma talks to a primarily Western audience in 1964. In 1966, Kusan Sunim of the famed Songgwang-sa temple in South Korea traveled throughout Thailand, Vietnam, India, and Nepal and eventually arrived in Southern California in 1972 to establish the first Korean Buddhist temple in Carmel, California—Sanbo Sa. Kusan Sunim was also responsible for establishing the first foreign branch of Songgwong-sa temple in Koreatown, Los Angeles. This temple, known as Koryo Sa, was established in 1980 and has a fully Korean clientele.[15] In 1972, the famed Zen master Seung Sahn Sunim arrived in eastern United States and opened the first Providence Zen Center.

According to Eui-Young Yu's 1988 study, there were three main avenues for the growth of Korean Buddhism to the United States: (1) the work of individual Zen teachers, with a mainly Western audience, (2) research and teaching on Korean Buddhism in America, introduced by scholars teaching in the United States, and (3) the increasing establishment of Buddhist temples for Korean immigrants following the Immigration Act of 1965. Sa Chal belongs in this final category. The first temple in Los Angeles established for first-generation Korean immigrants was Tahl Ma Sa in 1973. This temple complex replicates traditional Son temples in Korea and offers services for adherents on Sunday mornings. Fifteen more temples developed out of Tahl Ma Sa. The main difference between the Son centers targeting Westerners and the Korean Buddhist temples aimed at Korean-speaking worshippers is that the activities of the Son centers focus on meditational practices while Korean ethnic temples follow a more lay oriented model of a Sunday *pophoe* (worship service), devotional worship, and sociocultural exchange.[16] In the ethnic Buddhist temples, scant attention is paid to sitting meditation, the practice considered central in the Western-oriented Son Centers.

In the midst of the early introduction of Korean Buddhism in the United States, Sa Chal was established on March 10, 1974, after a Buddhist priest was invited from Korea to serve as the first abbot.[17] Located in a small apartment complex on South Ardmore Avenue, Sa Chal began to spread the Chogye order's lay Buddhism among Koreans living in America. Expressly opened to engage in missionary work in the United States, Sa Chal has served the Korean American community for almost thirty years. The current abbot, Abbot Lee, was installed November 1975 following the retirement of the previous one. Born in Korea in 1937, Abbot Lee became a monk at fifteen, attended the Buddhist Dongguk University in Seoul, and eventually established many Buddhist youth service and leadership programs aimed at modernizing Buddhism. While he did not originally intend to establish residence in the United States, he was drawn to Los Angeles to resolve tensions that had emerged under the first abbot. Nonetheless, Abbot Lee has remained the head of Sa Chal and has displayed a continued emphasis on the modernization of Buddhism to adapt to the needs of the Korean American community and the larger American landscape. Some of these changes include the use of pews rather than meditation cushions, the introduction of a choir and organ, and the presentation of weekly sermons. These transformations in worship are not, however, unique to Korean forms of Buddhism in the United States; they are also widely found in urban areas of South Korea. Since 1975, Sa Chal has enjoyed the unique position of having consistent leadership since the temple operates independently of Chogye order headquarters in Seoul.

Unlike many Chogye temples in Korea, Sa Chal is not directly under the administration of the main Chogye-Sa Administrative Headquarters established in 1955.[18] This main headquarters serves as the national administrative unit overseeing the twenty-five head monasteries in Korea and a number of Chogye-affiliated temples in the United States. Since the headquarters does not provide the abbot with a salary or financial backing, Sa Chal operates according to the particular needs of the Korean American community (e.g., by offering English-language classes, social services, and regular weekly services) and is overseen by a board of trustees. Resident monks are not offered any salaries and so rely, like many Buddhist monastics, on the generous support of the local laity. This accommodation to the Korean American community is, of course, necessary for the temple's continued viability. Other Korean Buddhist temples in the Los Angeles area, like Koryo Sa, function on a rotating system, in which a head monk is brought from the Seoul headquarters to preside over a temple for a number of years and then is replaced by another head monk. As such, membership at this temple remains small, with only seventy to one hundred registered members. Because of Sa Chal's consistent leadership over twenty-five years, the temple has enjoyed a stable flow of worshippers and a steady membership of about 720 registered families.

The first ten years of its development, from 1974 to 1984, witnessed a period of stabilization for the Buddhist community. During this early stage of growth, many monks were invited from Korea to preside over commemorative functions and offer dharma talks to the new immigrant community. In 1979, Sa Chal began to broadcast Buddhist teachings by way of the first local Buddhist radio show, airing every Monday twice a day. During the same year, the temple purchased one hundred cemetery plots in the nearby city of Glendale to offer to its worshippers for a fee. In 1986 the temple administration purchased its current 45,000 square foot four-story building and the Korean American Buddhist Community Service Center was established to provide social services to new Korean immigrants. In 1992, the abbot founded a Buddhist youth group in order to teach the Buddhist children.

For the past five years, Sa Chal has focused more on outreach to the Korean American community by establishing a branch temple in San Diego and a Korean American Buddhist program on local cable television. In 1997, the branch campus of Eastern Mountain Buddhist College in Korea was established at Sa Chal with fifty-four students studying to become lay Buddhist "missionaries"—those certified by the college to spread the Buddha dharma in the United States. Also established in 1997 was the Diamond Noodle Factory in North Korea, the funds for which are raised by the One Korea Buddhist Movement, USA, headed by the temple's abbot. In January 1999, Sa Chal increased its outreach to the local community by opening a Buddhist bookstore, the only one of its kind in Koreatown, and reconstruct-

SA CHAL CONTEXT, PROGRAMS, AND DEMOGRAPHICS

ing its first floor space into the Lotus Art Gallery, aimed at bringing more local residents to the temple. The latest venture initiated by Abbot Lee has been the first Buddhist preschool for local children, established in the summer of 2002.

DESCRIPTION OF NEIGHBORHOOD AND FACILITIES

Sa Chal is located in a mix of residential dwellings (some multi-family and some single-family houses) comprising both Korean and Latino residents. There are also many commercial businesses in the area such as Korean restaurants, Central American grocery stores, and variety shops. Across the street from the temple are three other religious centers—a Korean church, a Protestant church, and a Latino storefront church. If one moves east down Third Street, the area becomes much more Latino oriented, with markets exhibiting signs in Spanish. The temple is north of the heart of Koreatown. Yet, interestingly, in today's Koreatown most of the residents are no longer Korean but a mixture of Latino immigrants. It is only the newer Korean immigrants who tend to live in Koreatown for the first few years of their settlement and the elderly Koreans who can find affordable housing in the neighborhood.[19] There has been a steady rate of dispersal to the suburbs among Koreans living in Los Angeles following the attainment of economic stability. In fact, the number of Koreans living in the area designated Koreatown has dropped from one-third in 1972 to only about 18 percent of Koreans living in Southern California.[20] Although Koreans have steadily moved out of Koreatown, there is still a high percentage of those who continue to work in the ethnic enclave and attend religious services in the area.

Located on the northeastern corner of Oxford and Third Streets, Sa Chal is a highly visible seafoam green temple housed in a 45,000 square foot building. The first floor contains a small theater space, the Korean American Buddhist Community Service Center, a printing facility that is used both commercially and in-house, a guitar shop, a Korean acupuncture office, and a Taekwondo center. All of these shops are leased out, with rent paid directly to Sa Chal to offset operating costs. Also housed on the first floor is a classroom used by the Sunday Buddhist school for children, choir practice, and English classes during the week. The second floor includes two Buddha halls, one containing a golden Amita Buddha statue used primarily for worshipping the deceased and one containing three Buddha statues—a golden Sakyamuni Buddha flanked by a Medicine Buddha on the left and an Amita Buddha on the right. This room is used primarily for prostrations, silent meditation, chanting, and prayer and also contains a hundred tiny Buddha statues each lit up with a candle-shaped light bulb. Numerous paper lotus lanterns hang from the ceiling adorned with the names of family members and prayers made during the annual Buddha's birthday celebrations.

In the main dharma hall where Sunday services are held, an eight-foot golden Sakyamuni Buddha statue stands behind the pulpit atop an altar where worshippers can light incense and offer flowers and donations during the service. Along the wall behind the golden Buddha statue rests a huge engraved Buddha image which, when viewed up close, consists of hundreds of smaller Buddhas. On Friday evenings, the dharma hall is also used for special lectures. The dining hall houses a large seated wooden Kwan Um Posal image (many-headed Avalokitesvara Bodhisattva of Compassion) that sits in front of a painting of the same deity. At the foot of this image rests a small altar containing fresh flowers, incense, candles, and a donation box. The dining room has about fifteen long tables and folding chairs for the fellowship luncheon and is adjacent to a large kitchen. Inside the kitchen, a small table is usually set up for the monks and special guests to eat at in privacy. Off to the corner of the building in a separate hallway are residences for three monks and one empty room with a table for the weekly Buddhist Youth Group. The third floor of the temple houses the business office, and in the attic the abbot has his private apartment, which contains a study/library and opens onto his makeshift rooftop garden where he grows plants during his free time.

Sa Chal is the largest Korean Buddhist temple of the Chogye Order of Son [Zen] Buddhism in United States. Chogye itself is the largest consolidated school of Son in Korea and consists of both monastics and lay people.[21] In residence are four Buddhist monks from Korea who remain at the temple the year around. The administrative and ritual head of the temple is Abbot Lee.[22] The temple's support staff consists of the abbot's married younger brother, who is in charge of printing up weekly dharma pamphlets and helping with administrative tasks associated with the Buddhist college. Another lay worshipper organizes the weekly Buddhist radio show and hands out pamphlets during worship services. Another layman acts as announcer during the general worship service. The human service staff consists of a librarian for the Korean American Buddhist Cultural Library, a volunteer English teacher for adults who holds classes Tuesday through Friday, and the administrative director of the Korean American Buddhist Community Service Center. There are also two administrative coordinators for the Eastern Mountain Buddhist College branch campus housed within Sa Chal. Informal volunteer staff at the temple includes a rotating list of five to ten first-generation Korean women who prepare the Sunday fellowship luncheon. Two women in their sixties usually help the monks prepare food for themselves on weekdays and provide services such as arranging special foods for weekly memorial services for the deceased.

Sa Chal is a remarkable institution in that it has one foot in Korea and one foot in the United States; yet without this institutional vision the temple would not continue to be a viable community organization. One of its main activities centers on *pogyo* (referred to hereafter as "dissemination"), which Abbot Lee sees as one of the most essential jobs of Sa Chal.[23] Abbot Lee came to the United States because he thought of it as "an extremely democratic country open to all religions."[24] Thus he followed in the footsteps of pioneer monks Kusan Sunim and Seung Sahn Sunim. Seung Sahn Sunim is a well-known figure in both the Korean and Western worlds, for his ability to speak English has provided him with a diverse group of followers and he has concentrated on sitting meditation without singling out a particular ethnic group. Abbot Lee, on the other hand, has focused on helping the Korean American community, and since he does not speak English his ministry is tailored to this community alone. He has a much more public face than many of the other monks in the Korean American community and has transformed the temple from a small Buddhist institution to a renowned center with a newspaper, radio show, television broadcast, Buddhist cultural store, and now the Lotus Gallery.

Sa Chal has transitioned into its next stage of development where lay people are beginning to take on new roles in the congregation, and the temple continues to develop into a transnational site to administer to the needs of its primarily first-generation followers. With a view to the homeland of

SA CHAL CONTEXT, PROGRAMS, AND DEMOGRAPHICS

Korea and a view toward the future in the United States, Sa Chal provides for the social, psychological, and religious needs of the Korean American community. Its transnational focus keeps first-generation members in touch with their homeland (regardless of whether or not they ever return to Korea) by hosting numerous monks from Korea to give lectures and training to its members. In addition, Abbot Lee travels to and from Korea frequently, bringing news from the major Chogye order centers there. Although Sa Chal is not officially administered by the main headquarters in Seoul, Abbot Lee considers this relationship crucial for the development of Buddhism in the West. In addition, his close contact with Korean monks gives him even more legitimacy as a monk in the United States, since he does have important contacts with the Chogye headquarters. In this way, the temple mediates the process of immigrant adaptation, yet unlike many churches and temples Sa Chal also takes on a transnational role which may impede the process of full-scale assimilation.

EASTERN MOUNTAIN BUDDHIST COLLEGE

One result of the abbot's desire to disseminate Buddhist teachings in the United States was the establishment in 1997 of a Los Angeles branch of the Seoul-based Eastern Mountain Buddhist College. Administered through the main headquarters of the Chogye order, the college offers a two-year certificate course in Buddhist Studies to lay members. In addition to attending lectures by visiting Chogye scholar monks from Korea, students listen to taped lectures of the Korean monastic college professors, read textbooks published in Korea, and attend weekly Friday night lectures in sutra studies, Korean Buddhist history, Buddhist practice, and general Buddhist studies.[25] Currently, this branch school has over fifty students drawn from LA's twenty-five Korean Buddhist temples. Here students are given a rigorous course of study that accommodates their work schedules and are taught the essentials of Buddhism as established by the main headquarters in Korea. In addition to providing knowledge and understanding of Buddhism for practitioners, the school is part of Abbot Lee's strategy to again spread Korean Buddhism in the United States in response to the increasing numbers of Koreans who convert to Christianity.

By training Korean lay members in sutra studies and meditation and providing them with opportunities to obtain certificate degrees in Buddhist studies, Sa Chal is working to create its own staff of learned Buddhist missionaries in America. The mission of the Eastern Mountain Buddhist College administrators is to provide a fundamental education in Buddhist theory, doctrine, and practice that the laity can use to spread the dharma to others. While Sa Chal is not focused on training monks and nuns in the United States, its administrators are interested in training laywomen and men to become successful missionaries of the dharma.

THE KOREAN AMERICAN BUDDHIST COMMUNITY SERVICE CENTER

Abbot Lee has worked since the mid-seventies to increase the level of services offered to the laity with the understanding that his temple must be flexible enough to meet the needs of immigrants to a new culture. Thus, when Abbot Lee came to the United States in 1974 to take over as the abbot *(chuji sunim)*, he worked to establish the nonprofit Korean American Buddhist Community Service Center, which officially received nonprofit status in 1986. The center offers advice on housing, employment, SSI applications, and health care to recent Korean immigrants. It also offers a Korean cultural library, English classes to prepare for citizenship, and marriage counseling. This non-profit service center is quite remarkable within the Korean community, for there are few religious-based nonprofit social service organizations established by and for Korean immigrants in the local Koreatown area even among the more numerous Korean Christian churches. The main role of the center is to enable a smoother transition into mainstream American culture by providing psychological, economic, and social assistance to all who come through its doors. Yet, despite its visibility and openness to all who come, the center is underutilized; in fact, in an average month there are only about ten to twelve incoming clients.

LAY AND MONASTIC RELATIONS

As a fellow immigrant to the United States in 1974 who just recently became a U.S. citizen in 1997, Abbot Lee is very much involved in everyday relations with the laity of his Korean American congregation. Under his guidance, the temple has worked toward lay centrality and ownership of worship by training lay people in traditional practices such as leading recitations with the *moktak* (wooden gong) and leading prayers during services. There are three reasons for this continued interaction with Sa Chal's laity. First, like many other immigrant religious leaders, Abbot Lee is well aware that to continue attracting laity to Sa Chal the temple must meet the needs of the immigrant population. In the case of Sa Chal, access to religious and community services on an open schedule provides the laity with opportunities to ask the monks for advice, check out books from the library, and interact with other Koreans outside of home and workplace. Second, for the monastics, the laity are an essential component in their desire to missionize and spread the dharma to a Korean audience and then to a larger American audience. By training the laity in Buddhist rituals, the abbot hopes they will take on the further responsibility of teaching their own families about Buddhism. Finally, by including worshippers in the ritual processes they are recognized as leaders in the congregation. The structure of the services and the temple's adult education program demonstrate Sa Chal's seriousness about incorporating the efforts of the laity into the larger rhetoric of missionization in order to fulfill the Chogye order's desire to promote Korean Buddhism in the United States.

For the second generation, Sa Chal is looking toward a future in which young Korean Americans will be well trained in Chogye Buddhism. The abbot, like most of the members at Sa Chal, is well aware that for Korean Buddhism to survive in the United States the temple must reach the younger generations. The Buddhist Youth Group, Sunday school, and numerous cultural events at the temple are aimed at increasing the young persons' consciousness about Korean Buddhism and fostering their support. The first Sunday of every month, students attend the larger Buddhist worship service held in Korean. Since many students can speak and understand Korean, they are able to help the few U.S. born students who have trouble understanding the service. The second and third Sundays consist of lectures by teachers who introduce the students to textual readings and Buddhist history. The final Sunday of the month is a free day for students to organize a social event such as a picnic or skiing trip. Part of the reason for this free day, according to the abbot's informal secretary and translator, is that "we do not want to force the kids to practice like the Christians who make the kids study the Bible all the time. We want the kids to enjoy themselves and read whatever sutras they want and *choose* Buddhism."

Critical to the success of Sa Chal and Buddhism among the second generation is an awareness of their needs. For youth at Sa Chal, the main needs are social cohesion and ethnic solidarity and identity. Youth-group teachings are provided in English and special care is taken to integrate the youth into the weekly events at the temple. The Buddhist Youth Group functions through the help of elected student leaders who have often expressed the need for the temple to provide them a basic knowledge of Buddhist thought and practice. It is training that they claim they need in the midst of Christian student groups and their own devout Christian friends who often try to convert them. Confronted with similar competition from Korean Christians, the temple seeks to make Buddhism socially viable. This situation is further complicated by the fact that most Koreans in the United States have converted to Christianity, rendering Buddhists a religious minority. While Buddhists in Korea are still counted among the religious majority, this inversion of status in the United States exerts more pressure on the staff and devout laity at Sa Chal to missionize and develop Buddhist faith among the offspring of temple members. Without adequate cultural understanding, language fluency, and reminders of Buddhism for later generations, Sa Chal will not be able to make the transition from a primarily first-generation congregation to a second-generation one.

ROLE OF RELIGION FOR THE KOREAN IMMIGRANT COMMUNITY

Daily life at this urban Buddhist temple differs greatly from that of its sister Buddhist temples in Korea, particularly since Sa Chal has a regular monastic staff of four monks, or *sunim,* rather than an entire group of Korean monks in various states of training and practice. The distinctive character of Sa Chal is its lay centrality; in other words, daily life for Sa Chal monks revolves around attending to matters for its Korean American congregation rather than remaining isolated from the quotidian concerns of lay life. It is not uncommon to see one of the four monks visiting with lay practitioners who may stop by the temple on a weekday afternoon to pray in the Buddha hall and then have lunch with the abbot and other monks.

As the largest of the twenty-five Korean temples in Southern California, Sa Chal is host each year to the annual spring *Puchonim Oshinnal,* or the Vesak celebration of the Buddha's birthday, attended by the laity of all Korean American temples in Los Angeles County. Religious events such as the Buddha's birthday celebration also highlight ethnic culture and serve as a rallying point for the various co-ethnics in the city. The annual Buddha's birthday celebration typically is held in late April or early May and includes traditional Korean drumming and shamanic dance performances, a cross-temple choir performance, a young women's traditional Korean dance troupe, and a children's group playing traditional Korean instruments. Interspersed throughout these cultural events are periods of meditation and prayer held by the various monks and abbots as well as joint rituals of meditation, chanting, and beating of the *moktak.* In other words, the auspicious event of the Buddha's birthday in Los Angeles also becomes a period of ethnic celebration and preservation.

Since the Buddha's birthday celebration is the largest of all Buddhist celebrations by the Korean temples, the annual Korean ceremonies have an audience of approximately one thousand people, many of whom do not attend temple services on a regular basis. According to members of Sa Chal, this relative freedom of attendance is one of the positive aspects of the temple, resulting in less stress and guilt. The participants I spoke with often cited Buddhist independence and karma as the reasons why the temple was less rigorous in requiring consistent attendance, for the pathway to enlightenment was considered by many Sa Chal members as "up to them." Thus, while many participants usually attended on a regular basis, others felt that since Buddhism was about self-understanding, they were free to practice and worship at home if they chose.

Community rituals at Sa Chal can be understood as invoking memories of the homeland and reinvigorating community bonds. Korean American participation at the Buddha's birthday celebrations demonstrates that rituals have an important role in sustaining community identity through prayer, recitation, and song as well as an important part in the care and respect for the Buddha. While Sa Chal can be seen as a center celebrating Korean ethnicity, it also contributes to the renewal of self-esteem and healing for many Korean immigrants who may feel alienated in the host country. Through public rituals like the annual Year-End Celebration (which I observed in December 1998), Korean Buddhists are brought in communion as they sing the Three Refuges and recite the Heart Sutra, a ritual that sustains and renews the community by reorienting it toward its religious goals.

During this celebratory event, worshippers are encouraged to reflect on the past year's events and renew the community through a candle-lighting ceremony in which each member is bonded to the other by lighting his or her candle. When all the candles have been lit, the abbot offers a prayer to renew the communal spirit of the congregation and to provide members with the ability to strengthen themselves and clear away any negative karma of the past year. By lighting the candles and placing them on a wooden altar at the feet of the Buddha, the community heals the sorrows of the previous year and looks to the future for happiness, good fortune, and the strength to act without selfishness. A similar candle-lighting ceremony of regeneration takes place on the first Sunday of every month, when members are encouraged to renew their lay precepts.

SA CHAL SUNDAY SERVICES

On Sundays, events and services take place at Sa Chal from early morning until late afternoon. The following is the listed Sunday schedule:

9:00–10:45 A.M.	Prayer
9:00–10:45 A.M.	Korean School
10:55 A.M.–12:45 P.M.	General Buddhist Service
10:55 A.M.–12:45 P.M.	Sunday School
12:50 P.M.–1:30 P.M.	Lunch Time
1:15 P.M.–2:00 P.M.	Chorus
1:45 P.M.–3:15 P.M.	Sutra Reading
3:20 P.M.–4:00 P.M.	Family Worship (Introduction of New Members)

The early morning prayer group meets prior to the general worship service and is usually attended by twenty-five to thirty women wearing traditional gray Buddhist lay robes in the Sakyamuni Buddha trio dharma hall with Sakyamuni in the center of the altar flanked by the Medicine Buddha on the left and the Amita Buddha on the right. This prayer period includes sutra recitation and ritual prostrations led by the ritual monk. Although most of the worshippers at this service remain for the general service, there are usually five or six members who attend only the early morning service so that they can make it to work on time. The prayer and ritual service usually runs until 10:45 A.M., after which participants adjourn to the kitchen for some coffee and chatting before they enter the main dharma hall for the general Buddhist worship service. The Korean School is run primarily by one of the younger monks for the second-generation children between the ages of four and twelve.

The general worship service takes place in the main dharma hall, a large room with a golden standing Buddha image in the front. An altar at its feet holds flower and incense offerings. A typical service at Sa Chal begins with recitation of the Three Refuges, sung by all worshippers while standing in front of the golden Sakyamuni statue. Worshippers sing: "I take refuge in the Buddha, the Dharma, and the Sangha" in unison with the choir. After singing each of the Refuges, the ritual monk strikes the wooden gong and all the worshippers bow simultaneously in front of the Buddha. Each meeting of Sunday worshippers begins with this ritual recitation and signals the unity of all Buddhists. Taking refuge can be seen as the main ritual and belief system that brings together all Buddhists and marks off the time for communal worship at the temple.

Following the Three Refuges, worshippers move immediately into a recitation of the *Banya Shimgyong*, or the Heart Sutra, in abbreviated form. During this part of the service, worshippers stand with hands in prayer as they recite the sutra from memory, and some provide a more melodic recitation. Afterward, the oldest ritual monk who sits in the front of the room puts down the *moktak* and picks up the *chukpi*, a large wooden stick used in Son meditation to aid meditators in their practice. After the *chukpi* is struck four times, practitioners fall silent in meditation, which lasts for just a few minutes. The end of the abbreviated meditation session is symbolized by the monk striking the *chukpi* three more times and then the announcer/emcee informs the congregation that a prayer will be offered and that the abbot will give his *sulbop* (dharma talk).

The first three parts of the ritual sequence (the refuges, sutra recitation, and meditation) adhere to the traditional model of Chogye order Buddhism in Korea, although by standing rather than sitting. The remainder of the service, however, differs dramatically from the Chogye tradition since it is focused on active lay participation during portions of the service. Thus following the meditation session, two lay members usually walk to the front of the room to offer prayers and read a section of the Buddhist compendium while introducing the abbot's dharma talk. The abbot's sermons usually offer guidelines for daily living with little emphasis on explicating the meaning of sutra passages, a tendency that many male members of the congregation criticize.[26] During one talk the abbot discussed the importance of prayer and meditation with a pure heart and mind in order to be reborn in the Buddha's paradise, and he outlined the everyday causes of illness and advised the laity to take care of their physical health. He addressed this part of his sermon to the senior citizens in the pews, urging them not to eat too much or too little, lest they become susceptible to disease and the common cold. Through earnest prayer to the Buddha, he continued, worshippers can be healed physically, mentally, and spiritually.

During his sermon, the abbot took special care to elicit responses from the congregants and devoted most of the sermon to connecting Buddhist doctrines with contemporary matters, making the talk very personal by mentioning how he treats himself when ill. On a separate occasion, the abbot gave a sermon about the importance of praying with a clear mind and pure heart to help the congregants overcome the difficulties faced by living in a different cultural environment. By acknowledging their specific immigrant conditions, Abbot Lee offers them a self-generated means of overcoming the types of suffering specific to the majority of the congregation.

Following the period of the *sulbop* (dharma talk), the choir offers a hymn in praise of the Buddha as new worshippers and visitors are announced and welcomed and the abbot circles the congregation handing out Buddhist prayer beads to all newcomers. Worshippers line up to receive flowers from two volunteer lay people. Flowers are then offered to the Buddha in front of the main altar with a bow and short prayers as the worshipper places an offering in a donation box and then bows one more time in front of the Buddha. Once gathered back at their seats, worshippers sing the Four Vows, which consist of the following four verses: "I vow to cut all defilements; I

SA CHAL CONTEXT, PROGRAMS, AND DEMOGRAPHICS

vow to save all sentient beings; I vow to learn the Buddha Dharma; and I vow to attain enlightenment." Following the vows, members then turn to face the other congregants on the other side of the hall, greet them, and wish them well with the refrain, "May you attain Buddhahood in this lifetime." The service thus concluded, members gather up their belongings as all the grandmothers dash off to drop their purses on the tables to be first in line for the fellowship luncheon.

Much of Sa Chal's devotional life occurs inside the walls of the Buddha Trio hall. Votive lanterns dedicated to the temple members are one of the main informal devotional practices for the laity. In Sa Chal, these votive lanterns consists of rows and rows of miniature images of Sakyamuni Buddha, each containing its own votive light (bulb). By donating approximately three hundred dollars to the temple, a family can have a votive lantern lit in their name for the express purpose of attaining enlightenment in this lifetime, generating positive merit, and receiving a blessing from the monks. In return for these offerings, the monks bless the images each morning and evening with a recitation of the Thousand Hand Sutra *(Chunsoogyung)* chanted to the beat of the *moktak*. The morning blessing usually takes place from 4:30 to 6 A.M. and the evening recitation at approximately 7 P.M. Although the lay patron is absent, the resident monk still performs the daily ritual blessing.

During the week, the Amita dharma hall is filled with the sounds of the wooden gong as the monks chant sutras and bless the souls of the deceased ancestors. Large plates of Korean style sweet rice cakes, fresh and dried fruits, and vegetable dishes are offered during this service as sweet-smelling incense wafts through the air. According to traditional Confucian customs, this memorial responsibility belongs to the eldest son of a family. While many contemporary Korean Christians have dispensed with these Confucian ancestor rites of *chaesa*, Buddhists continue to perform the death-day anniversary for one's parents and elders.

ANCESTOR RITES FOR MRS. LEE'S MOTHER-IN-LAW

In April 1999, I had the good fortune to observe the ancestor rites conducted by Mrs. Lee, a member of temple, and her husband. The *chaesa* service was conducted in honor of Mrs. Lee's mother-in-law in front of the Amita Buddha altar in the late afternoon. A table full of various fruits and vegetables on white plates lined up on silver trays was placed in front of the altar space along with a makeshift ancestral tablet constructed of gold painted wood with the name of the deceased written in classical characters. Spread out in front of the Buddha were traditional Korean dishes such as prepared spinach, bean sprouts, pancakes, tofu, cooked acorn jelly, pan-fried noodles, and plates of fruit such as bananas, apples, grapes, dried persimmon, dates, and grapefruit. In addition, the Lee family had laid out traditional Korean white rice cakes covered with yellow bean and sweet white rice cakes made with sugar, pine nuts, and chestnuts. According to the Lees, there are no foods that one must set out. The importance lies in providing foods that the deceased particularly liked.

In a few moments, Mr. Lee donned a black Buddhist robe and was seated on a brown meditation cushion placed atop a woven plastic bamboo mat. As he sat down, he began reading from the ritual recitation book that lay open on a traditional Korean bookstand on the floor. As he recited sutras, he also beat the wooden clacker. Throughout the half-hour service, Mrs. Lee moved from bowing to pouring cups of symbolic wine from a clean silver teapot into a small silver cup which was rotated twice around the incense burner in front of the Buddha and offered up to the deceased. After emptying the previously poured cup of wine into a different teapot, she slowly poured a small amount into the silver cup, paused, poured again, paused, and poured again.

Mr. Lee continued to chant and beat the wooden clacker and his wife went off to the kitchen to pick up the soup and rice that were part of the ceremony. For the next five minutes, the two members chanted in unison the name of Amita Buddha for the sake of the deceased. While chanting, Mrs. Lee rotated a pair of silver chopsticks from one food offering to the other, each time symbolically tapping the silver chopsticks into an empty silver bowl six times before placing the chopsticks on another offering plate. As this rotation continued, Mr. Lee recited sutras. Later, during the ritual proceedings, Mrs. Lee came in with the hot bowl of soup and rice that were placed on the left side of the altar and offered with a bow to the deceased. Following this process, both husband and wife bowed in unison toward the Buddha with their hands placed in front of their foreheads. After this was through, Mr. Lee offered a glass of wine to his mother and proclaimed, "It is finished now." Mr. Lee then left the room and his wife began the next part of the ritual.

Taking an empty silver bowl, Mrs. Lee took a piece of each offering and placing them in the bowl, which was then filled with soup to symbolize the consumption of these offerings by her mother-in-law. She then removed each plate of food from the altar and placed them into a cart and wheeled the cart back into the kitchen, where she began to divide up the food for distribution to various members of the temple. This distribution and consumption was ritually necessary and important for merit-making. The main purpose of the ritual was filial piety and reciprocity. Although the Lees refer to this practice of worship as *chaesa,* or ancestor rites in general, it is in fact related to a Buddhist rite known as *shishik,* which is "offered to the spirits of the departed along with sutra reading and the intoning of Buddha's teachings in order to expedite their entry into Sukhavati."[27] Sukhavati, or the Pureland, is the realm of bliss presided over by Amita Buddha where individuals are thought to be reborn and guaranteed enlightenment and liberation from all suffering.

The monks at Sa Chal perform two general types of ancestor worship—the forty-nine day ceremony following a family member's death and the annual anniversary of the dead.[28] These rituals include the careful selection and presentation of specially prepared foods lined up in rows before the Amita Buddha altar, the burning of incense, bowing to the ancestors, and the recitation of Buddhist sutras. For many Sa Chal members, monks officiate at this rite of ancestor worship. For a single family, the forty-nine day ritual at Sa Chal can cost up to $2,000 and a *chaesa* rite for the anniversary day of the dead ancestor may cost between $300 and $500. These monetary gifts to the temple are one of its main sources of income. According to some temple members, Sa Chal has also effectively replaced the eldest son as the ritual officiant for ancestor worship for many Koreans and offers this service to those who request it, regardless of religious affiliation. In this manner, the temple accommodates its practices to the needs of its patrons and clients.[29]

While many families have their names engraved on plaques in the dharma halls and on the small votive Buddhas and request *chaesa* rites for their deceased family members, others wish to donate anonymous gifts to the temple in varying amounts. Thus each week small cash donations are made to the donation boxes placed below the Kwan Um Posal statue in the dining area, where fresh flowers and fragrant incense are usually laid out. The temple also receives cash and check donations of special thanks offered in gratitude for good fortunes that befell the donor. In addition, there are anonymous gifts of thanks to be used by the temple without restriction. These gifts are given freely and often anonymously, although some members' names will appear in the weekly newsletter as a sign of appreciation for their generosity. All of the above gifts are usually donated to the temple as a form of *dana*, or giving for merit and blessings.

LAY ASSOCIATIONS

One of the many associations developed for the laity at Sa Chal is the Pureland Association, a lay group of seniors over the age of sixty. This group was developed by Abbot Lee as a means of maintaining a sense of community among seniors and providing comfort, food, and services to the sick and lonely. Membership in the Pureland Association requires a one-time donation of fifty dollars and monthly gifts of five dollars per household. With these funds, members are able to provide in-house visits to seniors who are bedridden, visits to hospitals and convalescent homes, payment for medical services and medicines when necessary, and transportation to and from the temple for those who require assistance. In addition, Pureland Association members are entitled to purchase one of the temple's fifty plots in a nearby cemetery. If a member dies, the other members will often arrange for a funeral service and burial at the cemetery with the help of the resident monks. In addition, Sa Chal monks will also provide the forty-nine day ceremony and the annual anniversary rite for the deceased.

The Pureland Association has enabled many Korean American seniors to establish bonds with other Buddhists in the Los Angeles area, thus providing a necessary social connection, friendship, and encouragement for those who are ill and a means of coping with aging. By giving them a sense of security about having a proper Buddhist funeral, seniors who live alone

SA CHAL CONTEXT, PROGRAMS, AND DEMOGRAPHICS

can also take responsibility for their own care. Through informal visits and food delivery, members of the association help to comfort and encourage others and at the same time take on new responsibilities that may also enhance their self-esteem and sense of purpose in later life.

GENERAL SA CHAL MEMBERSHIP

Sa Chal has 720 registered families in its membership roster. While not all of these families attend the temple on a weekly basis, they are nonetheless an important part of the temple's organizational structure. Members are organized into twenty-four lay groups. Each group consists of a number of families, a strategy used to keep members in contact with one another through the aid of an association chair and also to help the temple keep track of important events and news from each family. In addition, all members are requested to volunteer to serve other members during the fellowship luncheon following each Sunday's dharma service, although it is always the women who prepare and serve this meal. All temple members are expected to attend weekly dharma services (although many do not) and volunteer or participate in one of the following: the Buddhist Youth Group, the Sunday school, the chorus, or the afternoon sutra reading and lay "training" sessions.

According to the abbot of Sa Chal, all of the members at the temple are ethnic Koreans, 93 percent of whom are Korean-born first-generation immigrants. Forty percent are between the ages of twenty-five and forty, 40 percent are over forty, 15 percent are between ages ten and twenty-five (which indicates that the second-generation and college-age students are either not attending any temple or are perhaps worshipping elsewhere in churches), and 5 percent are under ten years of age. In terms of the economic and professional status of members, the abbot states that about 60 percent are business owners and entrepreneurs (shop, restaurant, etc.), 20 percent are white collar workers (secretaries, managers, clerks, etc.), 15 percent are blue collar workers (factory work, delivery jobs, etc.), and about 5 percent are skilled professionals such as doctors, lawyers, and engineers. The above percentages do not include those who are retired or unemployed. From what I have observed, approximately 75 percent of members are female.

SA CHAL CONTEXT, PROGRAMS, AND DEMOGRAPHICS

FEMALE INTERVIEWEE DEMOGRAPHICS

Through snowballing methods of interviewing, I met and spoke extensively with twenty-five Buddhist women at Sa Chal in interviews lasting forty-five minutes to two hours. While I originally had no difficulty being introduced to and meeting women on my own during my first six months of field research at the temple, I required the active assistance of members at the temple to schedule anyone for the interviews. Thanks to the first few women who were interested and willing enough to spend an hour talking with me about their experiences in the United States and their religious practices, I was able to meet more and more female interviewees. Often, women would persuade fellow chorus members and friends to spend some time talking to me and would even explain to them some of the topics we discussed during the interviews in order to ease their tensions. What I noticed was that when I began the interview process with my female participants, they relaxed right away and were extremely forthcoming about their views and details of their lives. One of the obstacles I encountered during the two years I spent at the temple was that even though I would schedule an interview at a specific time, I would often be kept waiting an extra hour or two around the temple as the women finished their lunches, visited with friends, or just plain forgot about our interview times. Luckily, during these moments of waiting, I was usually able to strike up a conversation with other members of the temple, help around the kitchen, or observe rituals taking place in the dharma halls.

Of the twenty-five women with whom I conducted interviews, the majority (sixteen) were between forty and fifty-nine, two were younger than forty, and seven were above the age of sixty. There was a relatively high level of education among the women, with four having received graduate school degrees and nine who had college degrees. Twenty-four of the twenty-five women had children, and of this group, fifteen were married although four lived apart from their spouses, who usually remained in Korea. Of the eleven women who were employed, six were in the field of Eastern medicine or involved in small business ventures. The remaining five were wage workers in local shops or were childcare workers. Eight of the twenty-five women were retired at the time of our interviews.

SA CHAL CONTEXT, PROGRAMS, AND DEMOGRAPHICS

The majority of women lived in the local neighborhood of Koreatown (eighteen) and the remaining seven lived in the higher income suburbs of greater Los Angeles. Most of these women from the suburbs commuted to the temple every Sunday for at least one hour. Eleven of my participants spoke some English, while thirteen of the women spoke only Korean. The years of immigration ranged from 1970 to 1998, with the majority having arrived during the mid-seventies to the mid-eighties. Only two of the women I interviewed had been raised as Christians, indicating that they had converted to Buddhism in the United States.

All interviews were conducted either fully in Korean or in a combination of Korean and English depending on the interviewee's level of comfort. Interviews were held in the temple, in private homes, or at workplaces depending on the wishes of participants.

MALE INTERVIEWEE DEMOGRAPHICS

Interviewing a significant number of men at Sa Chal took substantially more effort since I had to ask just about all the male members if they would sit down for an interview. The process of scheduling was made more challenging by the fact that since there were fewer men than women, I did have to approach all the men and not just the ones to whom I had been introduced through mutual acquaintances. Of the men interviewed in this study, twenty-three were lay people and two were monks. The ages of the twenty-three lay men were between twenty-one and seventy-three, with the majority (eleven) between forty and sixty. Members of this study group had earned a high number of postgraduate degrees (ten out of twenty-three). Seven of the men who had done or were engaged in postgraduate work were in the field of Eastern medicine, a popular area of study among Korean immigrants in Los Angeles.

Sixteen of the twenty-three men were married, one was divorced, five were single, and one was widowed. Fourteen of the twenty-three laymen spoke some English and the remainder spoke only Korean. The majority were of the middle income bracket, with eighteen residing in the Koreatown neighborhood. The range of number of years spent in the United States was between one year and twenty-nine years, with the majority (seventeen) falling between ten and twenty years. Four men immigrated to the United States after 1995 and only two arrived in the 1970s. All of the men who participated in this research study were raised as Buddhists, unlike my female interview participants, two of whom were originally Christian.

4

Buddhist Practice and Self-Transformation

For Korean American Buddhist women, religious worship is directly related to the process of self-transformation. Paying close attention to women's personal stories shared during extensive interviews can illuminate how Buddhist idioms of self-knowledge, Buddha Nature, and karmic retribution resonate in women's struggles to combat feelings of depression and relationship discord. By invoking religious language to interpret life events, individuals work to reconstruct identities and enhance self-esteem. Through the telling of their stories and voicing their opinions, women also provide both an entry into the processes of gendered identity and strategies to counter power relations in areas where Confucian norms may dictate a more submissive behavior.

The process of narrating a self in an interview situation enables an individual to fashion an identity that highlights an ideal vision of herself that may have very little to do with her actual experience. Anthropologists James L. Peacock and Dorothy Holland have noted the differences between a life-focused approach which seeks to uncover something about the external reality of the story and a story-focused approach where the telling of the story is given primacy. Peacock and Holland advocate gathering information about the individual's life through a process in which "the *telling* of life stories ... is treated as an important shaping event in social and psychological processes, yet the stories themselves are considered to be developed in, and the outcomes of, the course of these and other life events."[1] However, Unni Wikan critiques the belief that narrative offers a privileged access to the self and advocates a study of individuals' lives that takes into account the *lived* predicaments and "the resistance life offers to people's efforts to craft themselves," which are often obscured by the telling of an event—that is, paying attention to the silences, the individual's actions, and the struggles that take place and constrain an individual.[2]

This very process the subject goes through in retrospectively ordering her life by way of conversation with others enables us to understand how she develops agency and reconstructs her life according to a particular ideal she may have in mind. Throughout this study, I attend to the act of narration and the individual's activities in the social world that may or may not conflict with the way she characterizes herself.

MOTIVATIONS FOR WOMEN'S RELIGIOUS PRACTICES

Buddhist teachings articulated as "finding and knowing one's mind" and self-realization have a particular resonance in the lives of Korean American women because they provide a socially recognized tool with which to interpret life events. As a formula for overcoming suffering, "finding and knowing one's mind" redirects the source of pain from uncontrollable forces outside a person back to the individual. As the women's narratives make clear, the reinterpretation of suffering as the result of one's own karma and ignorance enables women to become agents in their self-transformation, for by finding and knowing one's mind, women can reorder and redress the past.

Women's practices at Sa Chal include participating in the following temple activities in varying degrees: 9:30 A.M. and 11:00 A.M. worship services, private meditation, bowing and chanting, working in the kitchen to prepare the after-service lunch, singing in the choir, working in the bookstore and art gallery, and attending temple celebrations. Most of the Buddhist women at Sa Chal with whom I have had conversations cited "finding and knowing one's mind" and self-knowledge as some of the most important motivations for their worship. When I asked interviewees why they attended temple or why they were interested in Buddhism, one woman replied that "Buddhis[m] is about having control over oneself so nobody can tell you whether you should come to temple or not. I go because the [desire] rises from within my heart." Another woman stated, "the most important thing

BUDDHIST PRACTICE AND SELF-TRANSFORMATION

in Buddhism is to know how to control one's state of mind and how a person realizes oneself."

Mrs. Koh, a first-generation immigrant who participated in my study, offers comments that reflect the range of responses interviewees gave:

> What the Buddha dharma means in reality is that the individual must awaken. You can become a Buddha and I can become a Buddha. Since Buddhism is a pathway where I have to awaken myself, I am not going to tell other people to keep coming here to the temple. You have to know yourself and you truly have to look into your own heart and mind. So no matter if you go to this temple or that temple or stay at home, if you always think about the Buddha and study then the place that you are sitting becomes a dharma hall. . . . In religion, the mind is the most important thing: religion is an individual thing.

Mrs. Koh's beliefs noted above were common among the twenty-five women interviewed in this study who all agreed that ultimately Buddhist worship is a pathway to individual awakening that requires the person to rely on her own efforts both to attain enlightenment and to make changes in her daily life. Yet, while there exists the widely held belief that "religion is an individual thing," most women at Sa Chal attend temple on a weekly basis and take part in rituals and activities of a communal nature (only four out of the twenty-five women interviewees did not attend services on a weekly basis). Rather than sitting at home meditating, praying, and studying texts on their own, women at Sa Chal are quite diligent in their participation in temple worship services and as volunteers in the kitchen, bookstore, and art gallery. They also spend much of their free time in the company of fellow female Buddhists. What this signifies is that while women at Sa Chal believe that individually they have to work out their own enlightenment and their own problems, the temple provides an important context for seeking friendships, comfort, and self-validation—all within a co-ethnic religious community with a shared language and culture.

For some, like Min Kyung, a single woman in her mid-thirties, being part of a temple community helps overcome the sense of isolation and anxiety felt by recent immigrants whose adjustment to life in America has been

BUDDHIST PRACTICE AND SELF-TRANSFORMATION

difficult. During one of our interviews, Min Kyung described her arrival in Los Angeles seven years earlier as a single nursing student:

> I was so lonely I didn't know what to do ... so instead of crying, I started going to temple every day.... I really prayed a lot [because] I wanted to be strong for myself. Actually I cried a lot in those times because every morning when you wake up you realize that you are in a foreign country and you don't have anybody and you feel so sad, even though you came here out of your own decision.... But instead of [just] crying, I started going to temple everyday ... and I prayed a lot. I tried to do meditation and sometimes I would read the Buddhist bible and that made me very comfortable.

Like Min Kyung, many women at Sa Chal admitted that their interest and weekly participation in temple activities increased after immigrating to the United States, in order to find psychological comfort and inspiration on a religious and social level to persevere despite their difficult transition into American culture. Mrs. Song, another devout Buddhist, expresses similar interests in attending Sa Chal services: "I come [to temple] every Sunday. But if there is some particular reason—if I am unhappy or if [it is] one of those days when I am depressed and want to just sit and shed tears—I come to the dharma hall, sit in front of the Buddha, and [let] my tears flow down."

While Min Kyung states that she comes to temple to escape from loneliness and sadness by being in the company of other Koreans, she has attended Korean American Christian churches a few times as a new immigrant. Yet she explains that in a Buddhist temple she finds herself free to practice her religion individually without any intrusion into her private life from fellow members. She notes, however, that "when you go to church, they want to know everything about you; they ask you all those [personal] questions. When I go to [Sa Chal], of course some people who are sitting nearby you want to know about you, but most of them don't ask you much about your private life and also, I don't want to be asked!" Whether or not Buddhists at temple are less intrusive in one's personal affairs than Christians in church is difficult to assess, yet interestingly, many of the women in this study indicated that they prefer worshipping in a temple for the same reason—privacy.

BUDDHIST PRACTICE AND SELF-TRANSFORMATION

Min Kyung's desire for privacy derives from her status as a single Korean woman, something of an anomaly in the Korean community for a woman of her age because, as she puts it, "society thinks that you cannot be single by the time you reach thirty-three." Yet, because she chose to pursue her own career in the United States rather than having the two or three kids and being a stay-at-home mom, she also guards her personal life in order to protect herself from the constant barrage of questions she encountered at church, such as "Why aren't you married? Where is your husband? What does your husband do?" Throughout our interview, Min Kyung attributed the relative anonymity and freedom from scrutiny she experiences at the temple to Buddhist goals of "finding and knowing one's mind" and self-reliance. The maintenance of privacy in a religious setting is something she claims that "only Buddhists do," and is deeply tied to the doctrinal aspects of the Buddha Nature because one need not rely on others for self-awakening. It is for this reason that she believes people at temple tend to leave her alone.

Sa Chal women's identities are acknowledged first and foremost as Buddhists and not automatically as wives and mothers. Although Buddhist women certainly continue to recognize their primary roles as mothers and wives and may uphold the Confucian gender ideology, the temple enables women to focus on their religious identities in the company of other women. Such is not the case for the formal aspects of the Korean Christian churches studied by Ai Ra Kim, where a patriarchal religious institution gives divine sanction to Confucian gender norms that limit women to the role of care providers. In the church:

> Preachers exalt the self-abnegation of Korean women for children and others as akin to Jesus' death and resurrection. Most churches hold a special recognition program on Mother's Day, calling forth mothers over the age of sixty to the altar to face the congregation and receive gifts from the Women's Association . . . or Sunday School for their lifelong sacrificial devotion to the family. Through these rituals, churches implicitly and explicitly elevate women's sacrifice and portray other-oriented services as the priority in women's lives.[3]

Sa Chal, however, provides women with esteemed identities as exemplary Buddhist laywomen, or *posals* (female Bodhisattvas), regardless of whether they are nurturing mothers and virtuous wives. For example, during Sa Chal's twenty-fourth anniversary celebration in 1998, three women were awarded certificates of appreciation and gratitude for their perfect attendance record for over three years. The abbot and visiting monks from other local temples bestowed the awards and gifts upon them in the main worship hall. The women were called up to the front and publicly acknowledged for their devotion as exemplary Buddhist practitioners. Although one woman's modesty required her to be dragged to the front of the dharma hall by her friends, the Buddhist temple bestowed on her an important award defined outside of her status as a wife or mother. At Sa Chal, she adopts the identity of a dedicated laywoman and is henceforth defined by her religious devotion.

A large number of women at Sa Chal are also interested in attending temple for social reasons, for the Sunday schedule offers ample opportunities to meet with friends on the weekend. Thus, Mrs. Min, a woman in her late fifties who lives alone in Koreatown, explains that she comes to temple "out of habit and also because my mind gets stronger and I can relax and just enjoy myself when I come to temple. Here in America, I don't have many opportunities to meet my family so I come out to temple and can talk to lots of people." Choir member Mrs. Chang echoes her motivations for participation and states, "on the days that I go to temple, all day long from morning on, I am in a good mood and enjoy meeting with people." Thus, Sa Chal provides many women with a secure social life and ample opportunities to meet with friends.

Other women maintain that they come to temple for both social and religious reasons. Another study participant, Mrs. Kwak, explains:

> The main reason why I come to temple is to calm my mind. I just see the Buddha and my mind becomes more comfortable because I don't have any selfishness. I don't come to learn more about Buddhism but I do have [other] reasons for coming like meeting up with other Koreans where we can and do things together.

Mrs. Kwak's interest in coming to temple to calm her mind is shared by most of the women at Sa Chal who are interested in learning how to control their emotions through meditation and prayer. Hae Jin Rhee, a woman in her sixties, comments:

BUDDHIST PRACTICE AND SELF-TRANSFORMATION

> If Buddhism didn't make sense to me, I would not have become a Buddhist. Buddhist teachings have helped me calm my emotions and help me with my family relationships and my surroundings. When I was younger, I used to get so angry with my children when they behaved [badly]. My face would get all red and I would look like a devil with horns poking out of my head! But my kids would never listen to me at all. But then, once I began to learn to calm my emotions down, I started talking to my children and explaining to them how karma works. After that, they started to really straighten out.

This notion of calming one's mind also resonates with women who have turned to Buddhism because of a direct experience of suffering, like members Melissa Kang and Mee Soo Park. Melissa, who suffers from a chronic physical illness, says that she comes to temple for prayer and meditation because Buddhism "makes [one] feel peaceful" and because "praying to Kwan Um Bodhisattva really helps." She also notes that "Buddhism can help you cope with illness, philosophically at least," by offering a means of calming the mind and an explanation for the derivation of disease—karma.

Mee Soo Park, a woman who owns her own small business in Koreatown, has had similar experiences with her Buddhist practice, which she states increased only after she had undergone a particularly difficult time in her life. She recalls:

> I started going to temple because I came onto hard times and my business was going really badly. So I reached out to Buddhism even more. I went to meet the Buddha at temple because I had experienced actual suffering and it was then that I understood what his teaching meant. The Buddha taught that everything is related to karma and that everything that can happen in the future depends on your own mind.... My body's energy gets weaker and weaker because of my selfish mind ... and so I want to study [and calm] my mind and so that's why I come to temple regularly.

What is of utmost concern in this study is an attempt to capture those ideas and beliefs that most resonated in the lives of my interviewees. In this case, it is the interpretation of Buddhism for practical relief in everyday life much more than achieving a better rebirth or enlightenment. Most of the women claim that they participate in Sa Chal activities out of a desire to overcome

BUDDHIST PRACTICE AND SELF-TRANSFORMATION

loneliness, depression, and suffering, to be with fellow Koreans, to maintain their privacy, to worship the Buddha, and to calm their minds.

BUDDHIST PSYCHOLOGICAL HEALING

For Jin Soo Um, Buddhist meditation and worship enable her to view the problems in her life as resulting from her own misperceptions and give her the ability to "see things as they truly are"—impermanent and causally related to her own actions. Mrs. Um, a woman who converted to Buddhism following marriage, informed me during one of our many conversations that her religious faith developed out of a desire to combat a midlife crisis and deep depression that struck when she turned forty-five.

Born in 1947 to parents who "had no religion" aside from Confucianism, she admits that religion played next to no role in her life prior to marriage. One of four daughters, she attended an all girls' high school and was encouraged by her parents to pursue a nursing degree in college. After working for six years as a nurse in Korea, she decided to immigrate by herself to the United States when she was twenty-six to try to make more money and embark on a new adventure. An unmarried woman with a boyfriend back home, she arrived in California in 1974 and began studying for her licensing exam through the Korean Nurses' Association, an organization established to provide materials and educational assistance for Korean women seeking to pass U.S. nursing requirements. After six months of work, she returned to Korea to marry her boyfriend; the newlyweds returned to California a few months later.

Recalling her early experiences in America, Jin Soo Um explains:

> When I first came here, it was so interesting. I thought that my future was so bright and I wanted to make a lot of money! But at that time it was really hard. My husband came over with me and I got pregnant but I also had to work at night. Ugh! I worked the night shift so in the daytime I would sleep. It was a hard time you know; there just [were] not a lot of Korean people around at that time. In the morning my husband took my baby to the babysitter, and during the daytime I had to sleep for three or four hours. When I woke up I would go to pick up the baby and at night my husband took me to the hospital. . . . It was a really tough time.

BUDDHIST PRACTICE AND SELF-TRANSFORMATION

Although Jin Soo is proud of her work as a nurse and her contribution to her family's finances, she also looks back on this period as full of hardship. Her early immigration experiences illustrate the risks taken by a young couple in a new culture. A mother and a full-time breadwinner, she faced a tremendous financial burden and responsibility for making a smooth transition to life in America.

Her introduction to Buddhism has been a long progression from attending temple and occasionally bowing, without really knowing what she was doing, to her current practice of reading sutras every morning, praying, and attending Sunday services. She characterizes her earlier religious practice as follows:

> My husband's family members are very strong Buddhists. My brother-in-law used to be a monk. They are very devout, especially my mother-in-law. She prays in the morning at six o'clock, ten o'clock, and then at night, three times a day everyday! My house was very close to where Sa Chal used to be and so my father-in-law and mother-in-law went to Sa Chal. When I was pregnant, my husband took me to Sa Chal since he knew Abbot Lee. After going to the temple, my husband would pray and I had to follow him. He would say to me *Kido hae* [pray], and so I ended up at the temple once in a while. I also had to take my mother-in-law over there and pick her up. Whenever I would go to the temple, sometimes I would bow and sometimes I didn't because I didn't feel comfortable since I didn't follow any religion. I would wonder, "Why is there food, and fruit on the altar? Why do I have to bow?" I wasn't comfortable in the temple at that time, but I had to take my mother-in-law every Sunday. I didn't have much interest in Buddhism, so I just followed the family's religion.

Since Jin Soo did not grow up attending church or temple, she had no personal interest in religious practice aside from satisfying her in-laws, and admits that the early days of her temple participation were merely imitative. However, she claims that she found religion when her children reached high school age. She explains:

> When I was forty-five or so, I experienced what you might call a midlife crisis. I was lonely because I didn't have any of my own family here and I didn't

have close friends. When I had personal problems I wanted to talk to someone, but at that time I didn't have anybody. I had only my brother-in-law and sister-in-law, but I could not open my mind to them. That's why I kept it all inside. I wasn't working at that time so I just stayed at home and picked up my son and daughter from school. That's it. I didn't do anything else. . . . I was having a hard time because my son was a teenager and although he was very bright he started to wear really strange clothes. Every time I would try to talk to him, he wouldn't listen to me! Also I wasn't that happy at the time, but I didn't know why. I was depressed all the time and would cry every once in awhile for no real reason. My husband didn't know what to do. So I told him that maybe I needed to go to a psychiatrist because I was depressed and crying all the time. I was not happy and I told him that I had to go to the hospital. "Take me to the hospital," I told him and he said, "You'll be all right. You are just starting to get old. That's what it is." But I knew that something was wrong.

Rather than suggest that his wife seek professional counseling, Mr. Um urged her to practice Buddhism. Given that therapy still carries with it a social stigma in Korean culture, it is not surprising that her husband prevented her from obtaining the counseling she felt she required.[4] One day after spending a few more months alone at home crying and suffering from depression, Jin Soo came across an article in a Korean newspaper advertising the dharma talks of a well-known Korean Buddhist monk who was visiting Los Angeles. It was at this point that she says she became deeply interested in Buddhism and her life began to change for the better:

> I saw a Korean newspaper and went to the lecture at the temple for a three-day long dharma talk given by a monk and found that he was so interesting! He talked about Buddhas and other stories that got me so intrigued. After that, I went straight to the library and borrowed as many Buddhist books as I could, sometimes ten books, sometimes fifteen books. I just read books; I didn't do anything else! I'd read the books. I'd finish them and right away would borrow another book. Whenever a monk would visit from Korea to give a dharma talk I would go and listen. Before, I would just come to temple and bow, but actually I would say that I was not a Buddhist. I couldn't say that I was, because I didn't know anything about it. I couldn't even teach Buddhism to my kids.

BUDDHIST PRACTICE AND SELF-TRANSFORMATION

I can't [explain it], but for some reason it became so fascinating to me. The Buddha says that everything comes from inside. At that time those words comforted me because I realized that *I* made myself depressed. . . . I made myself upset over everything! At the same time, I also learned that I could control and change myself. *Then* I started to change my attitude toward my children, my husband and my family. That's why I became interested in Buddhism.

Mrs. Um's conversion story centers on a desire for a deeper understanding of Buddhist doctrines that she could use to interpret and change the course of her depression. She believes that being a Buddhist requires a true understanding of the teachings and practice, something she says she lacked during her early days of coming to temple. This desire to learn more about Buddhism on an intellectual level has led to an increase in her worship as well. Over the past two years, Mrs. Um has enrolled in the Eastern Mountain Buddhist College certificate program to obtain a more solid foundation and understanding of Buddhism, which she believes will increase her faith and her knowledge. More important, she explains, "I want to learn about Buddhism because I would like to become more comfortable. I want to feel comfortable all the time. You see, I am a very sensitive person and I become upset very easily so maybe [Buddhism] can help me calm down so that I can control myself."

Understanding the role religion plays in Mrs. Um's life requires paying specific attention to concurrent events in her life. The period of depression she refers to coincides with the 1992 Los Angeles riots, a further source of fear and anxiety for Korean immigrants blindsided by the eruption of violence and attacks on Korean-run stores. As a liquor store owner, she recalls trembling in fear and closing down her shop for days and she helplessly "cried all day long" as she watched the destruction of shops and mass looting. At the same time, her children were reaching maturity and she was not a constant influence in their lives. Because she no longer worked as a nurse, this particular stage in her life brought isolation, anxiety, fear, and her changing status in her family. At this critical juncture she found herself more open to Buddhism. She increased her worship to overcome feelings of helplessness after her children left the household and following the intense racial violence against Korean shopkeepers which made her question the wisdom of coming to America in the first place.

A self-proclaimed newcomer to religious devotion, Mrs. Um says she is attracted to Buddhism because it allows her to find the source of her suffering and the means to overcome that suffering—through self-reliance and "knowing her [true] self." She can translate a traumatic event into a positive learning experience and has found a community of Koreans who share similar problems and a common history. The temple provides her with a constant source of inspiration to strengthen herself when things "fall apart."[5] Religious practice becomes an active attempt to vanquish the stress and trauma experienced after immigration. By interpreting their personal struggles doctrinally, women like Jin Soo Um identify both the source of their problems and the antidote—themselves.

Through her study of Buddhism, Mrs. Um constantly works to develop confidence and self-reliance to avoid depression and life's emotional ups and downs. During the week, she listens to Buddhist lectures on tape when she drives in her car and on Friday evenings she commutes an extra hour to attend lectures at the temple. In addition to her intellectual practice, Mrs. Um comes to Sa Chal services a few times a month and tries to read the Diamond Sutra in the mornings. She has been struggling to perform the *Paekpalbae* ("One Hundred Eight") practice of ritual bowing every day although she says she has "already missed it a couple of times." Like many students I have interviewed at Eastern Mountain Buddhist College, Jin Soo takes classes because she desires to learn for herself and continue to recreate and restructure her life. She expresses very little interest in actively disseminating Buddhism among Korean Americans, although she would like to see her children become practicing Buddhists. Regretfully, she states:

> [My children] do not attend, not yet anyway. That is my job [to get them to attend]. When I come to temple, they don't want to come because there is nobody here to teach them and because there is nothing for them to do. People here speak Korean but my children were born here and speak English. They need to feel more comfortable in the temple but they complain that they are bored here.

One of the areas of greatest concern for this mother is that because her children are in college, the family has experienced greater tension, which she associates with the growing influence of Korean American Christianity on college campuses. Her own children have expressed an interest in attending church because they are attracted to the social interaction with other Korean American students encouraged by church organizations. Mrs. Um's eyes welled up as she described a fight that arose between her husband and twenty-one-year-old son over the issue of religion:

> For both of my children, during Christmas or Easter or whenever any of those [Christian holidays] came, their friends would say "Hey, let's go to church!" My children really wanted to go but I would say "No" and my husband would say "No, you cannot go because we are Buddhist, you cannot go." Honestly, I want to send them because if they went there it seems like they will learn something good. But my husband kept saying "No!" My husband says that you have to have the same religion in the family. If there are two religions, then you fight, especially because the Christians don't like the Buddhists. So you have to follow the same religion.... Really, living in America and raising kids is hard, especially because of religion. If they tell [Christians] that they are Buddhists, they don't want to be friends with them! When my daughter was in kindergarten, they talked about religion in the classroom and most of her classmates were Christians. She told them that our household believed in Buddhism, and not one of her friends in the class wanted to be friends with her after that! I still remember that.

For women with college-age children, a conversion to Christianity signifies a break from parental control and a generational rift between parents and children. While women are encouraged to find their children interacting with co-ethnics at college, they also struggle to fulfill what they envision as the responsibilities of a mother—to instill traditional and religious values. The accessibility of church groups on college campuses brings anxiety, for although they offer a context for instilling Korean cultural values, they also detract from the parents' ability to influence their children's religious upbringing.

Although her son will probably continue to attend church, Jin Soo has been able to share some Buddhist teachings with her daughter over the telephone and by sending her books at college. She makes the extra effort to reach out to her daughter, something she couldn't achieve with her son. She states:

> My daughter is in college but all her friends go to church and it seems that they always ask her to come along. She doesn't actually go to church but she says to me, "Mom, I don't go to church but there is always a meeting, a spaghetti party, or a pizza party and so they [Christians] constantly invite me to come along." During final exams, a bus comes and takes students to church and they support the kids with food and everything. So, ever since she left home, she doesn't have friends. She is lonely, so she calls every day and sometimes she cries on the phone. On Sundays, all the students go to church but she has no place to go. She is having a hard time, so whenever I call her I talk to her a little bit about Buddhism.

By teaching her daughter about Buddhism, Jin Soo hopes to avoid the gap that has developed between mother and son and help her resolve her feelings of alienation. Her daughter's situation illustrates the complexities of religious minority status within the same ethnic group. While Mrs. Um has no interest in converting to Christianity like many Koreans she knows, she works hard to learn as much as she can about Buddhism by attending classes so she can encourage her daughter to embrace the family's religion and maintain familial ties.

Mrs. Um's religious practice also has led to a kind of inward-gazing subjectivity in which her own happiness takes on greater importance, especially since her children have reached adulthood. Her temple participation gives her an active social life and interaction with members who share similar experiences. Furthermore, since she attends without her husband, she is received as an individual without primary reference to her husband. Sa Chal provides an opportunity to forge a new narrative in reaction to difficulties experienced in the United States. In other words, a Buddhist identity represents and creates an individual capable of reinterpreting past suffering as the result of one's own actions.

In becoming true Buddhists who see things as they really are, women employ the working of karma to redress past misfortune by taking responsibility for its development. Buddhist women's strategies of self-actualization find the origin of suffering not in an external source like husbands and children but in an internal cause—the unawakened self. This shift from an outside force that fragments a coherent sense of self to an internal source symbolizes a transition into an actualized self that identifies a troubling phenomenon as a mere slip in perception. The ignorant individual who allows herself to become angry and depressed is subdued by the Buddhist self who takes responsibility for her own karmic hindrances. This mental shift in perception then leads to very practical results as women find the strength to rework less than ideal relationships. The influence of the religious doctrines of self-knowledge and Buddha Nature in negotiating selfhood is unmistakable. It is clear that the power of self-knowledge and its benefits in daily life have a practical result—making life easier to manage. Women like Mrs. Um must work to reaffirm their statuses in the household and foster relationships within the family while making *their own* lives matter. Not only does membership in Sa Chal offer a sense of belonging to a community, but also a means of coping with obstacles in the development of a distinct female subjectivity.

While the decrease in a mother's influence on her children may be experienced as disorienting, religious activities offer a way to mitigate an attenuation of self-worth. By pursuing higher education in the Buddhist college, Sa Chal women fill their lives with self-enhancing intellectual pursuits as well as new avenues of communication with their adult children through religion. While education offers an opportunity to focus on one's intellectual development and recast oneself as student and *pogyo-sa* (Buddhist disseminator), ritual chanting and meditation transfer the cause of suffering to the internal machinations of an unawakened self. Utilizing doctrines of karma and the Buddha Nature, Sa Chal women begin the task of "purifying their hearts" to overcome failing relationships, depression, and illness by seeking an ideal vision of themselves as Buddhists working toward enlightenment.

BUDDHIST IDENTITY AND SELF-RENEWAL

That a Buddhist identity can renew a self fragmented by everyday living is perhaps best exemplified by Christine Chin's story in which religious worship helps center a life that had "fallen apart." Christine is a fifty-two-year-old mother of four children from two separate marriages, both of which ended in divorce. Born in 1947, Christine was a poor and uneducated daughter whose health was so bad that she was forced to withdraw from school and spend most of her childhood at home. Her family life was further complicated by her father's "taste for alcohol," which made her mother's life difficult as well. In 1970 Christine left Korea at the age of twenty-three after marrying her first husband, a close friend of her older brother. Although she did not speak a word of English when she arrived in California, Christine helped support her family by working various jobs in retail, gardening, housekeeping, and toy sales where all she "needed to know was simple English, nothing too difficult and just enough to know what customers wanted."

Christine was raised in a Buddhist household although she never went to worship services regularly. Following her marriage she converted to Christianity and began to attend a small Korean church in Los Angeles in the early 1970s. She explains, "I was married and figured that I should just follow my husband to church. People didn't really go to church out of a strong faith or anything but because there were few Koreans in LA that one could meet at the time." Although she spent four years attending church services on and off, she never considered herself a Christian, for she "just had no interest in Christianity." Christine marks 1974 as the time when she began to refocus on her Buddhist background and attend Sa Chal services. It was also in 1974 that Christine's personal life began to unravel as she was struck with multiple problems in her marriage that culminated in her husband's leaving her. Because she was living in a new culture, she lacked a social network of support and was forced to support herself, her children, and her eighty-two-year-old mother, who had just immigrated that year. Describing this period of crisis, she explains:

> After getting divorced, my life was really difficult because during the first year my children ended up going to live with their father in Georgia and I was on my own. I could not deal with my divorce and ended up cursing my husband for divorcing me because I ended up on welfare and food stamps. I was extremely bitter! I was so angry with my children and when they came back I blamed them for everything because I had to work even harder every day! I used to yell and scream, "what did you kids ever do for me?!" I didn't know where to place the blame at the time and I suffered so much because of my

children and my ex-husband. I used to be so angry all the time and must have looked really frightening! As soon as I would come home from work at night, my children would just disappear and they wouldn't come home again until after I fell asleep. That's basically how I ended up at the time.

Since her husband did not offer her financial support, Christine was forced to support the entire household on low wages, for she could not speak English adequately to get a better paying job. Having to support the family on food stamps and welfare checks was a tremendous humiliation for Christine, who had no other choice. As a result of her anger and embarrassment, she blamed her suffering on others—the husband who had left her for another woman and the children she had to feed and clothe on her own.

During the year following her divorce, Christine says that she relied on resentment, blaming others for her problems, and acrimonious behavior to cope with the newfound stress in her life. The result was alienation from possible networks of support in her friends and family. It was during this period of loneliness and desperation that she revisited her Buddhist roots by joining her mother at Sa Chal once a week. Through her Buddhist practice, Christine has learned to make dramatic changes in her life by taking responsibility for her suffering, a process requiring many years of hard work and dedication along with continued financial and emotional distress. Describing her decision to attend Buddhist services, she narrates the following experience:

> One morning after working at the coffee shop, I was drinking my cup of coffee that I was in the habit of drinking alone every day. As I sat there drinking it, I suddenly thought to myself, you know, I really shouldn't be suffering like this by myself. Why should I be so alone? So I went along with my mother to Sa Chal to worship. After awhile, I started going on the weekends because after the divorce and my kids leaving, I realized that I had to focus my mind. I didn't really know anything about Buddhism but I needed to do *something* with myself because I was so bitter. In the beginning, I went to temple without a thought of anybody else; I only thought about myself and my own pain. I never even considered anybody else's problems.

She continues:

> After I started reading the Buddhist sutras and listening to the dharma services, I finally began to understand the power of Buddhism and how it is possible to come to a realization of oneself and change one's circumstances. I began to see how I blamed everybody for my problems but now I know where the fault actually lies—myself. I used to curse my children because I had to raise them and I was so angry because my husband left me. I would just curse everybody. As I went over to the temple one morning it dawned on me that actually, all of this is actually my own fault. My children were just as attractive and good as anyone else's children, but they weren't raised in a household where people treated them well and looked after them. I began to worry about how different they would end up in the future. What sort of child should have to grow up in a home where the parents have split up, they have to live on welfare, and have a mother like me? I really contemplated the situation and came to the realization that I was being selfish and that I was responsible for making both their lives and my own miserable. From that moment on, I was so apologetic to my children and have since come to my senses.

Once Christine started to attend Sa Chal, she made the important discovery that one's karma plays a crucial role in shaping one's life and she began to teach herself to care for others and alleviate her own pain by working in the temple. On weekends, she would pray, light incense, read the sutras, and sing in the temple's choir and went about the daily task of taking care of other members in ways that she had not previously done at home. For example, every morning before the nine-thirty service began, Christine would drive over to the temple to make coffee and cake for other members. She began to clean the bathrooms in the temple, pick up any garbage left in the dining halls, and even fix Korean style dinners for the few single men in the temple. By focusing on others in the setting of the Buddhist temple, Christine began to discipline herself into caring for others as though they were her own children. Through her efforts, she began to understand that the laws of karma were always in effect so that if she did something kind for others, she would earn their respect and they would begin to treat her kindly.

Central to her religious practice is the desire to "be in a place where you can learn and be in the presence of other people that want to learn more about Buddhism as well." As such, she has found that the best form of worship is to "help out in the temple and just be with people rather than going to pray all day long and turn my prayer beads." For this laywoman, religious worship means *doing* and an active engagement in activities that bring her into relationships of care with others. After a few months of worship and participation in a religious community, she states:

> I finally realized that all good things would come to me if I did good things toward others—this was my religious awakening. Everything has changed since then. When I used to go to temple, I would never pray for anybody else because I was so stubborn. But then I realized that other people like my mother, my younger sister, and people in the temple were actually beautiful people and did not deserve my hatefulness. So I came to embrace them and in the end they came to appreciate and embrace me as well. Because I am happy and pleasant to them they don't dislike me anymore. I have found that even though I am alone and trying to make a living through some difficult times, I no longer look at other people who have more than I do with jealousy and wonder why I can't have the same things. Even now, if I didn't work for a month I couldn't even make my car payments, and yet I now get up in the morning happy, go to work, and take pleasure in the fact that people appreciate what I cook for them. Buddhism helped me see that self-realization can change your life.

Self-realization for Christine entailed seeing herself as culpable for her divorce and for the resultant anger and hatefulness that dominated her life. By removing the obstacles of suffering from external forces like poverty and divorce to the results of her own karma, Christine has transformed herself from what she sees as a hateful and angry mother into a woman who had finally found happiness. Or so she thought.

A few years after her first husband left her, Christine remarried and found herself divorced yet again. After an extremely complicated separation, she was forced to give up custody of her third son from her second marriage. At the same time, her teenage daughter had become extremely rebellious and ended up single and pregnant. These two traumatic events then led Christine to seek the solace of a Zen center, where she retreated for eighteen months to put her life in order and help her withstand the constant challenges in her life. She explains:

> My daughter had gotten pregnant and at the time I was so angry and humiliated that she would end up an unwed mother. At first I really wanted her to get an abortion, but then my daughter turned my own Buddhist teachings of responsibility against me and had the child. My other children were gone—one was taken away with his father to Austria, another ended up in the army and the other went down South. Basically I was alone so I decided to go and live like a Buddhist nun by going to a prayer mountain [Zen retreat]. I went to an American Zen center in the mountains where I could devote myself to the Buddhist lifestyle. I stayed there for eighteen months and after three months I shaved my hair and wore nuns' robes. I worked the grounds there and would turn my rosary beads and offer prayers at sunrise. I read a lot of books up there and followed the teachings of the Buddha as best I could. I had no money back then but I learned to really think of myself as the richest person in the world. After being there for a while, though, I wondered how it was that I could actually be doing anyone else any good. I figured that it would be better for me to cry together with people when they were sad and be with people when they suffered so I packed my bags and came down from the mountain. After that experience, I have devoted myself to Sa Chal.

During Christine's retreat from her everyday world, she devoted herself to a religious life by becoming a Buddhist nun—an act symbolic of renouncing her negative past and engaging in self-healing. Her decision to enter a Zen center retreat in the hills of California was a way of creating a new narrative for herself following a traumatic life in America. The Buddhist way of life gave her back a sense of purpose and centeredness after failing to live up to Korean cultural ideals of a life well lived.

At this time, Christine's life embodied all the characteristics Korean cultural norms repudiated—divorce (twice over), welfare reliance, bad mothering, and unwed pregnant offspring. By entering the retreat and adopting a Buddhist identity, Christine rendered her life more meaningful by learning to interpret her suffering as an object lesson on the workings of karma theory. However, her adoption of a Buddhist identity as a nun should not be viewed as an escape from the trappings of samsara and everyday life. Rather, through her retreat from the everyday world, this fifty-two-year-old-mother put her life in perspective and saw her circumstances as controllable in the end. A Buddhist identity offers a time to recreate and re-center a life gone awry by offering a narrative of self-reliance and the ability to mend the past. Rather than retreating from her life, Christine left the Zen center ready to embrace her past and make amends for a better future, for she believes that in order to be a true Buddhist one must be in the presence of others and face life with all its challenges. Pondering the course of the past thirty years of her life, this laywoman who has "been through hell and back" has found equilibrium. She ended our conversation with the following comments:

> I have a lot of regrets from my past because had I known and understood the Buddha's teachings early on then maybe my ex-husbands could have met different wives and really found happiness. Maybe I wouldn't have been such a terrible mother to my children. Nowadays, I am really working on cleansing my heart. My family had truly been broken up and they were so angry with me for what I had done. But now whenever I see them, I always express to them how sorry I am. Cleansing my heart is really what Buddhism is about. I have to purify my heart and show this heart to other people. A person doesn't need money for that. If you look at Buddhism, it is all about your fate. Because of your fate and your karma, you don't have to constantly wonder why things have happened to you, why people marry, why they divorce. If you just realize that this is your fate and your karma, then you won't suffer too much in your life. You should just realize your wrongdoings and change your behavior for the better. You cannot change your past karma but you can certainly try to do better in this life. I am not ashamed by all the experiences I have had, and the wealth that I have in my life now is health and the aid I can give other people by sharing my experiences.

Through her Buddhist worship, Christine created a self whose story is worth sharing. It is a tale of a woman once embittered by the suffering inflicted on her by others who learns to overcome pain and anguish through Buddhist teachings of karma and self-reliance.

BUDDHIST PRACTICE AND SELF-TRANSFORMATION

PUBLIC AND PRIVATE CONCERNS ADDRESSED THROUGH DUAL PRACTICES

Miruk Chon Yorae Bul . . . Miruk Chon Yorae Bul . . . Miruk Chon Yorae Bul . . . Miruk Chon Yorae Bul. . . . (Tathagatha Maitreya, the Future Buddha)

Mrs. Jung faces the white wall of the small dharma hall with her hands clasped in supplication before her chest as she repeatedly calls out the Buddha's name. After a few more recitations, she gets up from her meditation cushion and explains: "Sometimes when I get so angry that I don't even want to bow or meditate in the presence of the Buddha, I chant like this in front of a wall and it helps me fully calm my mind. By focusing my mind like this. I surrender all its negative thoughts as an offering to the Buddha."

Waking every morning at 2:30, Mrs. Jung leaves her suburban home and drives up the empty freeway for half an hour until she arrives at a small unmarked dharma hall in a quiet residential section of Koreatown, Los Angeles. At three A.M. she begins her two-hour chanting of the Diamond Sutra *(Keumgang Gyung)* followed by a recitation of the Buddha Maitreya's name until six-thirty while her two children and husband remain asleep at home. After her practice, Mrs. Jung returns home to fix her children's breakfast and drives her husband back to Koreatown to work. Despite getting up so early and her multiple commutes to the city, she sees her rigorous recitation schedule "as a pleasure," for it provides her with the "strength to calm the mind" and control her emotions when her children misbehave, her husband ignores her, and her mother-in-law visits from Korea.

Maitreya Buddha has a central role in her desire to "find inner peace" in her "chaotic world." Describing the importance of giving or donating her mind to the Buddha, she explains: "In practice, one recites or chants *Miruk Chon Yorae Bul* . . . to feelings that arises in mind from time to time [*sic*]. For example, as a person screams at the microwave, two obvious feelings form in the mind: anger and frustration. Rather than acting upon those feelings, he or she surrenders them to Buddha, taking them out of the mind." While chanting the name of the Buddha Maitreya is ultimately aimed at attaining an enlightened mind, it is for the name's efficaciousness in transforming everyday problems that members seem to recite.

Mrs. Jung is not the only Buddhist present at the dharma hall before sunrise. On an average morning she conducts her practice in the company of seven or eight other women. Although all the female participants are married with children, there are never any men present during the predawn service. Instead, the women leave their homes when it is still dark and gather to worship every morning among friends and confidantes often without their spouses' knowledge or consent. While Mrs. Jung claims that men do not attend early morning services because they are "more devoted to their jobs," she also admits that many women like herself are compelled to participate in order to cope with the marital discord that complicates their lives.

On Saturday evenings, the larger twenty-member group known as the Diamond Sutra recitation group meets in a private residence for its regular service; this time there are four or five males in attendance and some children, who occupy themselves by running around the backyard. Although this dharma center shows no outward indication that it is a place of worship, its interior has been renovated to accommodate a meticulously polished dark wooden floor for sitting, a meditation hall with an altar flanked by numerous copies of the Diamond Sutra, and piles of yellow satin meditation cushions. Unlike the more traditional Korean *bopdang* (dharma hall) represented in more public Korean style temples in Los Angeles, the recitation group's altar lacks a Buddha statue, for as the group's male leader indicates, "the most important aspect of Buddhist practice is the recitation of the Diamond Sutra to achieve one's own enlightenment, so we don't need to look at the Buddha." Rather than bowing down in front of an image, members of the Diamond Sutra recitation group believe that "studying" (reciting) the text itself is the most crucial and efficacious aspect of worship; thus in the *bopdang* the Diamond Sutra takes center stage. Mrs. Jung explains, "we don't have a Buddha statue because one's own mind is a Buddha and besides, we see the Buddha when we see the Diamond Sutra."

Members of this group choose the Diamond Sutra because it represents the group's belief that by reciting the sutra, one polishes or cultivates one's mind. As Mrs. Jin explains: "This sutra or scripture contains Shakyamuni Buddha's preaching on the Enlightenment. It is considered the most important sutra in Buddhism. In order to get a beautiful diamond, a craftsman needs to polish it well. Our minds are similar in a way that the minds can be so mindful, if we carefully cultivate them."

There are no monks or nuns in residence at this center. As the group's lay leader remarks, "in a temple the abbot is the middle man between you and the Buddha, just like in the church. Here you are one on one with the Buddha." Religious worship is thus self-mediated for members of the Diamond Sutra recitation group. They believe that individuals are responsible for their own enlightenment and do not require the assistance of religious virtuosos. This desire for ritual agency finds doctrinal legitimacy in the oft-quoted Buddhist idioms of "knowing one's true self" and "the Buddha Nature" which give these women the claim to self-knowledge as a means of self-healing without the need for a monastic specialist.

On Saturday nights, members of the group gather for a meeting that typically consists of a thirty-minute sutra reading followed by a fifteen-minute recitation of the Buddha's name. Subsequent to the ritualized session, members gather for an informal hour of discussion to "calm and surrender the mind to awaken the Buddha Nature," as one member puts it. After the sutras and meditation, cushions are returned to their original places and the meeting turns into a "testimonial session" in which members sit cross-legged on the floor around traditional foldout black Korean tables.

This casual and intimate setting enables lay followers to share their problems experienced throughout the week with regard to their families, friends, and work in "a safe environment away from the scrutiny of monks and other strangers" that prevails at more public Korean temples in Los Angeles. Here in this quiet residential home, members openly express their anxieties arising out of marital discord, economic hardship, and conflicts with their increasingly Americanized children. In this alternative to the formal Sunday worship at the larger temples, members are empowered to voice their vulnerability in the context of a religious environment as they share the ways that chanting the Buddha's name and reciting the sutras has had a positive impact on their daily lives. As Mrs. Jung explains:

> We share the unpleasant feelings we had throughout the week and try to dissolve those feelings. For example, I might share how I had a negative mind and was angry and fought with my husband. After talking abut it, we pray so that I may devote myself to developing a stronger mind so that I can let

BUDDHIST PRACTICE AND SELF-TRANSFORMATION

go of negative thoughts. Rather than constantly demanding to know why my husband was deliberately making me angry, I would end up realizing. "Oh, actually I am the one at fault here." Then you end up realizing that even though you might think that someone else is always to blame for your bad situation, in fact, the cause is your own. You realize that you yourself are the one with the negative heart and *then* you learn how to understand people because you see why it is that they are acting the way they do. For ten years I struggled with my husband and I worked to dissolve my bad feelings through the teachings by surrendering them to the Buddha.

The testimonial session becomes an opportunity to interpret the source of one's troubles as one's own misunderstanding and ignorance, something treatable by a reliance on Buddhist chanting to awaken the mind and refocus the self.

The efficacy of prayer groups as a medium for self-expression and transformation has been well documented in R. Marie Griffith's study of evangelical Christian women. In her ethnographic account of women's testimonials in the Women's Aglow Fellowship, Griffith discovered that the intimacy of the prayer group created a refuge where members could speak of troubles at home and reinscribe events of their lives in the company of others. More important, through prayer-group interaction and testimonials, "women teach each other how to deal with those kinds of pressures" in the home by offering examples of their own triumphs expressed in the religious language of submission.[6] Although Mrs. Jung's act of surrendering her negative thoughts to the Buddha to recast herself as the source of her troubles resembles the process whereby Aglow women surrender their wills to God to rework domestic relationships, an important distinction remains. This distinction in the act of surrender and submission hinges on a doctrinal matter of significance in understanding Buddhist women's agency.

Members of the Diamond Sutra recitation group are encouraged to surrender negative afflictions to the Buddha Maitreya in order to cleanse their minds and take control of their emotions. This has the further benefit of transforming relationships with spouses. However, because women incorporate the doctrine of Buddha Nature in their narratives, they also maintain their potential for enlightenment and Buddhahood. As such, surrender of negative emotions is directed toward the Buddha and further engineers their own path to Buddhahood. While the express purpose of this act is a better relationship with one's spouse, the woman does not explicitly apply the language of submission to her husband that Griffith's study of Aglow women indicates.

For female members, the recitation group can also be a venue for freely expressing hardships endured in the home in a supportive environment outside the presence of their husbands. Whether through the Saturday testimonial session or informal conversation, women help each other get through difficult times. Mrs. Jung explains, "people who come to me are usually unhappy so I share my own experiences with others and offer what I have received through the teachings to help them come to terms with their problems and find happiness like I have." For example, before the Saturday evening meeting begins, a group of six or seven women arrive around five-thirty to prepare dinner. During one Saturday session, four women sat on the floor in the kitchen preparing burritos as they chatted, joked, and talked intimately about their families.

As the women stuffed the tortillas with homemade Korean style salsa and beef, one woman began to discuss the Buddhist tenet of viewing all people as if they were Buddhas. Smiling, she turned to her friends and said, "Well, I looked at my husband and tried to envision him like he was a Buddha, but you know, after I did that I stopped and thought to myself, No way! The Buddha couldn't possibly look as bad as that!" Laughing out loud at her joke, the women rolled their eyes and nodded in agreement that, yes, looking upon one's husband as a Buddha can be one of the most challenging things a woman must do. In the intimate setting of preparing meals, a job usually undertaken by women in most Korean religious institutions, women commiserate, laugh, and find the strength to endure troubling relationships.

While such gendered space provides an opportunity to ridicule and thereby resist male dominance, I do not wish to suggest that these everyday practices reflect a romantic subversion of hierarchies that are upheld in other, more public settings. Rather, I want to draw attention to the complexities of gender identities that are discursively constructed and assertions of selfhood that are, as Dorinne Kondo contends, "rhetorical figures and performative assertions enacted in specific situations within fields of power, history and culture."[7]

A further indication of the complexity of gender relationship in this Buddhist setting can be found in the comments of the lay leader of the recitation group on women's potential for enlightenment. During his introduction to new members earlier that evening, the leader discussed the special importance of Buddhist prayer for women and claimed that the Diamond Sutra recitation group "does not acknowledge that the female Buddhist is spiritually equal to the male Buddhist. To become more like a Buddha, you must first be a man because the Buddha was a man." He continued, "the female Buddhists believe and agree with this. They just pray that they will be reborn as men." As soon as he stated the group's "official" position, a brief silence ensued and the women suddenly began to laugh at the leader, acknowledging that while some Buddhist texts may make such proclamations, they themselves did not internalize such gender discrimination. Yet at the same time, the women did not vocally challenge his remarks. On a separate occasion I asked his wife if she agreed with her husband's view on women's capacity for enlightenment. She replied:

> It's not the man's body that we really need to have, but the man's strength of heart. Women are always hanging on to men and relying on them too much. For example, see this garbage can here? A woman would try to lift it and think to herself "no, I can't do that!" But a man would not think that way. In a sense, having a man's heart and strength of mind is the more important thing for us.

Her response illustrates her belief that it wasn't women's bodies per se that were cited as hindrances, but more a certain weakness of mind which could easily be improved by an increase in religious practice.

Anthropologist Sherry Ortner refers to sites of gender resistance and stricture as neither the exertion of a free female agency nor the complete dominance of patriarchal structures in women's lives. Ortner argues against the romance of resistance in indexing any free agency and argues for an "embedded agency" that sees individuals as acting against while remaining within structures of power. It is her conceptualization of everyday practices as a "serious game" that proves most useful in decoding the scenario at the discussion group's meeting. She comments:

the idea of the game—the serious game—is . . . meant to resolve a number of problems in a broader theory of practice that arise particularly from concerns that animate feminist, minority, postcolonial subaltern theorizing. One is the necessity for retaining an active intentional subject without falling into some form of free agency and voluntarism. . . . [I]f we take the methodological unit of practice as the game, rather than the "agent," we can never lose sight of the mutual determination(s) of agents and structures: of the fact that players are defined and constructed (though never wholly contained) by the game.[8]

At seven sharp, members of the discussion group gather and bow in unison in three directions, take a copy of the Diamond Sutra and a meditation cushion, and sit on the floor. Within a few moments, members begin to read the sutra out loud. The recitation continues for at least half an hour as newer members struggle to keep up with the rigorous pace of group recitation and the veterans maintain the mental focus and physical endurance necessary to breathe and recite simultaneously. Throughout the recitation session, Mrs. Jung's voice emerges powerfully from the bellows of her body to cue the less experienced who fumble along as they attempt to coordinate turning the text's pages, breathing, and chanting. As the voices meld together in a constant pace, members are enjoined to cultivate calmness and "polish the mind," to escape from personal turmoil.

Thirty minutes later, the group's lay leader picks up a bamboo meditation stick *(chukpi)* and announces that the reverential reading of the text is complete. The sounds of the *chukpi* striking his palm signals members to rise from their cushions onto their knees and fold their hands in prayer to begin chanting Maitreya Buddha's name repeatedly: *Miruk Chon Yorae Bul . . . , Miruk Chon Yorae Bul . . . , Miruk Chon Yorae Bul.* For at least fifteen minutes members face a wall or keep their eyes closed as they melodically invoke the Buddha's name. In chanting the name, members offer up all negative thoughts and karmic hindrances to Maitreya Buddha, who then cleanses their impurities. Again, the sound of the *chukpi* indicates that the session is finished. After bowing in three directions once again, members collect their cushions and arrange them in two piles at the rear of the *bopdang*. The men unfold the short Korean tables in long horizontal rows and women set out paper plates and cups for the informal dinner. Once members are seated around the table on the floor and the food has been set out, the leader offers the food to the Buddha and members again recite *Miruk Chon Yorae Bul* twice out of gratitude.

All the members of the recitation group are first-generation Korean immigrants who share similar circumstances—language problems, extended work hours, changes in their social status, and alienation. During the testimonial sessions, however, a newcomer can share a frightening story in the context of the others' experience, and they will help her reinterpret the cause of her suffering as herself and urge her to take responsibility for her struggles. The newcomer is then urged to "surrender these anxieties to the Buddha." In so doing, she learns to transform experiences of suffering into something meaningful and ultimately surmountable. Religious observance and discussion guide women to adopt proactive measures to challenge life's vicissitudes and engineer a transformation of the self and relationships with others. As Mrs. Jung explains:

> You know, I used to always try to change the way my husband acted, but I realized that it was impossible to change him. After reading the sutras and chanting the Buddha's name, it became obvious to me that I needed to change myself and that if I changed the way I act toward my husband, then he too would treat me better. I realized that I was, in a way, making my husband act that way because I showed him an unkind face and was always angry. Now, whenever I really need my husband to help me, he knows that I am genuinely asking and now says, "Okay sure." My relationship has gotten a lot better. I don't get as upset as much and I try to understand my husband and have more patience because women's hearts are prone to cry and become angry. But I don't do that anymore because I calmed myself down. Before, my emotions would just get in the way but now I am able to gather my thoughts and express them better.

The recitation group member's narrative of self-transformation coincides with the strategies of weakness documented by Helen Hardacre in her study of lay Buddhist women of Reiyukai Kyodan, a Nichiren-based organization in Japan.[9] Hardacre notes that by utilizing strategies of weakness (extreme deference and subservience to men), Reiyukai women assert their power within the acceptable metanarrative of Japanese culture that dictates female submission to male authority. Affirming family values and extreme female deference, these wives strategically draw their spouses into closer relationships of emotional dependence. Just as a Reiyukai wife can manipulate her spouse into terminating an extramarital affair by silently enduring humiliation and triggering his guilt, a Korean woman is encouraged to tacitly persuade her husband to treat her better by responding to him with kindness and deference. A key distinction, however, is that guilt and repentance do not play a role in the Diamond Sutra recitation group's ideology. Rather, women are taught that they may change relationships by relying on their own strength to cope with suffering rather than eliciting guilt from another party. In addition, they are encouraged to overcome crises by being persuaded to see that they themselves have played a role in the development of the problem.

Through informal testimonials, members of the group share intimate details of their personal lives that are kept private in other public settings. Because members may feel alienated in larger social settings with co-ethnics, some seek the intimacy of the testimonial sessions that cultivate strong relationships of comradery and mutual trust. This lay bond eventually becomes highly guarded and respected, even more so than a relationship with a monk. One woman even admitted that she keeps her participation in the recitation group hidden to avoid the criticism of others who might view their practices as illogical and irrational. Some members indicate that they simply do not wish to share their personal experiences with too many other people (husbands and mother-in-laws included).

For Mrs. Jung, a thirty-seven-year-old mother of two, the Diamond Sutra has empowered her to overcome the isolation she felt as a non-English-speaking immigrant in 1992. Like many Korean women, Mrs. Jung changed her religious affiliation from that of her natal family to that of her husband's (Buddhism). Yet, she claims, "it was not until five years ago when I first began to read the Diamond Sutra that I even considered myself a Buddhist." When she arrived in California, she felt "stuck" and extremely lonely in Burbank since her husband was attending dental school full time in Los Angeles. At the same time, she was left at home with an infant to raise and forced to cater to the needs of her in-laws, whom she admits she could not get along with because her mother-in-law was constantly "nagging" her. Trained as a concert pianist in Korea, Mrs. Jung never wanted to immigrate to the United States and suddenly found herself in Burbank without friends or her own family. Her anxieties and isolation led her to resent her husband and question why she married him in the first place. Eventually, she states, her constant loneliness led her to obsess over whether her husband even loved her. Plagued with loneliness and doubt, her early immigration experiences were extremely dislocating.

"Luckily," she recalls, "around this time, I came across a copy of a Korean Buddhist book called *Polishing the Diamond, Enlightening the Mind*, written by a monk from South Korea.[10] When I read this book for the first time, I began to cry and cry and I just couldn't stop crying and I suddenly felt as though I knew the master all my life!" As soon as she finished reading the book, Mrs. Jung claims she became a "true" Buddhist and began to work toward making her life more enjoyable and less anxious. Rather than trying to change those around her with whom she was always angry (such as her husband, she adds), *Polishing the Diamond, Enlightening the Mind* enabled her to see that it was *she herself*—her deluded mind—that was the culprit of her suffering. Hence, if she learned to let go of her deluded thoughts, she would be able to alter her personal relationships. "By surrendering my negative mind to the Buddha and constantly polishing the diamond [the mind]," Mrs. Jung maintains that she has transformed herself from a depressed, angry woman into a loving wife and good mother who even learned to treat her in-laws with a purer mind and heart. She states:

> I finally understood the idea of cleansing one's mind through the Diamond Sutra. It was originally because of my bad relationship with my mother-in-law that I sought religion. Before, I used to think that my mother-in-law didn't understand me or even like me at all. She used to be angry with me all the time, but not anymore. The relationship has changed, but really, it is me that changed. I believed things were different because I began to try to understand her. Now, even she recites the sutra!

In return, she has experienced the benefits of changing her behavior since her husband and children are now naturally drawn to wanting to treat her well. Her children pay more attention to her requests, and her husband is now more emotionally attentive. In fact, she claims, "because my husband saw the dramatic change in my attitude, he too became a devout Buddhist and now is a leader in the recitation group." Mrs. Jung is also quite proud that she has been able to influence her in-laws in a positive way by introducing them to the teaching, for now her in-laws love her.

By reading the sutra and reciting the Buddha's name, she has learned to avoid responding to her negative emotions. After offering her mind to the Buddha, she claims that her family began to respond more positively to her because she had managed to surrender her negativity and "wrong attitude." Her own status in her family has risen because her children are impressed by her religious devotion and have come to "really respect" her. She is pleased that her children are learning about Buddhism through her example but will not force them to become active Buddhists, for she firmly believes that Buddhism is about "self-knowledge." Her kids should choose their own religion because "they have their own lives to live." Despite experiencing marital stress, isolation, and distress over having to negotiate a new culture and raising her children in the United States, Mrs. Jung has been able to transform her life through intense religious devotion in the company of others. For Mrs. Jung, chanting the sutra is not a one-time deal; rather "you have to constantly polish that diamond!" Even now when she feels depressed, she just opens the text to any page and reads. "Somehow," she says, "it always turns out to be something relevant to my problems."

BUDDHISM FOR MY FAMILY AND BUDDHISM FOR MYSELF

One of the women who participates in the recitation group's dawn services is Mrs. Han, a forty-two-year-old working mother of two who immigrated to the United States in 1981. While she has attended Sa Chal since 1985 with her husband and her mother-in-law, Mrs. Han admits that she does so only out of respect for her in-laws and her husband's demands. Raised a Buddhist, she did not begin to worship regularly until her marriage and subsequent move into her Buddhist in-laws' home. Like many Korean women I have met, Mrs. Han has suffered throughout her marriage because, as she says, "Korean women have a particularly hard time because of their husband and because of their in-laws you know. They have more worries than men because they have to live with in-laws, which can be extremely difficult."

BUDDHIST PRACTICE AND SELF-TRANSFORMATION

Prior to joining the Diamond Sutra recitation group, Mrs. Han admits that her health was suffering and she felt depressed and angry all the time.

She recalls that in 1993 she felt perpetually anxious and exhausted, so she turned to the temple's pianist, who invited her to a meeting of the recitation group. After her first worship service, Mrs. Han states emphatically.

> I found myself there. I really found the kind of practice that I knew would help me. I found my heart here in the Diamond Sutra. Since then, I have been coming to the recitation group Mondays through Fridays before working in the Wilshire district. Every morning before I go to work, which starts at 6:30, I go to the *bopdang*, read the sutra, and recite the Buddha's name.

She describes her first experience of recitation and chanting as one of "complete surprise and shock because I went to the group with an intense headache but oddly enough it disappeared immediately after reciting the text." Following her initial experience, she brought the text and accompanying chanting tape home and began "to practice regularly to study my own heart." She continues, "After reading the text the first time I developed a strong desire to come to the recitation group—to find the right state of mind." Mrs. Han cites this specific moment in her life as the time when her family relationships changed for the better and claims that she has:

> become calmer and much less angry. I used to be upset all the time and I would get so angry with my husband and he would get so angry with me. But after coming to the reading group and praying, I have learned to calm my mind down toward the people that I hate and I have learned to let go and accept the negative past. Reading [the Diamond Sutra] has enabled me to calm myself down.

Through her recitation practices, she takes responsibility for changing her negative relationships on her own, for "my husband didn't change at all. It was me that did the changing."

Interestingly, Mrs. Han is forced to hide her attendance at the reading group from her husband and her in-laws, who seem to take offense at her trying something outside of their family tradition of going to Sa Chal. Yet she manages to attend every morning discreetly on her way to work. Her husband, a semiregular Sa Chal member, forbids her to go to the meetings because he thinks they are cultish and too focused on one text alone. Even her mother-in-law forbids her, for she believes that whatever free time Mrs. Han has should go to her two teenage children—a boy sixteen and a girl thirteen. Ironically, her children know that she goes to the recitation group yet they keep this knowledge from their father and grandmother. In this way, Mrs. Han believes that she has bonded with her children secretly and influences them by bringing them to the group whenever she has the opportunity. She hopes they will come to the recitation group more often in the future even though they also attend Sa Chal. She tells them that if they ever are having a particularly hard time, they should read the sutras and chant *Mirok Chon Yorae Bul*. However, like many Buddhist parents, she never forces them to go to temple but hopes that eventually they will follow her example.

Had I not taken the time to listen to women's conversations through this research project, I never would have learned of this alternative to the "official" temple-based religious activity. What I originally thought was a loose noncommittal religious practice that allowed people to come to temple on Sundays "if they felt like it" turned out to be the opposite: religious lives that are deeply committed, but outside the public domain. Hence, women like Mrs. Jung can come to the Diamond Sutra recitation group to address problems in their immediate lives and eschew the hierarchy and formality of the temple for matters of intimate concern. Because they do not wish to lay bare their innermost concerns and risk vulnerability in the reserved social setting of Sa Chal, these women have sought alternative religious spaces. Members of the Diamond Sutra recitation group believe that individuals are responsible for their own enlightenment and do not require the assistance of religious virtuosos. This desire for ritual agency finds doctrinal legitimacy in the oft-quoted Buddhist idioms of "knowing one's true self" and "the Buddha Nature," which give these women the claim to self-knowledge as a means of self-healing without the need for a monastic specialist.

Since members of the recitation group choose to remain members of the larger temples in Los Angeles like Sa Chal, the two forms of worship appear to function in mutually enhancing ways. A dual membership in Sa Chal and the recitation group offers both a recognized participation in the larger Korean Buddhist community and a more private (and perhaps more effective) worship that allows for personal change and consolation on an intimate level. The recitation group has had such a profound impact on members' lives that the twenty plus members were motivated to raise enough money to purchase the group's current worship home.

Mrs. Han works in an ethnically mixed office in Koreatown and followed her husband to Los Angeles nineteen years ago. Although she tells me that she never wanted to leave Korea and hated living in the United States with her in-laws, her religious worship has helped her combat her depression and anger. Mrs. Han feels well adjusted to life in America and now can speak both languages. Furthermore, she has "armed [her]self with the strongest possible weapon—the mind." She states that she is very proud of the recitation group, and while she does not want to "missionize" since she feels she still needs to keep working on her own problems, her life has certainly improved. In fact, she says that often Korean women come to her and ask about the group or ask for some advise presumably because they have noticed how calm she is. While she does not feel comfortable with the notion of *pogyo* (dissemination), she does try to teach people and urge them to read the sutra whenever they can.

As a testament to the change in her personality, she describes how after a month of practice, her husband came home one day and looked at her and proclaimed, "You seem much happier these days. What's going on? Do you have a boyfriend or something?" She laughs as she tells the story of how by learning to calm her mind and no longer look at her husband angrily, he too has been calmed by her influence, "for if I look at him calmly and softly, how can he possibly get angry at me?" Mrs. Han claims that many women at Sa Chal are in a similar situation and that is probably why there are more women who come to the temple to worship. She believes that women have more grief because they are burdened with raising the family, living with in-laws, working long hours, and dealing with "husbands who think they are better than anyone else." She believes that male arrogance makes men too embarrassed or proud to come to the temple for devotional practices:

> You see, men like my husband tend to practice religion through the intellect by studying the Buddha's teaching. But I don't think that is enough. You also have to pray, but men think they are too good to bow down to the Bud-

dha or look like they are too attached to the Buddha especially in the company of women. So a lot of times, men may pray at home, but they certainly won't in front of others. As for me, my personality is best suited for prayer and for focusing on finding one's mind. It is better to change oneself and act positively, for it is more effective. But . . . well, I guess that both are important together but my husband studies Buddhism too much without praying, which isn't a good thing.

That she thinks women are more religious because their hearts are stronger and their problems greater implies that men cannot always provide what women need. "That," she says, "is why women seek out religion. That's why I come." Thus, although her husband may try to control her, she resorts to duplicitous measures by pretending to go to work earlier so as not to explicitly resist the familial and cultural gender hierarchy while going about her business of recitation. Many wives like Mrs. Han will attend Sa Chal on Sundays but then go to the recitation group "to really find yourself or when you really have a problem."

Mrs. Han finds solace at the recitation group among her peers. The only husbands who come to the group apparently are ones dragged there by their wives. Because her husband forbids her to go to the recitation group, Mrs. Han can never attend the Saturday evening services although she occasionally lies and says that her friends have invited her out to socialize. She says that she learns from the shared stories of the six or seven women who attend the weekday morning session, especially since they have similar problems. Mrs. Han and others are aware that monks and people like her husband are suspicious of the group and "some even say that the group is related to shamans." Some monks are also believed to disapprove of the group because it could potentially take away members from their temples. Because the monks at Sa Chal do not approve of these women's practices, which do not rely on the monastic authority in terms of ritual, the women are not able to engage in a ritual recitation program in the early mornings at Sa Chal. Yet rather than choose one over the other, Mrs. Han believes that a combination of the two is fine. She can go to the temple to appease her husband and socialize with her temple friends and not raise the misgivings and gossip of others. She adds, "sometimes coming to the recitation group can be really difficult because the practice itself is so grueling and besides, sometimes people can get lazy and that is probably a good time to go to Sa Chal."

For someone like Mrs. Han, going to Sa Chal on the weekends might appear at odds with her daily morning services at the recitation group. However, Sa Chal membership engages her in a public form of religion where she visibly demonstrates to her husband and mother-in-law that she is a virtuous wife and obedient daughter-in-law. Her early morning recitation group visits symbolize a more private form of religion, where she says her true heart lies. The larger public temple enables her to maintain an outer face of obedience and propriety as she chooses not to challenge but seemingly acquiesces in the desires of her husband so as not to embarrass the family. By maintaining her membership at Sa Chal, she does not raise the suspicion of other temple members who might gossip about her going to "that cult" because "everyone in the temple talks, you know." Through her participation in both private and public places of worship, Mrs. Han recreates and reenacts many selves as she shuttles between them.

Religious identity and the work involved in fashioning a self that has conquered suffering afford Buddhist women the opportunity to take responsibility for lives gone awry. That religion is often viewed by practitioners as women's work in this contemporary Buddhist community does not account for one of the primary motivations for attending temple in the first place—a desire to rework the self. Women's religious participation has consistently been viewed through the lens of Confucian ideology by practitioners and scholars of Korean religions alike who equate women's religious impulses with a desire to maintain the family's well-being. While women are defined and define themselves vis-à-vis their spouses and children, they also construct for themselves Buddhist identities that actively strengthen their resolve to improve their confidence, self-valuation, education, and agency and, at the same time, do so while remaining wives and mothers. The life conditions of Sa Chal women are often beset with troubles related to religious conversion, ethnic minority status, middle age, and gender. Buddhism provides a culturally acceptable framework for interpreting those troubles through the rhetoric of karma, self-knowledge, and Buddha Nature to render them solvable. By acknowledging their own culpability in severed relationships, illness, depression, and discord, women take the steps necessary to change their lives by controlling what had hitherto been viewed as outside their control. That is, women imbue significant and traumatic events with karmic meaning and learn to see themselves as key players in life's affairs. By taking an active role in the unfolding of unpleasant events, women change the plot and their interpretations of the outcome of their life stories by dissolving the forces behind karmic hindrances.

A methodology of resonance illuminates how individuals endure and order their experiences and the stakes involved in narrating a life according to culturally viable lines. The power of a Buddhist identity lies in its ability to resolve conflict as the individual strives to establish a critical relationship between her religious system of ideas and her "lived predicament." By casting and narrating one's experience through the lens of karma theory, Buddha Nature, and "knowing one's mind," women initiate a transformation of the self in which lives that eluded them and created suffering are given Buddhist significance. The women's stories I discuss in this chapter share a remarkable resemblance to the conversion narratives in the lives of evangelical Christians studied by Peter Stromberg. Stromberg's study of the performance of conversion stories notes that the actual telling of the story is in itself of utmost importance in the efficacy of transformation. Like the Buddhist in my own study, Stromberg has found that social actors come to a coherent sense of themselves through the deployment of canonical language to resolve their personal conflicts. That is, individuals create a semblance of order from their fragmented lives through recourse to doctrine "to create a meaningful link between the symbol system (Bible) and his or her own experience."[11] In other words, a relationship of immediacy established with and through canonical or doctrinal language creates a change for the individual narrating her story. The conversion story thus articulates how the workings of religious ideology impinge on the person.

Buddhism as practiced by members at Sa Chal does not include an official use of the conversion narrative per se. Nonetheless, individuals come to order their lives by creating a relationship to Buddhist canonical language that both promotes individual agency and reestablishes unseemly behavior as the inevitable result of what takes place when a person acts without knowledge of doctrine. The women in my study have acted in ways that are conditioned by karma, which casts culpability for misdeeds back on themselves, yet at the same time they employ the canonical language of self-knowledge and Buddha Nature to deem their lives transformed. Nonetheless, these women's identities are not completely solidified or necessarily changed for the better. In fact, the narrative project of both myself and my interviewees offers the chance, as Kondo puts it, "to find meaning in the chaos of lived experience through retrospectively ordering the past. It is a kind of Proustian quest in which the ethnographer [and participant] seeks meaning in events whose significance was elusive while they were being lived."[12] Their identities are constantly constructed and changing; however, it is the description and narration of events that are equally important in coming to a coherent and positive sense of self.

5

Buddhism—An Anchor in an Uncertain World and a Source of Independence

In his examination of religion as lived experience, Robert Orsi proposes that studies of religion take as their primary focus the social actor or worshipper who is embedded within and acts upon the cultures and communities that he or she inherits. That is, an ethnographic person-centered approach to understanding religion reveals how individuals "appropriate religious idioms as they need them, in response to particular circumstances." Viewing religion as both inherited and improvisational, Orsi points to the dynamic, highly personal, and idiosyncratic nature of religious involvement where individuals deploy religious meanings to transform and reinterpret life experiences to render them endurable and intelligible.[1] This chapter examines how such religious idioms and practices offer Korean American Buddhist women strategies to adjust to a new culture (1) by indexing the homeland left behind and (2) by providing the inspiration and rationale for breaking from tradition to "make it on one's own." Both strategies of adjustment are utilized by women in this study as a means of developing self-esteem.

For some women at Sa Chal, temple membership and a Buddhist identity act as symbols of the homeland that encourage an alternative pattern of adjustment to full-scale integration into a new cultural milieu. Religion provides these women with a sense of comfort and belonging to a familiar community by alleviating some of the stresses of immigration and anchoring women in a traditional setting that references the security of what they left behind. Buddhism, like Christianity for Korean American Christian women, thus helps them adjust to large-scale changes in their lives by offering psychological comfort as a home away from home. In this way, religion can be said to offer a salient means of coping at a crucial moment in their lives when, as Pargament and Park put it, "people strive for significance in stressful times in ways related to the sacred."[2]

A central component of this process of coping through religion can be "finding and knowing one's mind," which provides women with an opportunity to rely on themselves to develop methods of adaptation. In other words, despite the alienation they feel living in the United States, many women at Sa Chal seek to better their lives first by acknowledging that although they experienced tremendous loneliness and isolation in their new country, they were inspired to change these negative experiences through Buddhism. Of the women whose stories I present in this section, all sought meaningful positions in the temple as volunteers that they could not find elsewhere; in this way they learn to see themselves as agents in their own process of coping and they develop self-esteem by taking on responsibility for the temple's smooth functioning. At the same time, such strategies can have the unintended consequence of exacerbating feelings of isolation not only in American culture but also in the smaller Buddhist community for those women who are particularly shy and withdrawn. By relying on the temple as their primary social world outside the home, many of these women experience the temple and their Buddhist identities as an anchor in an uncertain world and avoid integration into American society. They become solely reliant on the temple as a small ethnic community where they need not worry about learning English or adjusting to American cultural values. Thus, while many women find psychological comfort in the temple, their lack of integration in the larger Los Angeles community sustains the feelings of insecurity they experienced when they arrived in the United States. As a result, it may be said that for some, the Buddhist temple isolates them in a small ethnic community, making it nearly impossible for them to make the transition into living as a Korean American. Interestingly, Ai Ra Kim notes that a similar phenomenon of isolation exists for women in Korean American Christian churches who are unable to speak English and do not work outside the home.[3]

On the other hand, Buddhist ideologies of self-knowledge and self-reliance can enable some women to adjust to life in America by furnishing the courage to venture outside the social setting of the temple into the working world. In this case, a Buddhist identity based on "finding and knowing one's mind" offers women a chance to recreate their identities from housewives and caretakers to "Americans making it on their own." The latter half of this chapter presents the stories of two women who have actively chosen to leave their previous lives as housewives behind in order to pursue their own American dreams without depending on men for social, economic, and psychological security. In so doing, these women actualize the independence they associate with both Buddhist doctrines and American culture.

For these women, religion serves as a means of finding legitimacy by asserting an identity that offers the strength to forge ahead while endeavoring to create nontraditional lives in the United States. In many ways, religion may help justify life choices that run counter to prevailing gender norms and contribute to the development of assertiveness as women recreate their lives in America as individuals instead of wives dependent on and defined by husbands. In this manner, many women find self-fulfillment defined by a new set of criteria where they judge themselves by their independent financial and social accomplishments fostered by and interpreted through their Buddhist teachings. Buddhism offers a protective community among co-ethnic Koreans as a means of holding onto a positive sense of self and a chance to try something new and "become American" or independent in the United States.

SEEING THE WORLD THROUGH BUDDHIST-COLORED LENSES

Mrs. Lee stands outside the temple's print shop wearing the traditional gray lay Buddhist robes *(bopbok)* and a large wooden Buddhist rosary she has worn every day for the two years I have know her. As I approach the temple, she turns her head away. As she says, she does "not like to talk to people." I quickly greet her with a bow and say in a loud voice, *Anyounghasaeyo Possallim!* (Good Morning Bodhisattva). Immediately this lay women who resembles a nun turns around and says, "You know, it really is surprising that you want to talk to me. I don't like to talk. Why would you want to talk to somebody crazy like me?" Mrs. Lee's response reflects her surprise that anyone should find someone like her worthy of conversation or even interviewing.

Feminist scholar Beverley Skeggs notes that the interview process can be a positive experience for many women who believe that their lives are not interesting enough to discuss. While the position of researcher creates a hierarchical relationship between the researcher who shapes and limits her study and the participant who responds to preplanned questions, this does not preclude the possibility that the relationship can be experienced as beneficial. In her study of community-college women, Skeggs found that "students' sense of self-worth was enhanced by being given the opportunity to be valued, knowledgeable and interesting. . . . This challenges the idea that the researched are *just* objects of a voyeuristic bourgeois gaze."[4] Anthropologist Kamala Visweswaran, however, characterizes ethnographic encounters as betrayals—that is, the betrayal of a universally understood comradery between researcher and participant based on gender. Such comradery is a privileged relationship in which the interview participant will offer knowledge out of trust based on gender. Visweswaran thus argues that acts of silence like Mrs. Lee's may in fact be read as a marker of her resistance *and* capitulation to my position as researcher.[5]

Mrs. Lee usually chants Buddhist sutras alone on Friday evenings in the large Buddha hall of Sa Chal to the sounds of her own *moktak* (wooden gong). An indispensable part of the daily life of the temple, Mrs. Lee prepares food for the resident monks and alternates working in the print shop with her husband and praying in the dharma halls upstairs. On special occasions, she prepares Korean treats like *o-gak bab* (five-grain rice), sets tables, and lays out food for temple guests, yet she rarely participates as an active member in any of these events. This extremely reticent fifty-one-year-old woman usually avoids the 11:00 Sunday service and keeps her distance from most people at the temple.

Mrs. Lee can generally be found working alone in the kitchen wearing her gray robes, woolen cap, and red rubber gloves to prepare *kimchee* and other Korean vegetarian dishes. Her heightened shyness has the unfortunate consequence that other temple members refer to her as "crazy," "strange," or "rude," a situation that exacerbates her sense of alienation.

Accustomed to her way of not speaking to others personally, I was surprised when one Friday morning she invited me into her print shop to chat. As soon as I sat down at her desk, which was scattered with scraps of paper with Buddhist mantras and songs written all over them, Mrs. Lee demanded that I hide my pen, paper, and tape recorder from her sight. She then explained, "I don't really know anything at all, but since you have been so nice to me and said hello to me every day, I feel sorry about [not talking to you]." After a few more minutes of small talk, she warned me again, "I don't even know how to pray! Please excuse me! I am sorry." Consistent with her exaggerated self-deprecation and modesty, Mrs. Lee then related the following:

> Even a person like me [pointing to herself] appreciates the Buddha's teachings. For a long time I studied Buddhism and said that I was a Buddhist. In the Buddha's time, there was a deaf mute person and he couldn't speak a word.... Now why did he become a deaf mute? In this person's previous life, people would ask him about the nature of the Buddha's teachings, but he would be so modest that he would merely reply, "Oh I don't know, I don't know, I don't know"... and so that became his karma. In his next life, he was reborn a deaf mute. So from what the Buddha says, even if you know just a tiny bit or the smallest amount of the dharma, if just that much has matured in your mind then don't just say that "I don't know, I don't know." Instead, even if you only know a little bit, then transmit and disseminate just that much to the person who doesn't know the Buddha's dharma. This is what the Buddha said. Based on that, I have developed strength and forced myself to spread the Buddha's teaching to people whose karma I [am related to], even though I don't like to talk.

This laywoman is quite cognizant of her marginal position in the temple community, yet her use of this Buddhist story enables us to understand how the enactment of a Buddhist identity encourages her to try to interact with others. Through her narration of the Buddha's teachings, Mrs. Lee rationalizes her unusual act of speaking in the company of others (myself) and claims that her desire to speak to others is always motivated by a desire to spread the Buddha dharma. By recalling the story of the deaf mute, she encourages herself to develop confidence in what she considers her lack of knowledge and compares herself to the deaf mute with his constant refrain of "I don't know, I don't know."

Realizing similar tendencies in herself, she tries to overcome her low self-esteem by acting on her responsibility to teach the dharma lest her future bring a fate analogous to the deaf mute's. Mrs. Lee thus realizes that in order to overcome her personal troubles, she must learn to rely on herself and offers the Buddha's story as an analogy and model to learn from. Finding inspiration in Buddhist teachings, she takes "what little [she] knows" and deems herself capable of transmitting the dharma by casting me in the role of the one who does not know the Buddha's teachings. By interpreting our conversation as a dharma lesson, she endeavors to create a self worthy of speech. Telling her own story by way of a Buddhist narrative enables her to construct an identity that both reflects her anxiety and offers the chance to challenge her usual self in favor of an ideal self who speaks confidently.

Oral historian Sherna Gluck points to the importance of ethnic or class similarity as well as gender in doing interview-based research. She maintains that the nature of an interview can change depending on whether or not the woman being interviewed feels a sense of affinity with the interviewer. As such, reading subtle cultural cues is very important, as are body language and vocabulary. She notes:

> the collaboration between the interviewer and interviewee results in more than new "historical documents." It allows for the creation of a new literature, a literature which can tap the language and experiences of those who do not ordinarily have access to such public expression except perhaps through the more anonymous form of folk culture.[6]

Anthropologists in diverse ethnographic fields have noted that the process of narration in the research situation creates a dialogical reality whereby both researcher and participant engage in projects of utmost concern to the self.[7] In discussing the shifting and overlapping role of the researcher in creating sites or opportunities for the crafting of identities on the part of interviewees, Dorinne Kondo reflects on her own ethnographic research:

> We [researcher and informants] participated in each other's lives and sought to make sense of one another. In that attempt to understand, power inevitably came into play as we tried to force each other into appropriately

comprehensible categories. This nexus of power and meaning was also creative, the crucible within which we forged our relationship.[8]

But what conditions have contributed to Mrs. Lee's self-deprecation, shyness, self-imposed silence, and eventual interest in talking with me?

Like many Korean American women living in a new culture, Mrs. Lee struggles to make sense of her environment. Like all immigrants in a new country, she must adjust to her inability to speak or comprehend English, her new entrance into the work force, and changes associated with her role as a mother and a wife. Based on the twenty-five interviews I conducted with the female members of Sa Chal, language barriers, financial burden, concerns over their children's acculturation, and confinement within the Korean ethnic enclave were cited as the most common sources of anxiety and stress.

One of the central concerns of Korean immigrants in America is the issue of generational status inversion, where the children in the household are cast in the role of navigating the new culture but at the same time are held to the sociocultural standards of the homeland.[9] Many women in Mrs. Lee's age group (early to mid-fifties) admitted that they suffered from the coming of age of their children, who then left the house for college or marriage. Furthermore, according to social worker and sociologist Young In Song, "[s]tringent sex role teachings, which are apparent at birth in Asian countries, can cause women to mainly identify themselves by their reproductive and maternal functions rendering adjustments hard to manage."[10]

Not only did Mrs. Lee leave Korea, where she comfortably raised her children, and move to a new country completely unprepared to speak the language, she also had to contend with changes in her status and identity as a full-time mother. While women in Korea must also face their children's eventual independence, the transition for immigrant women may be further complicated in the host country since they often have limited resources in their own language that "correspond to their actual needs and functions as they confront the midlife phase of life."[11] Thus the experience of moving to the United States coupled with the passage into midlife can lead to a crisis in personal identity for a recent immigrant.

Mrs. Lee does not dwell on her life in Korea, although she indicates that she happily passed most of her time at a Korean Buddhist temple in Seoul, where she knew Abbot Lee, "who was like a Buddhist superstar" back then. Through her work as a youth leader she met and married the abbot's younger brother and immigrated to the United States in 1983. She arrived or, as she puts it, was "dropped down" into Los Angeles, a place that she "vaguely remember[s] yearning for and thought would be filled with parties all the time." Upon arrival, however, she immediately began working and was forced to adjust to a new culture whose language she could not comprehend.

Although her husband believes that she prefers living in the United States, she admits that her life here is less than satisfactory for "who works these kinds of hours in Korea?!" She continues, "when I was in Korea, I was a housewife. I raised my children, took care of household affairs, and did just that. I didn't do any special kind of work or anything because I put my children's education first." Currently, she and her husband reside in Koreatown and work seven days a week. Since they do not speak any English, their daily lives are restricted to an ethnic enclave while their children are capable of navigating life in America more successfully. As a result of linguistic and cultural barriers, this couple has experienced a downward social and economic shift that necessitates Mrs. Lee's employment.

According to sociologists Kwang Chung Kim and Won Moo Hurh, married female Korean immigrants tend to work despite the "traditional expectations that married women do not work." Since a high-proportion of Korean married men become self-employed, they require affordable labor. In their analysis of the work experiences of 334 female interview participants, Kim and Hurh conclude that the employment of immigrant women produced anxiety for those who continue to view themselves first and foremost as homemakers: "Korean women are socialized to stay at home full-time after marriage. From this perspective, employment of immigrant wives is a sudden role addition in their new environment without any adequate preparation.... Their stress is further aggravated by the unpreparedness of their husbands and other family members to adjust to the employment of their wives."[12]

Not only is Mrs. Lee required to adjust to her minority status and lack of cultural tools for living in America, but she must also contend with working outside the home to engineer the family's economic stability. According to Kim and Hurh's study, such a woman experiences the double

BUDDHISM—AN ANCHOR IN AN UNCERTAIN WORLD

burden of taking care of the home *and* working. Since Mrs. Lee's traditional responsibilities define her as a housewife, she is expected to perform most, if not all, of the household duties in addition to working with her husband every day. And as the wife of the younger brother of a famous Buddhist leader in Korea she probably had greater social prestige in Korea, where the Buddhist population continues to outweigh the number of Christians.[13] The smaller circle of Buddhists in Los Angeles and her new employment status have made immigrant life a challenge:

> Everyone says that life as an immigrant is difficult and everyone sympathizes with it. Of course it is difficult! First of all, the country's structure and the Western style of living are so different. America is so big! Our Korean community is so small in comparison, which makes everything here complicated. Here, you are responsible for yourself and for making a living. But bearing responsibility for yourself is no easy matter; there are very few people who can do that right away. My English is really deficient; I only know broken English. I have lived in this society for fifteen years.

Life in America is clearly not what she hoped it would be. It is in this context of disappointment and dislocation that we can begin to ascertain the complex motivations compelling Mrs. Lee to participate in a religious life at Sa Chal in the solitary manner that she does. She finds strength and consolation through religious teachings and practice to heal her psychological wounds like many of her fellow worshippers. However, in her study of Korean immigrants engaged in small business enterprises in New York, anthropologist Kyeyoung Park has found that for some women, immigration and entrance into the labor force can be seen as freedom from traditional social constraints. While many of her female respondents related their new job status to a desire to make an equal contribution to society and their families, these women did not experience a rise in status in the household.[14]

Unlike many immigrants who flock to temples and churches for fellowship, Mrs. Lee does not reach out to the religious community to socialize in her native tongue and rely on co-ethnic networks of support.[15] She immerses herself in her religious practice at the expense of creating social relationships with her fellow Buddhists in response to anxieties following her migration. As a result, she responds to challenges in her life through the doctrine of the Buddha Nature by an abstract interpretation of all things potentially threatening to her. Commenting on her experiences of living in the United States, she explains:

> These foreigners [Americans] have a lot of good qualities I suppose. In reality I don't think that there are any truly bad people; that's my philosophy anyway. Everybody has the Buddha Nature. I believe one thing about the nature and qualities of the Buddha—that is that the world that we live in, the entire natural world, and the immutable principle [of the world] ... entirely consists of the Buddha Nature. The most important thing is the Buddha Nature. Oh, but please excuse me, I don't really know anything! But even though I don't know anything, I always turn my heart and mind toward the Buddha. Because of that, negative thoughts don't really affect [me]. The nature of Buddhism is so deep and profound. There is nothing that doesn't contain the Buddha Nature. The entire world, a great river, an ion, and the cosmos are all part of the Buddha's world.

Mrs. Lee challenges her lack of confidence when discussing the Buddha dharma and illustrates how religion enables her to make sense of her life. Her view of all things disagreeable, when infused with the Buddha Nature, enables her to transform her life by adopting a religious perspective that sees all things as devoid of actual harm to her. An extremely shy and reticent woman, Mrs. Lee finds solace living a life of service to the temple but chooses to remain apart from the community. At the same time, she feels marginalized from American culture, a situation that contributes to her reliance on the temple. Yet we see from her comments that Buddhism offers her the courage to live in a new culture as she reinterprets stressful situations through the lens of Buddha Nature, thus rendering them nonthreatening. This process of religious interpretation to heal a fragmented self is not without its difficulties, as witnessed in her attempts to check her own speech as she resorts to her usual exaggerated deference and self-denigration.

Like many of the participants in Ai Ra Kim's study of Korean American women in the church, Mrs. Lee makes "no distinction between religious and secular life: a religious life itself is [her] daily life."[16] Religion plays the central role in her life at the expense of social interaction. She explains that she avoids large functions in the temple because "people talk way too much" and recognizes that other temple members criticize her unusual behavior. Illustrating Ai Ra Kim's point that the "more religious the women are, the more they seem to avoid the outside world," she retreats to chanting and meditation to avoid personal confrontations.[17] For this *posal*, silence, semi-monastic behavior, and style of dress create a safe haven away from the gossip of temple members and a retreat from American society at large. Although Mrs. Lee explains that she wears her Buddhist lay robes in honor of the Buddha, the robes also represent a semicenobitic lifestyle as she devotes herself full-time to the Buddha's teachings to avoid the gaze of others. She has thoroughly submerged herself in a life of religious devotion. For this Korean American Buddhist, religious identity becomes the critical means of coping with experiences of dislocation and dissatisfaction heightened by the conditions of immigration.

While Mrs. Lee's religious participation is predicated on being alone in the company of others as she struggles to find solace in her life, Helen Yim's case illustrates a woman's struggle to find relief in the company of co-ethnic Buddhists. Her struggle, however, is no less complicated. Helen, like many women I met at Sa Chal, attends temple out of loneliness and isolation, yet she suffers from anxiety over being in a social setting like the temple where she desires to meet more potential friends but cannot seem to do so as successfully as she would like. Like Mrs. Lee, Helen moved to America with an expectation of prosperity. She recalls:

> I thought that America was a paradise, that there were no tears. I thought that it was a perfect country. Each time I watched television, I would think that the American women were so pretty! But when I got here, it was not like that at all! There were so many unattractive American people, and it was dirty. There were also a lot of thieves! I really thought that America was a paradise and that it was great, so that's why we came here. But in America there are a lot of problems, lots of people crying, lots of divorced people. We didn't know that about America. [My husband came here] for better chances, but he could not speak English. Everybody in America would speak to us and it would just sound like "blah blah blah" to us. We would ask them

BUDDHISM—AN ANCHOR IN AN UNCERTAIN WORLD

"what did you say?" But they treated [us] like ... fool[s]. Nobody hired my husband because he couldn't speak or understand English.

In Korea, Helen was a pharmacist with her own business and "made big money!" Her husband was successfully employed as an engineer yet could find work only as a part-time mechanic in a bike shop in the small town where they first lived in America. While her husband worked in the bike shop and studied to become a car mechanic, this new immigrant stayed at home with her three children and hardly ventured outside.

Helen Yim's early experiences in the United States were characterized by heightened loneliness since she could not speak English and was afraid to drive her car around the Los Angeles area. By her own account, she spent most of her time by herself. Although raised a Buddhist in Korea, Helen could not locate any Buddhist temples in her immediate neighborhood and did not begin attending temple until fifteen years after she immigrated in 1975. Further complicating her Buddhist practice, she married into a Christian family.

Helen explains her difficult situation and comments, "my husband's mother is Christian and she didn't want me to practice Buddhism. Christians only believe in one God, Jehovah, and think that he is the only god. They believe that Buddhism is nothing." In an attempt to appease her in-laws, Helen attended Christian churches a number of times yet felt that in the church, "everything was about comparison. It was very tiring going to church and having people compete all the time. They all talked too much. I like it here at temple because everybody is gentle, very calm, and they don't talk much." In an effort to avoid personal competition with other Koreans in the church, Helen decided to attend Sa Chal, where she believes that for the most part "everybody is very kind and calm, without too much fighting."

Young In Song's study of the patriarchal structure of Korean immigrant churches provides insight into the competitiveness that Helen apparently experienced during her church attendance. According to Song:

> The "status-anxiety," which stems from the marginality of Korean immigrants in American society tends to exist within a church. Immigrants who are unemployed, discriminated against and oppressed by the white major-

ity in American society tend to consider the immigrant church as a place where their desire for recognition can be satisfied.... Korean immigrants accord high esteem and status to lay leadership positions such as elders and deacons or deaconesses. On the whole, the internal conflicts which lead to schisms are directly correlated with the heterogeneity of characteristics of the congregation, status alienation of the immigrants, and the vested interests of Korean clergymen and lay leaders.... Competition for lay leadership positions among Korean men usually evolves into fierce struggle among candidates which frequently accompanies f[r]ictional exaggerated strife within the congregation.[18]

Rather than allow such rivalry to exacerbate her feelings of estrangement in America, fifteen years later Helen opted to return to her Buddhist roots.

In addition to her worship on Sunday mornings, Helen now attends the temple's Buddhist college every Friday night in order to receive her *pogyo* (dissemination) certificate to begin spreading the dharma in the United States. Because she never received any formal training in Buddhist practice yet considers herself a Buddhist, Helen now wants to study the historical and doctrinal foundations of the religion. In addition to filling her time with worship and school, she volunteers as the temple's librarian five days a week, and says that her religious participation comes from a desire to combat boredom. She explains, "I was bored, the kids were grown and I didn't have anything to do so I just figured that I should go take a class" and also come to Sa Chal. A fifty-nine-year-old mother of three, Helen does not wish to work for wages and chooses to fill her time volunteering at the temple and taking care of her home. In this way, she finds self-fulfillment and a sense of pride in providing for the needs of the temple through her work.

Religious participation offered Helen a way of finding meaning in her life after she moved from a position of economic and social comfort in Korea to isolation and insecurity in the United States. When she was a young mother of three, she found her primary fulfillment as a full-time mother, but when her children were married with children of their own, she was compelled to find a new means of defining herself—as Buddhist lay practitioner, Buddhist university student, and temple librarian. All of these new roles contributed to her development of self-esteem.

BUDDHISM—AN ANCHOR IN AN UNCERTAIN WORLD

When asked about the meaning of Buddhism and her motivation for studying its doctrines, she referred to her experiences at the church:

> They [Christians] are exclusive and think now that "Only *my* God, Jehovah is the one." Christians today still believe that Buddhism is only about dancing shamans and ghosts and that only ignorant country folk and illiterates believe in it. I have to study Buddhism more, so that I can answer to things like that. Otherwise, I wouldn't have any confidence.
>
> The one thing I have learned lately is that Buddhism is self-discipline and a religion based on spiritual enlightenment. Some of the faithful [Christians] are like slaves. Christianity is a slave religion because they say that underneath God they are all slaves. But Buddhism teaches that we are all Buddhas, so we always look up and the Christians always look down on themselves. Christians all think that only God is the boss. They always say that they are sinners, but that's not what Buddhism is about. Buddhism teaches that everybody is a Buddha and that people all have the Buddha Nature. That means we have to be good and take care of everybody, even beggars. But if we look at it carefully, Christians say that only the people who believe in God are good and that nonbelievers are going to hell. So that's why they are so exclusive. They are very simple.

Helen's comments indicate a strong resistance to the dominance of Christianity in the Korean American community and a strongly held desire to spread the Buddha dharma among some female Buddhists. Yet we may also view this strong resistance as an indirect way for a woman to voice her dissatisfaction with her Christian mother-in-law. Helen's characterization of her relationship with her in-laws as somewhat strained and ambivalent may be a contributing factor in her diatribe against Christians. In this context, a woman can safely express her anxiety and resistance to her in-laws by associating them with the exclusive Christians whom she deems both threatening and simplistic. By claiming a Buddhist identity in contradistinction to her in-laws, Helen finds an opportunity to work through personal conflicts stemming from her married life by invoking religious symbols and language. Citing the distinctions between Christians who view themselves as subservient to an outside force, Helen creates a sense of independence and pride in self-reliance garnered through Buddhist teachings and practices where the individual is the boss of her own destiny. In this way, she contributes to a positive sense of self where she knows that as a Buddhist she relies on her own decision making and does not have to rely on others to change her life.

In addition to working out relationship issues with her in-laws, Helen focuses on learning about Buddhism to reconnect with her daughter, who—like herself—has married into a Christian family. Her daughter's marriage and non-Buddhist identity are a source of distress for Helen, who fears a loss of intimacy with her daughter. Her participation in the temple provides a context for creating a new role for herself as a Buddhist missionary who can then disseminate the teachings to her daughter. Since her children have all left the house, she no longer has to work or take care of her children and has become more active in Sa Chal. Helen's increased religious participation reflects a combination of religious commitment, a desire to participate in the spread of the dharma, and the hope of finding a new venue for her energies. Hence, her motivations include a desire to renegotiate her status from that of a young mother to that of a woman in a midlife stage of development, for "[t]his change initiates the so-called "empty nest" stage when women experience an attenuation of childrearing responsibility."[19] Her dedication to studying Buddhism establishes a new way of sustaining a mother's influence in her married daughter's life—through the inculcation of religious values.

Helen's struggles to find fellowship and new meaning in her midlife status in the temple setting dictated most of our daily interactions during my field research and also indicate that her desire for companionship and support in the temple has not been met. Throughout my two years of temple interviews, Helen repeatedly urged me to refer to her as "Mom" and envisioned our relationship as a possible catalyst for her own daughter's conversion to Buddhism. For example, during our second interview Helen dialed and redialed her daughter's home phone number at least ten times in the hope that I might teach her daughter about Buddhism in English since she herself could not seem to do so successfully. Despite her continual redialing, Helen was unable to reach her daughter and became visibly distressed. After hanging up the phone, she looked at me and told me that I was just like her daughter and asked me once again to call her "Mom."[20]

While the temple seems to enable Helen to overcome isolation, loneliness, and boredom, she struggles to integrate herself comfortably in the social circle of fellow Buddhists. Although I chose to participate in these scenarios out of respect for her, it became more and more obvious that, as Kondo also experienced, "informants were hardly inert objects for the free play of the ethnographer's desire. They themselves were, in the act of being, actively interpreting and trying to make meaning of the ethnographer."[21] As I tried to understand Helen's motivations for practicing Buddhism to study the role of religion in self-preservation, she was trying to make sense of her own position in the temple through me.

Like Mrs. Lee, Helen's religious practice partially helps her endure changes in her midlife status and new life in America. While Mrs. Lee attempts to isolate herself from the gaze of others, Helen endeavors to belong yet restrains herself from attaining a potential social network. Both women, however, approach the temple and religious life as a haven away from environments where they feel displaced. While many studies of the impact of the church in Korean American lives have focused on how the church enables women and men to adjust to living in a new culture, they routinely neglect a focus on personal idiosyncrasies that detract from a more generalizable study of religion's mediating influences. A focus on the individual person, however, provides opportunities to reveal the complexities of trying to make sense of the disorderliness of life. Observing actual experiences of *being* Buddhist in Korean America shows the difficulty in using religious identity to expose the intricate negotiations of selfhood that take place in community. That is, co-ethnicity and shared religious practice do not guarantee positive experiences of adjustment for members of Sa Chal who seek solace in their religious organizations.

Hae Soo Cho's story represents the experiences of many elderly women at Sa Chal who join the temple out of a host of concerns including the desire to overcome loneliness and socialize in a co-ethnic, co-religious environment. Hae Soo Cho rides the bus or walks to Sa Chal three or four days a week where she rotates volunteer shifts with other *posals* in the temple's bookstore. Occasionally she brings along her five-year-old grandson, whom she looks after while his parents work. At the temple her grandson is free to roam around and spend time with the monks, a relationship his grandmother hopes will continue in the future. The daughter of farmers, this sixty-six-year-old woman was raised a Buddhist and eventually married into a Buddhist household. Currently, however, only two of her five daughters consider themselves Buddhist. Three of her daughters converted to Christianity prior to immigration and her remaining two Buddhist daughters are too busy with work to have time to attend the temple, although she maintains that "they practice in their minds." Hae Soo expresses no regret over her daughters' conversion to Christianity since she remains actively involved in their lives. She does admit, however, that Buddhists who convert to Christianity "don't have strong faith."

It has taken ten years for Mrs. Cho to adjust to living in America, although she originally immigrated to join her daughters. "In Korea," she says, "I was a mother and yet had no children there. What was I supposed to do with myself? So I just came over" (in 1988). Her initial experiences in the United States were characterized by loneliness heightened by her inability to speak English and her fear of leaving her daughter's home. For many elderly parents like Hae Soo, the desire to be closer to their children acts as the primary catalyst for their emigration from Korea. Once in America, many of these grandparents discover increased poverty, loneliness, a lower status in the household, and unpaid labor as their grandchildren's babysitters. In addition, most Korean immigrants who arrive in the United States in later life find it nearly impossible to learn English and therefore to perform such tasks as applying for Social Security, finding a low-income apartment in a neighborhood where they feel comfortable, and obtaining proper medical attention.

Despite these struggles to adapt to life in America, a measure of satisfaction and self-esteem can be attained by participating in social organizations. In a recent study of retired Korean American senior citizens, Young In Song found that life satisfaction and mental adjustment were primarily found in religion, which "can also serve as a supportive network for the development of leadership for this subpopulation, in providing opportunity for validation of self-esteem, and in offering psychological and spiritual encouragement and hope for a more dignified life."[22] Like the church, Sa Chal provides a support system that validates the participation of its aged female members.

Although Mrs. Cho appreciated Los Angeles's sunny skies, warm weather, and abundance of flowers when she arrived in the United States, she found that she was often depressed:

> In Korea I used to take care of myself, but being at my daughter's house made me feel really sad. I developed this strange sense of being an outsider and would cry a lot. It wasn't that my daughter did anything wrong. I didn't have any purpose. I just lived there and they would give me money. I came over to my daughter's house and just ate what they gave me, otherwise I would just wash the rice and make food. That's how things ended up. I was old and the relationship was disappearing. I just didn't have any fun living here. So I thought, am I just bored? Why was I so sad? I kept thinking about going back to Seoul....
>
> Since I always looked like I was going to cry, my daughter told me that if I wanted to return to Korea, she would buy me a ticket to go back. But I told her that I wasn't leaving and that I had no desire to go. I had to start thinking about living here. Why should I go to Korea again? I am not a one or two-year-old child. I came this far hadn't I? It was because I stayed at home alone and didn't have anybody who understood me. There was no one there to talk to because my daughter would go to work at the store and I was always alone. So I started to pray to the Buddha all the time, I read the sutras and bowed. That would take up about two hours of my time. After two hours. I would just sit there and think about my friends and hometown and my family back in Korea. But I really had to start thinking about living here. Why did I need to go to Korea again? Eventually I started going to my daughter's store and helped out by running errands. Even though I didn't really know where anything was, I would walk around and look for it. Soon a sense of ease began to emerge in my mind and I developed self-confidence. From then on, I would go just anywhere without any problems.

Following this adjustment period and newfound ventures outside the home, Hae Soo decided to take English classes "to develop more independence." After taking classes and becoming a citizen she applied for welfare assistance and found herself an apartment close to Sa Chal. Moving into her own place near the temple transformed her views of living in the United States, and now she confidently says, "I really think that it was good for me to come to America. Maybe I have some kind of karmic rela-

BUDDHISM—AN ANCHOR IN AN UNCERTAIN WORLD

tionship with America. I don't really think much about going to Korea anymore."

According to Mrs. Cho, her religious participation increased as a way of coping with depression and boredom. Now her daily life revolves around the temple, where she comes to meet friends, worship, and volunteer. As a result, she has also strengthened her religious commitment:

> I used to come out here each week and would sit quietly reading Buddhist texts. After doing that, I started learning more about Buddhism and now my faith is even stronger. After learning the sutras and how to meditate, I began to purify my mind. I used to say that I hated this person or that person . . . but eventually those bad thoughts would disappear and I realized that I didn't really hate those people. Then I started to change my perspective and do good things for people. If I have something good to eat, then I will give it to someone else, half of it anyway. That's the kind of heart one develops in Buddhism and I try to live with that kind of heart. Each day I ask myself, what good things have I done? Since I am a Buddhist, I don't have any discomforts. You have to observe and purify your mind. I believe in Buddhism for myself and come out to temple for myself to cleanse my mind. It's not for the sake of anyone else. Buddhism is about purifying my own mind! After studying I will become awakened, so that's why I study the doctrines. It's not for the sake of others.

This grandmother's religiosity is not motivated by a desire to pray for the well-being of her family. She has become an independent woman who no longer spends her time waiting for her daughter to come home. She has a newfound focus on her personal development and self-confidence by venturing out on her own and devoting her life to Buddhist worship.

The three women's stories depicted above demonstrate how religious identity can contribute to self-transformation and actualization during difficult periods of transition. Sa Chal provides a space for immigrants to a new country and women in their middle years to enact new roles for themselves as Buddhist missionaries and *posals*—roles that are not contingent on being wives and mothers. Their experiences of living in a new culture are fraught with tension and apprehension because they have not learned English and chose not to attend Christian churches, which they considered too demanding of their time and their privacy. As my interviews with these women illustrate, Sa Chal does not overly impinge on their personal lives and offers them a place to go when they are bored or lonely.

Through active roles as Buddhist missionaries and exemplary lay practitioners, women's lives destabilized by immigration and midlife transitions are given new meaning in a context where they focus on themselves and develop "self-knowledge." While Mrs. Lee completely devotes herself to a semimonastic life, Helen Yim studies to become a Buddhist missionary and struggles to fit into the social life of the temple and Hae Soo Cho overcomes her loneliness and finds meaning through daily worship. Religious identities can enable women to develop self-esteem and self-reliance; however, these experiences are by no means uniform or always positive. The social setting of the temple can also highlight the feelings of alienation, loneliness, and scrutiny that complicate positive views of the self.

BUDDHISM AND THE CONSTRUCTION OF A NEW AMERICAN IDENTITY

For the women described in the previous section, a Buddhist identity resulted in full reliance on the temple for emotional and social support, although with varying degrees of success. However, not all women at Sa Chal have relied on their religious identities to retreat from active participation in mainstream culture. My interviews with a number of female *shindo* (worshippers) indicate that immigration to the United States can have a positive impact on women's self-esteem, particularly when new experiences are mediated through Buddhist idioms of self-knowledge.[23] While sociologists of Korean American churches claim that immigration leads to the reconstitution of gender hierarchies in the home and church, I have also found that immigration provides women opportunities to assert and create identities that involve an inward-gazing subjectivity aimed at enhancing the self. Thus some women at Sa Chal have chosen to immigrate on their own and willingly become self-providers by seeking employment opportunities they did not have in Korea.

In their efforts to find new identities as doctors and businesswomen rather than as wives, these women indicate that Buddhism provides them with a doctrinal justification (self-reliance) for the remarkable shifts they have made in their lives. Buddhism plays a further role in their resistance to female subordination by providing a sense of security and incentive while they cultivate a spirit of independence. Women's increased self-esteem through labor-force participation following immigration has been studied by sociologist Pierrette Hondagneu-Sotelo, who found that married women's spatial mobility outside the home increased their sense of authority and autonomy in the home.[24] In my own research I discovered that it was primarily the unmarried, separated, or divorced women whose self-esteem grew in response to increased labor participation, although I do not wish to imply that women who were alone were inclined to fill their time with work. Rather, I have found that women were more inclined to stay unmarried, separated, or divorced in order to work and fulfill their own versions of the American dream, largely defined as economic and social independence.

According to recent studies of women's roles in the Korean Christian church, however, Korean women's lives inside their homes and religious institutions remain subordinate to men. Yet like many Buddhist women interviewed in this study, Korean American Christian women often silently resist male hierarchy behind the scenes while not outwardly challenging male dominance, in order to maintain family structure.[25] In works documenting Korean American Christianity, immigration is held to include the inevitable transplantation and reassertion of Confucian values that remain unchallenged even in the United States. This reliance on Confucian patriarchy is said to provide both status enhancement and assurance for men who have experienced status anxiety in the United States. Women, on the other hand, are said to be encouraged to uphold the hierarchy and fulfill their roles as obedient wives, mothers, and symbols of the homeland. Even though a woman may obtain a higher paying job than her husband, she will remain secondary in status by continuing to perform all household duties as the caretaker of others. Yet this transplantation of Confucian cultural norms is by no means uniform. In the following section I present the stories of two immigrant women and the process of self- actualization each one undergoes as they follow their dreams of "becoming someone else" in the United States. In so doing, I argue that religious participation can provide the inspiration to forge different narratives for the self in a new cultural milieu.

"WORKING ON MY OWN"
—MRS. OH'S STORY

Mrs. Oh sings in Sa Chal's choir and spends much of her free time during the week volunteering at the temple and meeting with her friends since she lives only a block away. Although she is married and has three grown sons (all of whom live in Korea), she decided at age of forty-nine in 1997 to move to the United States on her own "to see what it would be like to live here." After all, she says, "I have always liked America." She currently lives alone in a small rented room in the guesthouse of a Korean family's home in Koreatown. The room she rents barely accommodates the two of us as we sit and chat on the floor while sipping roasted barley tea on her day off. Mrs. Oh's bare room resembles that of a temporary dweller. There is a single futon mattress on the floor, a small low table, a lamp, and a black lacquer wood vanity that holds a few personal items. On the wall, a Buddhist calendar marks the special events of the month, and a single photograph of her sons is the only visual reference to life back home. Mrs. Oh claims that she eventually plans to bring her husband and sons to America after a few more years of establishing herself. However, she states, for now living alone is "no problem for my family because my children are all grown and do whatever they want and take care of themselves. Even if their mom was in Korea, they would all do their own things American style."

Although Mrs. Oh came to the United States to pave the way for her sons to follow, her solo immigration also reflects an attempt to assert an independent life and identity outside of what Korean culture offered her. She remarks that in Korea, "I just stayed inside with the family because I was the woman in charge of the household. I came here first to establish myself and then after a while of playing around on my own I thought that I should just continue to live here. That's how I ended here." Here the decision to immigrate marks a divergence from the ideological norm for many Korean women, for immigration signifies an opportunity to reject her position as *an saram* (inside person) or *jip saram* (house person), and make it on her own.[26] Interestingly, she does not divulge any information about her husband who remains in Korea except to say that he "just works and does his own thing."

Mrs. Oh's decision to migrate to the United States is directly related to her view of American gender ideology, which she prefers to Korea's Confucian gender norms. She explains:

> In America, women and men can live fully on their own—that's the big difference between America and Korea. In America, women can work hard and move up, but in Korea there aren't any women that have worked that far yet. Only the people who are poor are seen to be working, so unless you need to, women do not work. Women in Korea work because they are too poor. In America, if you play around, then it looks like there is something lacking in you because if you are smart and on your own are active, then you will work. If you don't it's sort of a deficiency isn't it? America is where you do your own thing for yourself. If you get rid of women's rights and can't live on your own, that's Korea. Since Korea has had a long-time Confucian culture for over two hundred years that tradition has just been passed down. Because we have received those teachings, Korean women are supposed to be inside [*an saram*] and they are not supposed to go outside. In America, since it is a more enlightened country, women have to go out and participate and so, no matter what, women work as hard as men. In Korea, women are on the bottom and men are on top. In America, women are on top and men are on the bottom, so they participate hard and they work for a living.

This married woman's motivation to immigrate to America reflects her own version of the American dream where women's roles are validated in the public space of work, something she could not achieve in Korea, where she was defined by her position as housewife and mother.

Sociologists Pierrette Hondagneu-Sotelo and Silvia Pedraza have separately noted that women's migration indicates a desire to transform gender relations within the household. Hondagneu-Sotelo's study of Mexican undocumented immigration found that women's migration provided opportunities to increase women's spatial mobility beyond the household, since women became major contributors in establishing a family's successful transition to America by obtaining jobs and seeking out sources of support like health care and social services. Thus migration for women became a "circumvention of patriarchy."[27] Pedraza notes that "[f]or the women themselves, the act of emigrating also became a way of escaping total dependence on their husbands," a primary motivation for leaving the homeland.[28] These studies do not, however, account for women like Mrs. Oh who are married with children yet choose to leave their families behind while they seek to fulfill their own immigrant dreams.

There remains a tension, nonetheless, because Mrs. Oh emphasizes her responsibility as a mother in her claim that she came to America for her children; however, at the same time she considers life in America more liberating for women who can make it on their own and take responsibility for their own lives. It is in the context of this conflict between her traditional role as mother and wife and her new single life in America that her religious participation plays a significant role in her immigration story. A Buddhist identity and temple participation enable her to fulfill the desire to spend time in America on her own precisely because the Buddhist temple symbolizes Korean culture and the homeland where she can spend time with co-ethnics and friends. At the same time, her Buddhist participation enables her to develop self-knowledge on a religious level that she then associates with her independence in America. Interestingly, Mrs. Oh employs a comparison between Buddhism and Christianity to elucidate her reasons for coming to the United States on her own:

> What the Buddha taught is that I have to cleanse my mind, and it is my mind that is the most important thing. But Christians believe that they have to pray to Jesus a whole lot and develop goodness, then they will feel comfortable. People who believe in Buddhism intimately live according to our karma. The difference between Buddhism and Christianity is that Christians have to follow and know Jesus ... but Buddhists think that "I have to follow myself."

Here, Mrs. Oh deploys religious meaning to make sense of her personal decisions in the framework of religious doctrine. She describes both life in America and Buddhist teachings through the language of self-reliance, whereas Christianity is seen as a reliance on an external source of support—Jesus. Mrs. Oh makes this association in opposition to some scholars and practitioners alike who assert that Christianity is more modern and therefore more American.[29] Buddhism for Mrs. Oh advocates independence in one's life, a meaning that she invokes to describe her unusual journey to America.

Her immigration can be seen then as an assertion of autonomy that challenges Korean cultural norms on womanhood. In this context, Buddhism rationalizes her radical decision doctrinally and offers a community of co-ethnic female friends where she finds a home away from home, for although she has fulfilled her dream of working and living alone, "in America . . . you have to struggle and work. No matter what you do, you have a job and so you have to work." Mrs. Oh is proud of her decision to move and struggles to make ends meet on the small salary she earns preparing food in a Korean grocery store. As she works to be independent, she also devotes herself to the temple by singing in the choir, praying, chatting with friends, and visiting on her days off. Since she has been a Buddhist since birth, Buddhism is something she already knows and feels comfortable with even as she tries something new in her life. She is either at the temple or at work, for "[e]very Sunday I go and when I don't have to work I go and pray in the morning. There's not a lot of people during work days, only on the weekends."

Despite her self-reliance, there remains throughout her narrative a conflict between wishing to maintain autonomy in the United States and upholding some aspects of the "traditional Korean woman" to avoid drawing too much attention to herself. She reflects this conflict in the way she invokes Confucian gender ideology in her narrative of religious practice. While she sees her immigration as an act of resistance and a repudiation of her previous housewife status, Mrs. Oh invokes gender rhetoric to describe other aspects of her life that assert her "Koreanness" so that she does not appear too exceptional in her behavior. Thus she describes Buddhism as woman's work, since historically Confucian tradition dictated that men should maintain public lives through work and not engage in religious activities (especially Buddhism):

> [In Korea] only the wife goes to temple. If a hundred people go to temple, then the husbands don't even make up ten percent . . . only mothers and women go. Buddhism is like that. Ever since early times, women believed more than men did. [Women] would pray for the sake of their families, their children and their husbands. Women did all that. That is our tradition.

According to our country's Confucian teachings, mothers were always doing things for the sake of the family. That teaching has been passed down as it is up until now. The husbands go to the office. In Korea, women don't go to work so men end up going out to work, so they can't go to temple. Women don't work and have free time, so that's why they can follow the prayer schedules on the first of the month and the middle of the month.

Ambivalence in narratives of gender ideology also indicates that religion and gender are highly contested and contestable in Mrs. Oh's life. Her story articulates her desire for the autonomy that instigated her immigration and illustrates the way a Buddhist identity reinforces and doctrinally justifies her unusual decision to leave a family behind. Mrs. Oh neither wholly internalizes nor rejects Confucian ideology but is both constrained by and resistant to it. It is her religious identity that provides the most practical opportunity to challenge and maintain traditional gender norms simultaneously.

JANET LIM—BUDDHISM AS A QUEST FOR SELF-AGENCY

I don't know what loneliness is, I don't feel lonely. I have no time for loneliness, but I like it. Perhaps I enjoy being all by myself. I like it better when I am alone, I don't like when things are too noisy.

Of the twenty-five women interviewed in this study, Janet Lim's story best illustrates the power of a Buddhist identity in shaping a woman's individual agency, independence, and self-narration. When examining Janet's life story, there are two separate images that she offers—as a woman wronged and as a woman fighting for justice. These are the details gathered from the events in her life as she chose to tell them: she married at the age of twenty-one, abandoned her dream of becoming a prestigious professor, moved to the United States to follow her first husband, supported him, and gave up a child whom she has not seen since. Janet's story continues: after her first husband left her, she worked a variety of odd jobs, remarried, and was left by her husband for another woman. Currently, Janet is raising her second son on her own, working on her degree in Eastern medicine, and is a defendant in a lawsuit brought against her by the president of her university. Those are the difficult events she has faced since immigrating to Los Angeles in 1973.

To hear her narrate those occurrences in her life story evokes a different tale—that of an independent woman on a quest for authenticity and justice who relies ultimately on herself as the arbiter of all decisions in her life. Lawrence C. Watson and Maria-Barbara Watson-Franke define life histories and narratives as retrospective personal accounts orally elicited and recorded as texts. Rather than using personal accounts and oral histories as supplements and data test theories, the authors argue that the individual life history offers perspectives on subjectivity and individuality. Life histories and narratives provide an opportunity to view a Buddhist individual's life within the context of numerous contradictions. Watson and Watson-Franke also argue that in the life history "the whole life course is seen from the point of view of the person as he is currently trying to make sense of his relationship to past events, and he may not remember or choose to emphasize the things that were once important."[30]

Janet describes herself as someone who never needed male companionship, resists the intrusion of others in her goals, openly critiques those against her, and advocates freedom of speech according to First Amendment rights in the United States. Janet was born a Buddhist, attended Christian missionary schools in Korea, went to church in America, abandoned the church, went to a Jingak (Esoteric) Buddhist temple, and finally settled at Sa Chal in 1992. Janet's narration of her life trajectory can be best approached retrospectively—that is, in her narration we are given a firsthand view of a woman reinterpreting the past events of her life experienced as a challenge to self-esteem into a tale of a woman's struggle for truth and self-reliance.

Although her narration is described as a story, it is not fictional. However, referring to her narration as a story enables us to see how Janet refashions an image of herself as resistor or agent rather than as a victim or mere respondent to life's vicissitudes. In other words, Janet's misadventures in life are reinscribed by her as events that she herself instigated out of a desire to be an independent woman unhindered by Korean culture, men, church, or temples. Furthermore, it is precisely this reinscription that renders her experiences endurable. For by retelling past events as she does, she casts herself as the main protagonist who abandons or conquers all things detrimental to self-determination. In the following section, I will show how Janet's religious identity as a self-knowing Buddhist provides the tools with which she reshapes and retells the events of her life to reflect a life that runs according to her rules.

Janet, forty-eight, grew up in a Buddhist household in Seoul that eventually changed its religious affiliation in the early 1960s. She recalls that during her childhood many of her neighbors came to her family's home to urge them to attend one of the many Christian churches that began "popping up all over the neighborhood." Eventually, her family converted to Christianity simply because "the temples were so hard to get to since they were in the mountains, and we had about forty churches or so in every city." As a result of the increased presence of Christian missionaries in Korea, Janet herself began to attend the local missionary junior high school, where she was "forced to pray each day." Yet somehow, she recalls, "I didn't really trust God or know Jesus because it [belief] was mandatory." One of the interesting tensions in Janet's life is that although she attended church from her adolescence until she was forty, she claims that she never really believed in what the church taught her; rather, she went "out of habit."

Janet later graduated from high school and was accepted by Seoul National University, the country's most prestigious school known for its academic rigor and the quality of its students. While enrolled in university, Janet had planned to become a physical education professor but she explains that as soon as she graduated, she met her first husband, who was already living as an immigrant in America. Janet then abandoned her hopes of becoming a college professor. Because her husband was six years older than she, Janet was urged to marry quickly, move with her spouse to the United States, and have children. In other words, at this point in her life, she says, "the man came first." Although she presumed that her new husband already had a job in the United States, Janet soon discovered that he would not work when they arrived in Los Angeles in 1973. Hence, her early experiences indicate a tremendous amount of struggle leading eventually to the dissolution of her marriage:

> I got homesick within the first three months. I cried every night because I wanted to go back. And then I got sick and I had a boy. He's twenty-four

BUDDHISM—AN ANCHOR IN AN UNCERTAIN WORLD

> now, I haven't seen him since I got divorced. I was so young when I got divorced. I was only twenty-six. Maybe it was time to get divorced. I didn't like anything here. I was sick and furious with his family. They were so rich but they didn't do anything for us! In Korean culture, the parents are supposed to help out their son or daughter when they get into hard times. They were so rich and they helped his older brother and sister a lot but not [my husband], and he didn't work! So I had to go to work and I got sick. I didn't feel like going on living with him. I just worked and did everything. I was a salesperson. I even worked with sewing machines but I did it only for a week. I couldn't do it any longer because it wasn't for me. I had no skills in this country; I could not speak English so I couldn't get a nice job or anything. I didn't like being hired to work for someone else. Maybe I have a bossy personality; I don't want to work for anybody else. I work for myself.

In her narration, Janet describes how she was bound by Korean culture to give up her plans to become a college professor and marry a man who ultimately left her no choice but to find a job to support the family. Besides believing that her in-laws should take care of the family financially, because "that's Korean culture," she found life in America much more complicated than she had expected. As a result of her frustrations, she became ill, eventually got divorced, and her husband was awarded custody of their son.

An important point to note in this narration is that Janet views her first marriage as something she herself no longer desired. Although she married originally because she thought she was supposed to, in the end she maintains that she decided for herself that marriage was not for her. Similarly, although she had no choice but to look for low-paying jobs, she also claims that she works for herself and does not want anyone telling her what to do—husbands and employers alike. Interestingly, Janet spent very little time talking about her first son, whom she hasn't seen since her divorce. When I asked her if she misses her son, she shrugged and replied, "Well, what can you do?"

After working on her own and moving back and forth to Korea in 1977, 1982, and 1984, Janet decided that she wanted to get married again. Although she experienced her first marriage as an unpleasant impingement on her aspirations, she admits that she got married for a second time because "I was so tired of being alone, I didn't want to have to go to work by myself.

You know how Korean [women] are. When they get married, they can have a house, eat and it is easier." In other words, Janet chose her second marriage as a means to create for herself a materially comfortable lifestyle where she wouldn't be forced to make a living, something that was denied her in the first marriage. She also thought that the second time around, things would be easier. However, years later, she found herself divorced once again.

When asked about the cause of her second divorce, she offered two conflicting responses. The first one was that her husband cheated on her and decided he wanted to marry someone else. When I asked her if she had grown tired of marriage and living with her second husband she replied:

> No, no, no! I thought that I could live with him until we died, so I never thought about divorce or anything. Then all of a sudden, he told me one day that we had to get a divorce because he had to marry some other lady. He told me all of a sudden! Of course, before he told me that, he didn't come home at night for maybe two or three months.

Janet's initial response indicates that she felt her husband had abandoned her without warning and cheated on her, something she neither suspected nor chose. Yet, after a few more minutes of reflecting on her second divorce, she reinscribed this event from one in which she was abandoned to one that she herself had psychologically abandoned first:

> Actually, *I* didn't want to be married anymore. [Even] he [my husband] said to me, "I didn't know that living by yourself makes you so happy; you should be alone." I was happy because I didn't have to do anything for him anymore. He had an affair with a woman, but I understand it because perhaps I made him do it because I didn't want to have a sexual life with him, not with anybody. I don't know why, but right after I got pregnant, I didn't want to sleep with my husband. So he needed to do something about his "nature" you know. . . . I have no objection to him because I understand him. He said he had to marry her. . . . I have a better life now. I can go to school [again] and I can work.

Janet recasts herself from a woman who was suddenly abandoned to an individual who had decided beforehand that she no longer wanted to be married. She claims that she did not want the responsibilities of being a wife and no longer wanted to have an intimate relationship with her husband. For her, the single life was the best option because she wanted to go back to school and work on her own again. She describes her divorce as amicable; in fact, she and her ex-husband see each other on almost a daily basis when he comes to pick up their thirteen-year-old son for school. Living on her own and working for herself proved to be more appropriate for a woman who desires to be defined by her own actions and achievements. Rather than defining her life through her husband, divorce allowed her life to take center stage once again.

For Janet, men are not a source of comfort because they are too "self-centered" and "arrogant," more reasons compelling her to live alone. Describing her views on the lack of male attendance at Sa Chal and other religious organizations, she rolls her eyes, shakes her head, and says:

> In Korea, [men] do not even go to church because they think that religion [is not] for them. They think that they are somebody else, you know; they want to be somebody else. They think they are so special so they don't want to go do religious things like [going to] meet God or the Buddha. Of course, they stay home, go golfing, and fishing.... They think they have some sort of [special] dignity and they want to have honor so [they don't bow or worship in front of the Buddha].

Janet finds men important as friends with whom she can have an equal relationship but not as husbands, for that is where gender hierarchy comes into play. Yet although she is a staunch defender of her own rights, she often exhibits behavior that signifies a complete deference to men in certain social situations. For example, I have seen her at Sa Chal's reunification meetings, where she is often one of the few women in attendance. In these social settings where Korean men usually sit around tables to discuss political matters in North Korea, famine relief, and reunification, Janet can often be found serving tea to all the men by herself and serving their meals. But how are we to interpret this submissive behavior from a woman who claims that she cannot stand male authority?

This scenario of exaggerated deference points to one of the strategies women like Janet employ to play at the "men's game" by upholding

BUDDHISM—AN ANCHOR IN AN UNCERTAIN WORLD

received gender norms of female deference in order to secure for herself a position in what is typically coded as a male activity—politics. Jean Lipman-Blumen refers to this exaggerated behavior as "micro-manipulation" of gendered relationships marked by the strategic use of behavior and rhetoric traditionally coded as female to offset gender hierarchies.[31] By serving tea, bowing, and preparing food, Janet does not violate gender norms or draw attention to her presence in an otherwise male locale. She acts in a manner that substantiates her presence, for it "makes sense" that she should be there to take responsibility for such female activities. At the same time, however, Janet gets to sit in on reunification meetings and voice her political positions in the company of men.

Another area where Janet expresses her autonomy and resistance to authority is in her religious practice. As mentioned above, Janet attended Christian churches until she was forty; yet she cites two particular reasons why she chose to leave Christianity and return to her original religious tradition (Buddhism). The first contributing factor centers on the Korean Confucian ritual of *chaesa*, or offering rites to one's ancestors.[32] While her family had been practicing such rituals since her childhood, her older brother had decided to cease offering *chaesa* rites to her dead parents after his conversion to Christianity. She explains:

> [Korean Buddhists] think that *chaesa* is very important, especially for somebody who goes to temple. In Korea, somebody who goes to church won't do *chaesa* because they think that dead parents are *guishin* (ghosts). But that is not the right thing to do; we have to do *chaesa* for our dead parents or grandparents. Christians don't do *chaesa*. They think that they are just [supposed to] pray . . . for the dead or the dying. I think that *chaesa* is a beautiful thing to do. In Korea they say that the daughter should not "take" *chaesa* for their parents, but I think that is wrong. . . . Even myself, I am the daughter of my parents, [but] I do the *chaesa* myself at home. Because my brother goes to church, he doesn't care about *chaesa*. Since I don't feel so good toward my parents if it's not done . . . I do it by myself at home.

Although ancestor worship traditionally belongs in the ritual domain of men, Janet resists such gender restrictions out of a sense of "what is right" according to her own conscience and not according to gender norms. Since her brother refuses to uphold the ritual worship for their parents, Janet becomes the ritual agent in "setting things right" for her parents.

The second factor contributing to Janet's return to the Buddhist temple was the resentment she felt over an intrusion on her decision making vis-à-vis the church. When I asked her why she chose to come to the Buddhist temple, she claimed that in Buddhist temples, "nobody seems to care whether or not a person has been married once, twice, or never." As she sees it, "Buddhists have an open mind and they can take [accept] anyone else, but if you go to church, they make you feel guilty. That doesn't make any sense." Since she has been divorced twice, Janet wishes to avoid the negative views against divorce that she experienced in the Korean churches.[33] For Janet, Buddhist teaching encourages one to work on one's own enlightenment and so the person in the temple is ultimately approached as an individual and not defined by her relationship to a spouse, something that also coincides well with her interest in self-authority.

A similar situation exists for members like Won Kyung Chin, Melissa Yang, and Sin Young Cho, women at the temple who are either separated or divorced. All of these women indicated that they enjoyed the relative lack of concern over their marital statuses and personal lives experienced at Sa Chal, and they attributed this to the fact that one need not be involved in a marriage in order to live as a good Buddhist. Instead, many women are approached first and foremost as pious laywomen rather than dutiful wives and mothers at the temple. Throughout my interviews with separated or divorced women at Sa Chal (seven out of twenty-five women, two of whom were twice divorced), I found that being Buddhist enables a woman to overcome the social stigma of divorce and provides a new support system following the dissolution of her marriage. Although divorce is still frowned upon in the Korean community, the Buddhist temple appears to buffer the criticism women might experience in other pubic venues like the church, since Buddhist women commonly do not attend services with their husbands or children.

Sociologist Siyon Rhee's recent study of the perception of divorce in Korean American communities indicates that divorce continues to bring disgrace to a family, with women bearing more of the social stigma for "failing" as virtuous wives. According to Rhee, the divorce rate for Korean Americans is relatively high compared with various other ethnic groups in the

United States at around 4.8 per thousand population. At the same time, the numbers are remarkably lower in Korea, where the divorce rate was noted at 0.6 per thousand population. These statistics indicate that in Korea divorce is still considered "something totally unacceptable, disgraceful, and shameful to the entire family."[34]

Ai Ra Kim's study of Korean American women and the Christian church notes that the stigma against divorce is no different in the United States; it is still considered "forbidden territory" that invokes shame and disgrace.[35] According to Kim, divorce takes on further theological significance as a betrayal of commitment to God and a violation of God's will; hence in the church, the attitude toward divorce among church members remains highly negative. Women in the church are thus encouraged to endure in their marriages not only for the sake of their cultural traditions but also for their Christian traditions.

Yet, throughout my interviews with temple members, choice and personal responsibility were cited as the primary agents in determining religious practice, and so one could not be judged negatively for worshipping on one's own. Women at Sa Chal attached no theological significance to marriage; commitment in a marriage was valued according cultural customs but not sanctified by the Buddhist tradition itself. Women may have felt embarrassed for their status as divorced Korean women but did not experience any guilt about their situations. In addition, since most of the members of the temple are women, there is little attention paid to viewing women in relation to their husbands, at least during their time spent in the temple. This situation also accounts for Janet Lim's desire to leave behind the scrutiny she may have experienced as a twice-divorced woman in the church.

Janet recalls her experiences with the church in Los Angeles as the main reason for her conversion to Buddhism:

> The reason I quit going to church is because I used to have a business in Koreatown in 1990 and the *chondo sa* [evangelizing woman] at the church used to come to me and say, "the reason why your business is not doing so well is because you didn't pay them [the Church] enough." She said that I didn't pay the church ten percent of my wages! I thought about that and asked her what it would mean if I sent the money to my parents, even one

hundred dollars a month. She then said, "you are stealing money that is for God, you are stealing it, so giving it to your parents is not good." Then I felt really bad. I used to pay [the church] ten percent of my wages. If I made four hundred dollars a week, I gave them forty dollars, that's ten percent, right? We had envelopes [in church] and I wrote my name on [it] and every week I paid them, every week! Then one day during the sermon, the reverend said out loud, "In my church somebody is paying only ten dollars, that's not a donation, that's not even ten percent." He meant ten dollars was not good enough! Then I decided to quit. I don't think that this is right. I couldn't give donations without finishing my payments. I think they are crazy!

Janet's biggest gripe with the church centers on money, the amount of which she contends should be up to the individual to determine and not the church. She also expresses anger and humiliation for being pointed out as someone who would not give the full ten percent of her income toward church tithes. Janet no longer attends church and even avoids socializing with Christians if she can help it. She prefers to spend her time with the "more open-minded Buddhists" she meets at Sa Chal and at school, where she is the president of the Buddhist student organization.

Janet also chose to attend Sa Chal out of an extreme dislike for married monks of the Jingak (Esoteric) and Taego (married) orders of Korean monks. She further maintains that, like church ministers, married monks are more corrupt and impure than the celibate Catholic priests and the monks of Sa Chal. Marriage would make monks more susceptible to cheating a person by threatening them with divination and besides, she says, "they always think of their families first and they can't think of other people's needs because they have to take care of their wives and children, so I don't really like them." Based on her reaction to the married Buddhist and Christian clergy, it appears that the unmarried, unfettered lifestyle suits both Janet's view of her self and her ideal view of her religious virtuosos.

As noted throughout her narrative, Janet does not believe in relying on others for her spiritual well-being. She enjoys the lack of proscription and the relative anonymity she finds at Sa Chal services, although she knows the abbot on a personal basis and attends most services anyway. Janet also feels comfortable in the temple because she does not feel judged for her two divorces and appreciates the generosity of Buddhists who give "freely because they want to and not because they *have* to." Janet's views of Buddhist practice center on the self in determining what constitutes right belief, a view she finds articulated in the temple as well. Perhaps it is her two marriages that ended in divorce that have influenced her religious views as well—as something that should be neither intrusive nor limiting. As she tells it, her past life experiences have compelled her to approach all matters, even religious ones, on her own terms according to her own preferences. In 1997 Janet embarked on a second career as an Eastern medicine doctor and continues to work in her business, a marketing company co-owned with a Buddhist friend and temple member. In light of her life story, we can interpret this latest endeavor as a result of her earlier quelled plans to become a prestigious professor back in Korea. For now, as she puts it, she has "no man standing in [her] way."

As noted above, a Buddhist identity fosters Janet's independence and enables her to reinterpret her divorces as proof of her desire not to be tied down. Being a Buddhist also teaches Janet to rely on herself alone for financial security. Thus she distinguishes herself from churchgoers who depend on others to take care of them. She claims, "the reason why the church has so many people is because many people go there for business and not for religion. They want to go make friends and get whatever they can from the church." But, she continues, "Buddhism is not that kind of a religion; we have to do things ourselves." Janet thus finds doctrinal justification for the choices she makes in her life and relies on her individual agency in making decisions.

In the women's life stories depicted in this chapter, I have attempted to illustrate how Buddhism functions as a support for women in two different ways. On the one hand, the symbol of the temple as a homeland provides some *posals* with a haven and solace away from the conditions of immigration that they have experienced as destabilizing. On the other hand, the Buddhist doctrines of "finding and knowing oneself" also provide a source of courage and a rationalization for women who have come to America and fashioned lives for themselves that challenge Confucian gender ideologies of ideal Korean womanhood—marriage and housework. By defining themselves as Buddhists they challenge Korean cultural norms and work to "make it on their own" in America without reliance on a man or anyone else. While Mrs. Oh and Janet Lim have sought to create new identities for themselves in the United States as women looking after themselves, they have also relied on Buddhist teachings of self-reliance and self-knowledge to interpret the choices they have made. Buddhism can thus act as a symbol of being at ease in the world by referencing a pre-immigrant life and, at the same time, as a source of inspiration for making choices that may run counter to Confucian gender norms.

6

Finding Male Selves: Men's Religious Practices

If I were married and my wife came to temple to pay her respects and prayed for our entire family, then I might think, "Oh, maybe I don't have to do that. My wife is doing it so why should I do it? I guess it goes back to the question of why guys have so much pride in themselves and they don't want to do certain minor things [like bowing]. I guess guys have a huge [amount] of pride in themselves so they don't want to go to temple and start bowing down. I see all these *ajushis* [middle-aged men] who come to temple and pay their respects, but some of them don't even [do that] and they just sit there in the corner! They drink coffee or talk among themselves to other *ajushis* with that certain position that they sit in. They always have their hands in the air [gesturing] or their hands upon their knees or on the table. And I always see these Korean *ajushis* reading newspapers and I think it's wrong! . . . It's really fascinating. If a couple goes to temple and they pay their respects at the same time, the guy kind of disappears and the woman participates in the ritual and prays. The guys just go outside to chill and have a smoke. [James Jang, twenty-two-year-old Sa Chal member]

The perception of the temple's worship hall as women's space indicates that religious practice at Sa Chal is deeply gendered. The delineation of the temple into male and female space is readily apparent when one walks through the doors of the worship hall for the 11:00 A.M. Sunday service. From the rear of the hall, one can see the backs of women's heads just peeking over the tall red plush velvet chairs of the pews. On this particular Sunday morning, a cursory look at the temple's Buddhist choir shows fifteen women and three men all dressed in long green satin robes. Of the approximately one hundred participants in this one and a half-hour service, fifteen are men. The choir members, abbot, ritual monk, general announcer, and the choir conductor stand at the front of the worship hall. Of the eight men in the pews, three elderly gentlemen have come with their wives; one middle-aged gentleman sits with his wife and explains the service to her since she used to be a Christian, and four men sit in the rear. The men in the rear have come alone to temple; three of them are visiting students who plan to return to Korea after graduating from their degree programs in Eastern medicine. Most of the women are grandmothers and housewives who attend temple without their spouses or their children and sit among their friends, whom they meet there every week.

While there are only fifteen men in the actual worship hall, there are another eight or so men present in various parts of the temple. Mr. Lee Jang Won is in his office above the bookstore working on printing materials for the temple, and Mr. Koh Moon Soo sits behind a desk in the foyer at the top of the stairs collecting weekly donations. Mr. Huhr wanders around the temple on the first floor checking on the new bookstore and the art gallery. Mr. Yang and Mr. Cho sit drinking coffee as they chat and read the *Korea Times* while a young father carries his baby back and forth in the dining hall to keep it quiet. Two resident monks wander in and out of the temple's various rooms to watch over things. The oldest monk usually sits with Mr. Koh and chats with members as they come to offer their donations, and the youngest resident monk generally supervises the activities of the dozen or so young children who come to the temple with their mothers.

The gendered space and larger percentage of women is typical of any Sunday at Sa Chal, especially when there are no outside speakers invited as guest lecturers and no special events like the Buddha's birthday to celebrate. The only times when the percentage of men outnumbers that of women in Sa Chal are during reunification meetings sponsored by the temple, where it is clear that these meetings are considered "men's space," and during meetings for the new College of Buddhist Studies aimed at training international missionaries. During special lectures given by guest speakers, the number of men nearly equals that of the women in the pews.

In an attempt to understand the separate male and female spaces and the construction of male religious practices at Sa Chal, this chapter examines the lives of those Buddhist men who take part in the temple's programs and services. In so doing, particular attention is paid to the processes through which men create meaningful roles for themselves in the temple and attempt to expand their influence despite their smaller numbers. That women comprise the majority of the weekly worship services is well acknowledged and expected by men and women alike. However, in an effort to expand their participation in ways that enhance perceived conventional male gender roles, the men also engage in a renegotiation of their identities following their arrival in the United States.

In many ways, men's participation at Sa Chal is deeply tied to a desire to raise their self-esteem by creating male spaces and social selves in the temple through a strategy of male inclusion that dictates a separation from women's roles and "women's religion." That is, men interpret Buddhist doctrines and idioms of "finding and knowing one's mind" as a means to reinscribe Confucian male identities and statuses challenged by the experience of immigration. By asserting that Buddhism is about self-knowledge and self-reliance, men at Sa Chal also see true religion as a male intellectual tradition defined by Confucian gender characteristics that equate maleness with political and scholarly activities which are then held to be superior to female forms of religiosity. In this way, men participate in those religious events sponsored by Sa Chal that reproduce traditional Korean male status roles.

In looking at the ways men assert their identities in and through Sa Chal's programs, two particular areas that receive a high percentage of male attention emerge: (1) political participation through the temple's reunification meetings and famine relief efforts and (2) scholarly activities through the temple's College. In many ways, religious activities provide a means of self-transformation and coping that articulate a positive male sense of self. Sa Chal provides an opportunity for men to develop a positive sense of self through activities that are coded as male. Through political participation, men at Sa Chal tend to assert a transnational Korean identity as opposed to a Korean American identity that increases feelings of low self-esteem

FINDING MALE SELVES: MEN'S RELIGIOUS PRACTICES

emerging from experiences of alienation in the United States. At the same time, men often define and assert identities based on an intellectual and rational interpretation of Buddhism which they distinguish from what they consider the emotional work of women's religion. As will become clear, men's desires for an intellectual Buddhism are enacted at Sa Chal as well as the struggles some men go through to valorize and renegotiate their positions in the United States vis-à-vis the temple.

PERCEPTIONS OF MEN'S AND WOMEN'S RELIGION

During my two years of research among Buddhists at Sa Chal, I often asked members to explain the discrepancy in men's and women's attendance at worship services. The varieties of responses offered were based primarily on references to the putative attributes of each gender. While some women claimed that men were too arrogant to bow down to the Buddha, others maintained that men were unable to come to temple since they worked all the time. Others believed that men chose not to attend temple simply because there were not enough other men around with whom they could socialize. Men, on the other hand, tended to claim that the temple's programs did not appeal to their intellectual curiosity nor provide them with enough opportunities for leadership roles. In many ways, these responses reflect men's desires to have more social prestige and responsibility in their ethnic institution similar to that of Korean Christian churches that reserve lay leadership positions as deacons, elders, and ushers for men.

Sociologists Eui Hang Shin and Hyung Park maintain that since Koreans have suffered in America because of their racial marginality, "Korean churches are the primary sources of comfort and compensation for Korean immigrants." Furthermore, the churches become very popular among the male population of Korean immigrants, for "[s]ince a great majority of Korean immigrants are deprived of status competition in the broader society, their competition supplies a meaning to life, [and] a means for feeling important."[1] Male Buddhists at Sa Chal are aware of the leadership and status competition offered by the churches and maintain that the temple should provide similar opportunities for laymen to take on some of the responsibilities for temple administration held by the monastics.

FINDING MALE SELVES: MEN'S RELIGIOUS PRACTICES

In men's responses, women were characterized as more faithful and more connected to the family's religious identity since they had more free time and because they had no other culturally acceptable means of letting go of stress. Female Buddhists were also held to enjoy the more devotional forms of Buddhism that the temple offered over a more intellectual, philosophical, and therefore male approach to Son Buddhism. Furthermore, women's practices at Sa Chal were associated with a lower form of religiosity characterized as emotional, sensitive, dependent, and oriented toward the good fortune of the family. Through this contrast between rational and devotional styles of worship, men at Sa Chal thus distinguish between a "higher" form of religion centering around more cerebral activities like meditation and a "lower," feminine form of practice based on physical activities such as prostrating, chanting, and praying in front of the Buddha during worship services. Since men were posited to be more interested in an intellectual understanding of religion, the body was viewed as secondary to the practice of meditation and "awakening the Buddha Nature." I found that in drawing these distinctions, men create a stereotypical view of women's religious practices as devotional although the women themselves do not see their practices as mere devotion. Rather, as noted in chapters four and five, women at Sa Chal are engaged in the construction of self-esteem and a process of self-transformation through their religious worship. In this way, men can be said to have a rather misinformed perception of women's religious practices as nonintellectual and devotional for reasons that derive from a stereotypical male Confucian view.

Through their contrast between men and women, mind and body, cerebral and devotional practices, men at Sa Chal also reproduce gender hierarchies that enable the construction of a male subjectivity vis-à-vis the homeland and conventional Korean cultural norms as a point of reference. According to many Sa Chal members, immigration has a tremendous impact on self-esteem especially for those who had positions of high Confucian social status and professional respect in Korea. Upon arriving in the United States, many male participants experienced limited mobility and inverted status and were unable to maneuver easily through the American system. I suggest that this downward turn in social, economic, and political status serves as a motivating factor for men's engagement in those activities sponsored by the temple that facilitate a strong psychological and emotional connection to Korea. Furthermore, these activities are generally aimed at the exclusion of women and directly influence the construction of a male subjectivity and reconstruction of male identity in America. Central to this reconstruction of male identity is the creation of a transnational identity which, as I show, enables men at Sa Chal to view themselves as Koreans rather than Korean Americans. That is, an individual asserts an identity through religious activities that establish a strong connection with the place of origin and constructs a distinctly male space for himself in response to the vicissitudes of immigration to the new country.[2] At the same time, in asserting a transnational Korean identity in the United States, many male members of Sa Chal further claim that by remaining Buddhist in the United States they remain more loyal and more "authentic" Koreans in contrast to their male counterparts in the Korean American churches.[3]

By participating in the temple's political activities, men at Sa Chal temple assert a transnational Korean identity that emerges as a direct response to their ethnic minority status in the United States and their religious minority status within the Korean American community. Throughout my interviews with male participants, I discovered that many members of Sa Chal do not even desire to become full American citizens; they are tied instead to an ideological translocal Korean identity.[4] Thus, for someone like Mr. Yang who immigrated in 1983, the idea of American citizenship holds very little appeal because he still considers himself a Korean and not a "Korean American." Even after living in the United States over fifteen years, he has yet to apply for citizenship and admits that he still pays "more attention to news and happenings in Korea than in America—Korean 70 percent and American about 30 percent." For some male members "becoming American" is the last thing they desire even though many of these men do not wish to move back to Korea. They keep themselves ideologically tied to the homeland as an identity marker even as they work for economic success in America. This transnational identification reflects the isolation many immigrants experience in the United States. As Mr. Yang aptly puts it: "For someone like me, I am just here alone with all my family in Korea. My mother lives there, my relatives are there and so even though I live here [with my wife], it's lonely and so you really have to worry a lot about yourself."

The desire to remain focused on Korea as a main source of identity and

FINDING MALE SELVES: MEN'S RELIGIOUS PRACTICES

reference despite living in the United States for a number of years exists as an option for many immigrants who have not experienced a positive sense of adjustment to life in the United States. For most of these men, a positive transition into American culture requires more than economic success and determination, which they seek at the temple.

"TO BE BUDDHIST IS TO BE KOREAN"

According to David Jeon, a forty-seven-year-old temple member who came to America in 1987, "to be Buddhist is to be Korean." Throughout our interview, he explained how Buddhism existed in Korea before Christianity, and he insisted that most of Christianity is derived from Buddhism, since he believes that the Bible contains passages very similar to Buddhist scriptures that were written "way before the time of Jesus." His comments equating Buddhism with an "authentic Korean identity" reflect not only his unquestioned Buddhist faith but also a more common disappointment and perhaps even envy of the increasing numbers of Korean Christian churches in the United States.

Currently he owns a marketing company that he runs with a fellow Buddhist member of Sa Chal and spends most of his time socializing and working with temple members. During the weekdays, male friends from the temple can usually be found in his office chatting, drinking tea, working on new business ideas, and discussing temple affairs. Like many men at Sa Chal, most of David's social life revolves around Buddhists at the temple. In addition to being an active member at Sa Chal, David is also heavily involved with the temple's famine relief efforts to North Korea and serves as a main administrator for the One Korea Buddhist Movement, USA. As an organization that raises funds for famine relief in North Korea, the One Korea Buddhist Movement is also tied to reunification efforts and established the Diamond Noodle Factory just outside of Pyongyang in 1998. The noodle factory is a joint venture between the abbot of Sa Chal, David, and his older brother, a Buddhist leader in South Korea.

As a main figure in the famine relief project and reunification endeavors within the Buddhist community, David devotes most of his time to the transnational Korean community and maintains significant ties to Korea by traveling back and forth to South Korea, the United States, and North

Korea. Although he has lived in America since the mid-1980s, like many of the men I interviewed he claims that he has no desire to become an American citizen or to obtain citizenship rights like voting or financial assistance in the future, for he still sees himself as "a Korean always." Another factor contributing to his refusal to apply for American citizenship is his sense of disappointment over his son's involvement in gangs and his disrespectful anti-Korean behavior toward his father. Furthermore, since the Los Angeles disturbances of 1992, David has developed a strong distrust of the U.S. government and the police department based on their slow response to the violence that erupted in Koreatown.

When asked about his involvement in the temple's efforts in North Korea, David expresses a widely held view among men when he claims that he became an important figure in the reunification and famine relief movement out of nationalistic pride. Over tea he explains:

> Because of the political motives of the Christians in Korea during the [Korean] war and the lack of nationalistic pride among Korean Christians who have been duped by Westerners and the Korean obsession with PX culture, Korean Christians in Korea and in the United States have lost their history and their culture. There is no philosophy among Christian converts! They were all obsessed with the material value of PX culture during the Korean War and the influence of the Salvation Army and other Christian groups who brought in specialty foods that later ended up on the black market. They also brought in special gifts for kids at Christmas time and ended up creating this love for Western things!

David argues that Korean Christians have been so heavily influenced by Western powers that even today they lack pride and a sense of loyalty to their own country of origin. In response, David has devoted himself to spreading Korean Buddhism throughout North Korea, South Korea, and the United States. In so doing, he also asserts his own identity as a Buddhist and as a nationalistic Korean in contrast to the Korean Christians who have, as he puts it, "betrayed their country." David then reiterates, "to be Buddhist is to be Korean," and, similarly, "to be Korean is to be Buddhist."

The notion of the betrayal of the Koreans was a commonly expressed sentiment among many of the participants in this study. I found that in

FINDING MALE SELVES: MEN'S RELIGIOUS PRACTICES

addition to blaming the West and Christianity for the lack of nationalistic pride among Korean Americans, the men's efforts at reunification and famine relief were heavily driven by memories of a past that still looms large in the minds of many Korean immigrants—the Japanese occupation of Korea from 1910 to 1945. David refers to this period as the "Japanese brainwashing of Koreans." In his view, historically the Japanese (even before the occupation) had criticized Korean Buddhist monks, and then during the occupation Korean monks were forced to marry like the Japanese Buddhist monks. David explained in an excited voice:

> During the occupation, the Japanese forced the monks to marry so that they couldn't rebel if they were tied down with wives and children! Because of this brainwashing, after the occupation, the Korean Christians like Syngman Rhee started criticizing all the monks' departure from celibacy which proved for Christians that Buddhists were not "pure" anymore! Then, since the Christians only believed in one god, the Buddhists were thought of as devils!

David thus equates Buddhism with a strong sense of nationalism and a Korean identity that has been undermined not only by Japanese imperialists but also by Christians attracted by the West. Interestingly, his equation of Buddhism with Korean nationalism seems to exclude the historical relationship between Korean Christianity in the United States and Korean nationalism in the early part of the twentieth century.

For men like David Jeon the establishment of the Diamond Noodle Factory can be understood in relation to the political desire for reunification between North and South Korea that is espoused by some temple participants, even if this desire is more ideological than acted upon. In fact, there are many who would like to "help our people" gain reunification of the two countries. As his friend Jae Woo, a Korean immigrant student, claims, "Every Korean wants Tong-il [reunification] at heart." For many Koreans in the Los Angeles Koreatown district, reunification plays a key role in their ethnic identification, for they see themselves as Koreans or Koreans living in America rather than as Korean Americans. As such, this transnational identification as Korean is related to the exertion of political agency among immigrants who do not have much political clout in the United States.

Although David never explicitly discusses his sense of dislocation, the fervor of his critiques against Korean Christians in America and his daily struggles with his son reveal some of the main motivations for his participation in Sa Chal. While he criticizes the Korean Christians for their material success and "selling out" to American culture, it is hard to see how someone who works seven days a week in his own business cannot be affected by the financial support offered by religious organizations outside one's own. These contributing factors have thus led him and others at Sa Chal to reject the notion of becoming American citizens and to embrace a more transnational identity.

One of the men I met with on quite a few occasions was Steven Lee, a bilingual member of Sa Chal who had recently started bringing his new wife to temple services. Although raised by Buddhist parents in Korea, Steven did not attend temple on a weekly basis until he arrived in the United States in 1971. His earliest recollections of Buddhist worship are as a small child who used to follow his mother to temple every once in a while, where "we just prayed to the Buddha." Steven's father also considered himself Buddhist but chose not to attend services. He explains, "my father never went to temple. . . . That is usually the case and that is the old family custom [in Korea]. Usually religion is the mother's job, not the father's. It's custom." Religion for the Lee family was very informal and as Steven puts it, "to tell you the truth, I did not think about religion until I grew up" and came to the United States.

Currently he is the only Buddhist among his seven siblings. One of his sisters proclaims no religion, and his second oldest sister and third sister converted to Roman Catholicism and Protestantism following their marriages. Two of his brothers choose not to attend any religious services, although one "is close to Buddhism" and the other "married a Christian." Similarly, he is the only one in his family to immigrate to America; the rest remain in Seoul working and raising their children. Steven did not start attending a Buddhist temple until a very traumatic event occurred in his life. Although he did not talk much about the incident, I learned that the death of his child from crib death in 1974 led him to seek the support of a temple in Los Angeles. At that time, he came across another well-known Korean temple called Tahl Ma Sa and sought the prayers of the resident abbot. However, after observing the struggles between the abbot and some rebellious monks, Steven soon left the temple.

FINDING MALE SELVES: MEN'S RELIGIOUS PRACTICES

His second attempt to attend Buddhist services did not take place until nearly twenty years later, in 1995 after his divorce from his first wife. Although he had known the abbot of Sa Chal for quite a while through joint reunification meetings, Steven did not feel compelled to participate weekly until the dissolution of his marriage. He explains:

> I was having a really bad time of things because I had just gotten divorced and I needed something. So I started coming to Sa Chal where I knew the Buddhist monk. That's pretty much why I started. I went for myself—not only for knowledge but to develop myself and make myself strong and concentrate on myself. I didn't just want to be a Buddha, in fact, I don't care if I can become a Buddha or not. I just wanted to live the right way. At the time, the main reason I came to temple is because I needed to build myself up. I was in a bad situation. I lost my family and I needed to make myself strong and build myself up again.

In many ways, Steven's reasons for coming to Sa Chal reflect those motivations that he attributes to Buddhist women:

> [W]omen are looking for something more; they have to have somebody to hear them and listen to them . . . and women have a harder time than men because they have children and they work. Men also work but they have a chance to go drink and talk and clear their problems up once in a while, but the women don't have a chance to drink or anything. It's customary for women not to do those things.

Despite his explicit gender rhetoric, Steven attends temple regularly for psychological comfort in coming to terms with the early death of his child, his divorce, and the change in his economic and social status after immigration.

Steven arrived in the United States in the early spring of 1971 with his first wife, a concert pianist who had dreamed of coming to America since college. Although he had no interest in leaving Korea, where he worked as a civil servant with an economic planning board, he gave in to his wife's desire to immigrate for "a higher level of opportunity and because she figured that the USA would be a wonderful land." Like many new immigrants Steven had difficulty adjusting to his new surroundings and did not speak English when he arrived. Though he had a high-status job in Seoul and a master's degree, he learned that his previous credentials carried little weight in the Los Angeles work force. At that time, he and his first wife deliberately chose to live in California instead of on the East Coast, for, "my wife's friends said that it was better to stay in LA because we were [Asian]. They said that LA was the best place to stay especially for foreigners." Yet living in Los Angeles proved to be very difficult for Steven despite the larger percentage of Asian immigrants, for as he discovered: "Of course, racism here is very very high. We were scared back then because some [people] would come and try to cheat us and push us to sell them stuff [like alcohol]. We also feared the whites [because] they really discriminated against the Orientals and, of course, we could really feel that."

Steven characterizes his immigration as a downward turn in economic opportunities as well. Fully expecting to obtain a high-paying job, he learned that even after he developed his English skills to fluency, he was still being passed over for jobs. He explains:

> White people [Americans] think with their noses high in the air. They even behave that way too. Ever since we [Koreans] came here we started our own businesses and worked for large companies. But even when we work, they always think that Orientals [*sic*] are not worthy of consideration for promotions. Really, I have experienced that before. I have argued with them and talked to them about it. I used to ask them, "hey, what's going on? I am the priority person here and I am the one supposed to be promoted." But they wouldn't consider me at all, even though I had a college degree, they wouldn't consider me for the promotion.

Steven currently does not utilize any of the skills he learned through his master's degree study in public administration. In this respect, his frustration with his status in the United States reflects what sociologist Won Moo Hurh considers a psychological crisis "when the immigrants perceive limitations to occupational and social mobility in their adopted country. Furthermore, the perception of the glass ceiling on one's occupational career is certainly a painful and demoralizing experience."[5] He does harbor some resentment and regret for having come to the United States, for he has been

FINDING MALE SELVES: MEN'S RELIGIOUS PRACTICES

unable to obtain a job that provides him with both security and pride. Pondering his situation in America, he claims:

> If I stayed in my country, I would not even work like this or have such a hard time. I started out here in labor work. I started as a box boy at a supermarket and then a warehouse man, and then a stock man. Well, I could not stand this kind of work. Then I became a real estate broker and then, well here I am now. If I had stayed in my own country, I am sure that I would have been in a better position than I am now!

Because of the instability of his most recent job as a lead abatement contractor, Steven was forced to move into his wife's office space, and because his job does not provide him with the economic and social status he desires, he recently decided to become a doctor of Eastern medicine like his wife. He has also been filling his schedule with classes at the local Eastern medicine college and at the temple's Buddhist college.

Related to his disappointment with his job prospects, Steven has also been actively seeking fellowship at Sa Chal with other men who may be in a similar position. As such, he often attends worship services with his wife and during the subsequent luncheon hour makes attempts to find other men to befriend. Yet meeting friends at Sa Chal has proven difficult, even though he says that he "couldn't stand being alone at the temple." Thus his desire for socializing among co-ethnic men has not been met, for as he puts it:

> You know, Koreans especially don't talk that much or smile at people much. They only keep to themselves. That is really difficult. . . . Many people here are kind and I am trying to make closer friendships with them, but not many people want to make close friendships here. Even though my office is only three blocks away, if I invited [members] to come to my place sometimes, nobody would come. If they came, then I could say hello and treat them to some tea, [but still] they won't come.

Steven has thus been very lonely at the temple even as he tries to become better acquainted with a group of potential peers.

While he has not found comfort among intimate friends at the temple, he has found a group of men who share a similar political interest in reunification, which Sa Chal's abbot actively supports. Thus, Steven does come to meetings sponsored by the temple and has had a lot of interaction with other male members who take part in the same activities. He is closely tied to reunification movements and transnational famine relief, giving him a tremendous sense of pride and notoriety in the Korean community that he has not found elsewhere. These projects enable him to create an identity for himself that is defined by the homeland rather than by U.S. standards of economic and social success, which he believes he cannot meet.

Like David Jeon, Steven has a strong sense of transnational identity, which suggests a direct relationship to the downward mobility he has experienced in the United States. We can see this relationship in his claim, "I am Korean, I am a Korean, I could not be an American. I am a Korean living in America." Through his weekly attendance at Sa Chal, Steven seeks to redress the psychological discomforts of personal dislocation. At the same time, he works to maintain a sense of high self-esteem through projects that reference his leadership and prestige back in Korea. Although he has tried to find emotional support among male members of the temple through personal friendships, he has been more successful by way of his participation in activities viewed by other men as specifically male—reunification meetings.

Mr. Yim is a forty-three-year-old man who immigrated to the United States in 1986. A graduate of the City College of Seoul, he claims that he originally came to America to study business but because of "Korean problems" got involved in political movements for reunification and could not complete his graduate studies. Mr. Yim states that he has been actively involved in Korean political activities for a dozen years, for he believes that "the biggest problem for Korea is reunification." As the former coordinator for the Korean Resource Center in Los Angeles for twelve years, he has recently decided to switch fields to Eastern medicine in order "to make more money" as an acupuncturist. A classmate of Jane Lim's (chapter five) and an alumnus of the same school as David, Mr. Yim's social world overlaps between the workplace, school, and the temple, thus demonstrating the tight bonds that some members of Sa Chal form (although Steven has been unsuccessful in this endeavor).

Currently married to a Korean woman who works as a shop clerk, he claims that he and his wife do not wish to have any children because "having children is seen as an obstacle in Buddhism, right?" When I asked him what he meant by this statement, he laughed and explained, "I mean, the Buddha had a son Rahula, but look what happened to him!" Using the Buddhist notion of the negative aspects of too many attachments, he conveyed to me that he did not want any other obstacles to get in the way of their financial and social success in America.

When I first met Mr. Yim, he was sitting on the couch in David Jeon's office with a set of large Buddhist mala beads in his hands. The son of farmers who never had a formal education, he says that he became politicized "at the age of twenty during the Kwangju Uprisings where I saw the tremendous cultural and class conflicts and could not believe what the oppressive government was doing."[6] He says that he was a staunch Marxist between the ages of twenty-five and forty. Currently forty-three, he divides his life into three periods according to religious affiliation—Confucianism, Marxism, and Buddhism. Describing his own history of religious practice he states:

> If we talk about religion, my concept may be different from everyone else's. I was a Confucian until I was twenty-five. After that, you could say that from twenty-five to forty I was a Marxist; that is, if you consider Marxism a religion. From forty on, a Buddhist, or you might say something close to a Buddhist.

Mr. Yim's current interest in Korean nationalism and reunification can be traced back to his early Confucian years. He started out as a Confucian based on family custom, but all along he believed that Confucianism was far too class based:

> On the farm, everything was about Confucianism. You had to bow to the elders, elders had to eat first, and things like that. I had to live by those standard because they were my family's virtues then. But when I became twenty-five, it was 1980 and the Kwangju Uprisings took place. I didn't understand why our people were killing one another. I started to wonder about the cause of the problem. Why did we have to kill each other? Where was the problem heading? That is when I became interested in class problems, for there was a difference of class between president Chun Du Hwan and the citizens

of Kwangju. I also started examining the situation with North Korea which we referred to as Red. By looking at these problems, I have concluded that there were really two main problems, nationalism and class issues. From those two issues, I determined that class issues were more important, which led me to Marxism.

Thus Mr. Yim decided to become a staunch Marxist to rebel against the class-based Confucian system he grew up in. In an effort to eradicate these class differences, he became a Marxist and worked toward reunification of North and South Korea. However, by the late eighties and early nineties, the Cold War had ended and Mr. Yim decided that Marxism was no longer viable or "in the main," although he was still attracted to its philosophy and potential as a religion. He explains, "if you see Marxism as a religion, it states equality. Equality is a good thing in terms of class. I really think it is a good thing but I don't think it is current enough as a way of solving problems."

Desiring a religion that eradicates class differences and is conducive to reunification, Mr. Yim at the age of forty-three began to profess a belief in Buddhism:

> By looking at Korea, it is going to be Buddhism [that makes change]. . . . Why? Because Buddhism has been around the longest. This is one of the reasons why I have chosen Buddhism to be the religion I am closest to and am currently going to practice. Buddhism was the first religion of Korea; I talk about the two together, Buddhism and nationalism. I speak of nationalism in terms of Buddhism because the religion is one of the oldest in Korea and the practices can thus solve the problems of nationalism.

Here Mr. Yim posits that since Buddhism arrived in Korea before Catholicism and before the Neo-Confucian Yi dynasty, it serves as the perfect symbol of Korean national identity which he believes is lacking among Korean American converts to Christianity. In this respect his views are reminiscent of David Jeon's belief that "to be Korean is to be Buddhist" and not a Western influenced Christian.

Mr. Yim's perspective on Buddhism also reflects the beliefs of many men at Sa Chal—that it is a highly logical and rational religion and one that makes

FINDING MALE SELVES: MEN'S RELIGIOUS PRACTICES

sense "on a philosophical level with the doctrines of karma." Devotional aspects of Buddhism such as prayer or chanting are women's religious activities to help them "wish for their well-being, but that's not the case for us [men]. We are more logical." Like Steven Lee, he believes that men "can find themselves a hobby like fishing, golfing, or drinking" to relieve stress, but women are more inclined to bow to the Buddha and attend temple on a regular basis to pray for a better life, because it would be inappropriate for women to be seen drinking and carousing in public. According to Mr. Yim, men do not need to go to temple every week. They have other venues for relieving stress. Furthermore, since he believes that men are more logical, a devotional form of religious practice will not suffice. He prefers to read Buddhist texts and meditate, for he views Buddhism as a philosophical religion and believes that he does not have to be in a temple to "think" about religion. He just "reads a book about Buddhism every two weeks" and tends to come to temple services when a special monk or scholar is scheduled to give a "real" dharma talk that appeals to the male intellect.

Mr. Yim has known the abbot of Sa Chal for over twelve years and has attended the temple sporadically during this time. He does not feel compelled to attend the temple, for it does not provide him with the mentally and philosophically inspiring dharma teachings that he believes the monks should provide. One of his main criticisms of the temple's abbot, in fact, is that he "doesn't ever teach anything very intellectual in the dharma talks. He doesn't study enough texts, that's what his problem is. . . . If the monks want to bring in more men and more second-generation members, then they have to study more."

He goes on to say that the temple should provide more services and programs that would give men opportunities to take leadership roles, otherwise after the current abbot dies "the temple will disappear" without any successor. When asked about the content of the abbot's dharma talks, Mr. Yim replied, "Well, you know, the immigrant community has a tough time and so they come to the temple seeking comfort, not really religious teachings, so that's what the abbot talks about." He continues, "I don't see the point in coming to the worship service to listen to that." Instead, he reads the Diamond Sutra and meditates. Thus for Mr. Yim the Korean temple provides women with a culturally acceptable space in which to work through emotional problems but fails to appeal to men's need for psycho-

FINDING MALE SELVES: MEN'S RELIGIOUS PRACTICES

logical comfort in a way that addresses their culturally performed "intellectual" and "high status" identities. In this way, he confirms the widely held belief among men that temples must provide opportunities and special programs that valorize the male ego.

TRANSNATIONAL IDENTITIES

While a transnational context has always existed for immigrants to this country, what is different now is that immigrants are aided by the immediacy of the homeland, which renders the narrative of "becoming American" nonessential to the development of an identity. However, as I note in chapter seven, paradoxically "being American" is still highly regarded, particularly because the highest values of American culture (independence and self-reliance) are deeply compatible with being Buddhist. Nonetheless, it is in the context of transnationalism that identity formation, agency, and self-esteem emerge for many male immigrants in their assertions of a Korean identity. In supporting famine relief and taking active roles in promoting reunification by attending meetings, staging protests, or even traveling to North Korea, many Korean American men are involved in an assertion of Korean identity and nationalism while continuing to live in the United States. Male support of such activities thus ties them closer to the Korean community and a strong ethnic identity. For many men at Sa Chal, the claim for identity and agency is made not as American citizens but as transnational Koreans—a response to the conditions of immigrant life often experienced as displacing. Thus in this context the Buddhist temple helps produce an alternative form of identity outside of any distinct claim to an American identity.

Viewing oneself in relation to the homeland through the temple provides an individual with an opportunity to express agency and confidence while living in the host country. In fact, some scholars even reject "immigrant" as an analytically appropriate term because it implies a "permanent rupture" from the homeland and obscures the everyday reality of life in the United States, which is tied economically, politically, and ideologically to the country of origin.[7] Through their participation in political programs at the temple, many male Buddhists in the United States are able to assert a political agency that they do not experience in the host country, given their minority status and inability to assimilate completely. When I polled members of the temple, I found that most men consider themselves fully Korean with very little interest in in-depth integration into American culture.[8] Many feel isolated from mainstream society or excluded due to racism and language problems. Upon arrival in the United States, many experience downward social mobility and are unable to maneuver easily through the American system. This downward status is one of the primary factors motivating an immigrant to continue to look back to the homeland as a source of reference and engage in transnational activities. Hence many men at Sa Chal actively support reunification and famine relief as a way of combating or offsetting their crisis in status in America.

Sociologist Luin Goldring points to a similar phenomenon in the Mexican American community, where Mexican immigrants look to and maintain close social ties with the country of origin by sending remittances, supporting local and political projects back home, and even returning there with gifts. Goldring outlines three main reasons for maintaining these transnational ties: (1) the immigrant is able to valorize social status within a transnational context, (2) the individual may change his or her own status in the host country by taking part in home-based or transnational activities and become "key players" in a different social context, and (3) transnational organizations may offer resources that permit the development of alternative hierarchies where individuals are viewed in relation to those back home rather than in the host country.[9] Despite the appearance of permanent settlement in the United States, such border crossings are an integral part of the immigrant experience.

Goldring's study further indicates that immigration and transnationalism affect men and women differently. For many of the male Mexican participants in Goldring's study, immigration brings both positive and negative results, yet for women these results are often experienced as beneficial to their self-esteem. For example, women often gain status prior to their own immigration because they are responsible for taking care of the household and family during their separation from husbands who migrated earlier in search of employment. In addition, many Mexican women find that working in the United States provides them with opportunities for advancement and enhanced self-esteem. For men, however, the social setting of the host country makes it almost impossible to retain their status, particularly when they lack the political power and agency they had in Mexico. A similar situation can be said to exist for some women at Sa Chal who indicate that they are less interested in transnational projects like famine relief than they are in the high satisfaction they find in working independently for a living in the United States. Others felt such activities were in men's domain and some claimed that they had no interest in reunification and would not support anything related to North Korea.

Similarly, Ai Ra Kim attributes the rise of male leadership and worship in Korean American churches to this lack of power in America, for the church provides a context in which men can reassert their agency and political power. In her study of the role of the Korean church in Korean immigrant social life, Kim asserts:

> Churches confer social status and positions of leadership upon adult members. This function is highly important, especially for men. Most Korean men, except for those in prestigious professions such as medicine, law and big business, find their social status has been denigrated after immigration; their traditional egos and pride become damaged. Korean churches help heal their psychological wounds by giving men recognition and power within the church leadership and bureaucracy through the position of lay-elder and lay-deacon, board member and trustee. Most of the staff and administrative officers of ethnic Korean churches are men. In particular, being an elder grants prestige and power to a man: elders exercise tremendous power inside and outside the church, and almost all elders are men. Also most of the celebrities in the Korean communities are elders of their churches. In this sense, men still control the reins of power in the Korean community. The church reflects traditional Confucian Korean cultural/social structure and system.[10]

Kim's work indicates that the religious institution plays a key role in sustaining Korean identity and gender relations despite the transition to a new country. While men may view the church as a source of power through the conferral of lay leadership roles, the Buddhist temple lacks specifically ritualized roles for men. Hence most men at Sa Chal occupy the few administrative opportunities available (e.g., volunteer accountant) or pursue leadership roles in temple-supported programs outside of the worship service.

FINDING MALE SELVES: MEN'S RELIGIOUS PRACTICES

This continued tie to the homeland enables many men at Sa Chal to alter their social landscape and actively engage in nationalistic or political processes related to Korea that they do not have access to in the United States. Thus, although men may be less visible at the temples and less inclined to worship publicly with the women, they are more willing to take an active part in reunification and famine relief than women are in Sa Chal. I do not wish to suggest that developing a transnational identity is merely a simplistic way to combat alienation but that perhaps such an identity has developed as one type of coping mechanism and method of adaptation that has previously been overlooked. Thus, as Kim says, transnationalism can be said to "resist or raise their [men's] social standing and validate their self-esteem." Although male members are said to be embarrassed to bow down in full prostration in the company of women, they are nonetheless active in Sa Chal's academic lectures and political activities. While these activities do not exclude religious and spiritual motivations, of course, they do indicate that men are involved in creating alternative practices more suitable to meeting their psychological needs.

BROADER IMPLICATIONS OF TRANSNATIONALISM AND RELIGION

By taking a leading role in relief efforts for North Korea through the noodle factory and by coordinating a support network between the United States and South Korea, Sa Chal provides a specific avenue for maintaining ethnic identity and active involvement in the homeland. As a new post-1965 immigrant institution, Sa Chal is by nature involved in transnational activities supported by members who cross national borders at least once a year and do not really consider themselves Americans; they are more tied to an ideological translocal Korean identity. Like the Italian Harlem church studied by Robert Orsi, the temple brings together immigrants and their children through ceremonies and services to provide an essential link to the homeland.[11] Unlike earlier immigrants of European descent, however, the new post-1965 Immigration Act Koreans are better able to transport themselves back to the homeland through telecommunications, computers, and airplane flights. This ability to exist almost simultaneously in the homeland and the new land has obviated the need for many new immigrants to even worry about full-scale assimilation in American society.

It is in the context of transnational immediacy that the cultural practices of identity formation, memory, and resistance can take place for many new immigrants. Excluded or marginalized from the American mainstream, new immigrants have sought different means of developing subjectivity outside the narrative of American citizenship. For Koreans at Sa Chal, the claim for identity and agency is made not as American citizens but as transnational Koreans. This claim for hybrid identity is a response to the conditions of immigrant life often experienced as displacing. In other words, for many recent immigrants, the ethnic congregation serves as the site for an alternative form of identity outside of the claim to an American identity.

There are ethnic stakes at hand in transnational famine relief movements that have implications beyond the material both abroad and at home, in the global *and* the local context. These implications have different meanings for the different parties involved at the temple and in the Korean community. In supporting famine relief and actively promoting reunification by attending meetings, staging protests, or even traveling to North Korea, many Korean American Buddhists I have spoken with are involved in an assertion of Korean ethnicity and nationalism while continuing to live in the United States. Through the Diamond Noodle Factory and the children's relief movement, Buddhists in the United States are able to assert a political agency that they do not experience in the United States, given their minority status and inability to fully assimilate. While there is a tendency to assume that all immigrants desire and follow the same trajectory to full-scale participation in American culture, and the benefits of citizenship embarked upon by early groups of European immigrants, this assumption does not take into consideration that such a trajectory is not easily followed by all immigrants, or even desired.

The continued tie to the homeland also enables Koreans to alter their social landscape in the United States and actively engage in nationalistic or political processes related to Korea that they do not have access to yet in the United States. As noted earlier, Sa Chal mediates the process of immigrant adaptation, yet, unlike any other U.S. based temples and churches, this Los Angeles congregation takes on the role of a transnational site which impedes what is often accepted as the eventual assimilation of the immi-

FINDING MALE SELVES: MEN'S RELIGIOUS PRACTICES

grant. What this emerging transnational identification signifies is that religion plays numerous roles in immigrant lives and that there are more processes at play than assimilation and ethnic enclaving for new immigrant congregations in the United States. Many members of the temple, following years of adjustment in Los Angeles, have been able to extend their gaze back home, a transition also reflected in the larger history of the Korean community in America. Immigrant religious organizations are self-reflexive in their response to congregational needs. Religion therefore reflects the patterns and demands of adaptation to the new land as well as the continued maintenance of religious and cultural traditions. In Los Angeles, the temple becomes the symbol of home and continues to mediate this relationship through transnational activities, thus bringing about a new function of religion.

BUDDHISM AS "INTELLECTUAL WORK"

I don't think that coming to temple every week is a factor in becoming a Buddhist because we are trying to be free from everything that entangles us. So if it is something that you dread (coming to temple every weekend), it is not worth it to come every week. [Lawrence, a twenty-five-year-old Sa Chal male member]

Strangely, men think that if they go to temple, they seem like they are somewhat backward because people think that those who believe in Christianity are more modern. If you believe in Buddhism, they think you are old-fashioned [but] men study the Buddhist sutras. The reason why is because in the past Korean Buddhism didn't have any sutras written in Korean characters and so they were very difficult to understand. Men are different because they have the type of personality that wants to learn from books. That's why more women come to temple . . . and they have more time. [Dr. Cho, a fifty-three-year-old Sa Chal member]

When I began my research and interviews with men at Sa Chal to determine how they viewed their own Buddhist practices, they drew a strong distinction between their own forms of worship and those of women. When I asked the men to elaborate on the significance of the female majority in worship services, most of them made reference to *Kibok* or "fortune-praying" Buddhism, which they applied to *all* women in Korea who were traditionally bound to look after the spiritual welfare of the family. The term *Kibok* Buddhism dates back to the period following the liberation of Korea from Japanese occupation in 1945 and the Korean War when women became active agents in restoring Korea's temples. A scholar of Korean Buddhism, Young-Ja Lee, has shown that women's participation in the development of temples brought about the term *Chima*, or Skirt Buddhism, a derogatory word referring to "women's activities" and "fortune-praying" practices.[12] Thus, even today men continue to associate women's practices with a lower form of religiosity.

As I noted earlier, however, most women interpret Buddhist teachings and their own practice in ways that point to their own self-edification. In fact, none of the women with whom I spoke ever characterized their own practice as mere fortune-praying for the sake of others. For example, seventy-two-year-old Mrs. Hurh, who moved to the United States in 1987, asserts that she comes to temple "in order to purify my mind." For this woman, who lives alone in Koreatown, "the aim of Buddhism is to become a Buddha, it is for oneself. The other important thing is awakening, you have to aim to become a Buddha." Mrs. Hurh acknowledges that *Kibok* forms of Buddhism existed in Korea but she herself correctly understands the true meaning of religion: "At first [in Korea], women were into fortune-praying Buddhism so they would pray to the Buddha for things and ask for their children to be wealthy. But more importantly, I have to awaken myself so that I can become a Buddha. If you want to become [a Buddha] then you really have to be awakened and learn the Buddha's teachings."

Like Mrs. Hurh, the other female Buddhists I interviewed all agreed that enlightenment and self-realization were their main motivations for worship—the same motivations cited by men. Not one woman indicated that her sutra recitations and prostrations were aimed at the well-being of her family members. Korean Buddhist women, contrary to the prevailing perception among men, engage in religious worship for a host of reasons centering on themselves as active agents in their self-transformation. In fact, most women agreed that awakening and Buddhist practice could only be done on an individual basis.

For Mrs. Hurh, the Buddha dharma is a profound teaching that most people would not be able to understand without an adequate study of its doctrines and sutras. That this intellectually complex tradition is not for the weak willed is why, she believes, many Koreans convert to Christianity following immigration:

> I think people convert because they didn't really know the Buddha's teachings. They really didn't know the Buddha dharma. If you just look at the skin of a watermelon, you won't know what it is. You don't know the taste or if it is sweet or sour. You don't know that the inside is red or what's in there, right? After eating it, you know that it is red, sour, and sweet. . . . People who know that much cannot convert. If you know just that much of the Buddha's dharma then you wouldn't be able to convert. There's nothing you can do. If you only look at the skin and don't eat it how are you going to know if it's sweet or sour? Those people will just convert because they don't know the [inner] meaning of Buddhism.

This grandmother has worked hard to fathom the Buddha dharma and has developed a mind strong enough to pursue the goal of Buddhism. There is no turning to Christianity for Mrs. Hurh, for she has tasted the core of Buddhism. Her view of her religious practice is at odds with men's perceptions of women's spiritual motivation, for she devotes her time to sutra readings and meditation aimed at achieving enlightenment.

Mr. Jang Won Lee has this to say about men's participation at the temple:

> Men don't believe in praying for help to solve their problems. Life is difficult and exhausting so in order to comfort their minds, men will go off on their own to get rid of their stress by drinking. But a woman can't let go of stress like a man because it looks bad in our culture. So women look to religion in order to alleviate stress and they seek out programs for support. We really need to change the programs [at Sa Chal] because men need to have some sort of relationship [with the temple] and participate more. It's a very practical thing to do, but the person with faith is really the woman. Men are not dependent and so don't rely on others. So Buddhism has to open up more activities [to attract men]. I don't know if it will increase their faith or not but men just don't want to go to temple and pray. They don't think about going in front of the Buddha and begging for things—women can do that

because they are more sensitive whereas men are a lot more intellectually oriented. If you want to have a lot of men come to temple then you have to have a program that matches men—a more rational program. Then the men will come. Men will listen to lectures but they won't come to temple and pray every weekend. So men have to have programs that are intellectual.... Right now the sermons in the temple are set up for women; they give sermons for women to set their minds at ease.... It's not that men don't have faith but they need to have their own religious activities.

Jang Won Lee sits at the desk in his temple office and explains why men do not attend worship services at Sa Chal, an explanation he believes lies in a lack of intellectual content in the monks' sermons. As a printer and administrator for the temple's new Buddhist college, Mr. Lee works tirelessly seven days a week in the hopes of establishing a strong missionization program to spread Korean Buddhism throughout the United States, yet he will not sit through a full Sunday service. As the former General Propagator of the Chogye order in Seoul, he set his eyes on America as a primary place to "provide immigrant Buddhists with a spiritual home." In 1983, he arrived in Los Angeles with his wife and two daughters and began to work with his brother, the abbot of Sa Chal. Originally, Mr. Lee planned to develop youth programs aimed at bringing in more second-generation Korean Americans to the temple since he noted that most of the worshippers' children tended to go to Christian churches to meet friends and speak in English with fellow Koreans like themselves. Unfortunately, Mr. Lee notes, he does not speak English, nor does the abbot, nor do the resident monks, thus language barriers have become the main deterrent in attracting more students to the temple.

Over the past three years, Mr. Lee has directed attention to the training of parents in order to develop a strong family base of Buddhism. As a result, he dedicates most of his time to administering the temple's Buddhist college, a two-year certificate program that trains students to become Buddhist missionaries in America. It is this program that he hopes will appeal intellectually to men and will motivate them to begin attending temple on a regular basis. For if more men attend temple, he believes that the children are likely to follow, and not only will the number of younger Buddhists attending temple increase with the increased participation of men but also the worship style of Korean Buddhism will change from what he sees as a female- oriented, "overly detailed ritualism" to a more *inclusive* form of worship with a solid foundation in the intellectual, doctrinal, and social aspects of Buddhism that appeal to men. "Unfortunately," he says, "very few of the existing monks and people leading the monastic life are capable of leading such programs." He then adds, "They may think that beating the wooden gong and chanting the name of Amita Buddha are what Buddhism is all about but that is not enough for you to propagate faith." For Mr. Lee, men in general have been excluded from the temple's worship services, which he feels cater only to rituals and not to textual and doctrinal studies.

In associating women with old rituals and men with more intellectual interests, Mr. Lee brings to light a connection of women with the Buddhism of the Yi dynasty in Korea, when the religion was persecuted by the Neo-Confucian leadership. It is to the men that he turns for a modernization of Korean Buddhism; more specifically, it is to laymen such as himself that he looks for change and the growth of Chogye order Buddhism. Like David Jeon, Steven Lee, and Mr. Yim, Mr. J. W. Lee associates Korean Buddhism with nationalistic pride. Yet he believes that Buddhism must modernize and move from a position as cultural monument to become a contemporary lay-centered missionizing religion if it is to be viable beyond the next ten years or so. Citing its history in Korea, he explains:

> Despite its long history of Buddhism, Korea—a country governed by the principles of Confucianism borrowed from China—fell at the end of the Yi dynasty. Korea was belatedly awakened by the foreign powers when she was colonized by the Japanese who had already come to grips with what was going on in the world. It was inevitable because Korea was too weak. After Korea was liberated, Christianity began to missionize aggressively and overshadowed Korean Buddhism, which had no time to awaken itself. Therefore, Korean Buddhism colored the traditions and history of Korea well, but failed to provide the Koreans with living cultural ideals that could be actualized in social life. This is our national history. So Korea was already taken up by others when Christianity and other foreign religions rushed [into] Korea in big waves after the liberation of 1945. Under the circumstances, the sense of sovereignty based on her own religion that guides the spirit of the nation

was buried completely in oblivion. When Korean Buddhism awoke from its hibernation and was struck with the idea that "this is not the way it should be" the young people had already been viewing it like an ancient cultural monument.

For Mr. Lee, it is now up to the laymen to change the future of Buddhism, for the monks and the women are mired in the ways of the past. By "just sitting there beating the wooden gong and praying for blessings and good fortune," they are "preserving Buddhism as a historical monument." In this way, Mr. Lee associates women's Buddhism with *Kibok* Buddhism.

For Mr. Lee, an intellectual male form of Buddhism offers a corrective over fortune-praying Buddhism and is a more viable form of practice in today's circumstances. While he suggests that men need more programs that appeal to their intellectual inclinations, he also draws attention to an important function that the temple's Buddhist college may have for developing a male subjectivity that caters to a need to feel scholarly and intellectual, and more important, change the face of Buddhism in America. While he believes that the Buddhism practiced by women in the temple may provide emotional healing, he also contends that it does not help men in their need to express their faith. He advocates instead:

> Men need to have programs that will bring them out here; otherwise, it is no fun for them. Most people will say that men won't come to temple because they can't understand Buddhism or because they don't have any interest, but I don't feel that way. We have to have a road for men, we have to open the doors for them.

As mentioned above, the temple's Buddhist college is aimed not only at creating more missionaries to spread Korean Buddhism but also at appealing directly to men's intellectual interests. Mr. Lee's comments do appear to ring true, for when I attended Friday night lectures at the temple, I noticed a consistently larger presence of male students than female students. Usually there are twenty or so students at these weekly lectures, only four or five of whom are women. The ratio of 75 percent men to 25 percent women seems nearly opposite to the 15 to 20 percent male attendance at general worship services on Sunday mornings.

One of the main obstacles, however, in opening the doors to men, according to Mr. Lee, is that you cannot force people to come into the temple, because "religion is an individual thing" that motivates one to worship only when one is so moved. As he puts it, "my belief in Buddhism is from within me," and a matter of individual choice. Thus, since one cannot be forced to go to worship like the Christians "who are really dependent on God," it seems nearly impossible to bring more men into the temple. Mr. Lee contends that for Christians, "all things are taken care of and helped by God so that's why they believe," but for Buddhists the locus of faith is oneself and one must rely on oneself to take care of things. Since the individual is the source of action, he asserts that one cannot impose one's faith on another. It is for these reasons that a man who is dedicated to bringing more men and more second-generation believers into the temple cannot get his own children to attend worship services, because "they feel that it doesn't fit their lifestyle, so they don't come."

His solution to this problem is that "we need to develop programs that would encourage their attendance," rather than trying to force them to attend. He states:

> We need to develop and brighten society and offer programs that men will be interested in. For example, we could offer something like Buddhist martial arts. If we don't develop the programs, Sa Chal will fail. Buddhism will never die, but if Sa Chal doesn't change its ways, it will fail. We need to concentrate on the young and [male members].... If we educate people and expand their knowledge, then we will expand; if not, we will fail.

Mr. Lee's comments cannot be adequately understood without paying attention to his experiences living in the United States as a male immigrant. As mentioned above, he works at the temple's print shop running off the weekly service pamphlets as well as the print work for the Buddhist college, and he has been working to expand the student body at the college. Based on my personal interactions with this layman, I have noticed that he has no interaction with non-Koreans during the workweek and spends most of his time with other Korean Buddhists at Sa Chal. That he does not speak English after living in the United States for over fifteen years has become his "burden." In fact, every time I would see him at the temple, he would ask me to translate works from Korean into English, make phone calls on behalf of the temple to English speakers, write articles for a temple newspaper in English, and teach more classes to the children. That he would request me to do all this work each time I saw him indicates the lack of support and help he has in making these projects more successful. In addition, on numerous occasions I have noted his frustration at not being able to speak English and not having the support in the Korean Buddhist community that he had in Korea.

As mentioned earlier, Mr. Lee served a major role in the development of youth programs in Korea and as the General Propagator for Chogye order Buddhism. His position in America carried much less social prestige, especially given the fact that as a religious minority in the Korean community, Buddhists seem much less inclined to actively spread Buddhism in ways that the Christians do. While it is commonplace to find Korean Christians standing outside the Korean supermarkets handing out pamphlets and tapes from their churches, most Buddhists are too self-conscious about being pointed out as different to engage in such activities.

I have noticed Mr. Lee's frustration with his own children as well, for although his wife often talks about how proud she is that her daughters are bilingual, Mr. Lee cannot get them to attend services or even help out with any of the temple's projects. At the same time, I could not help but note that in his critique of Buddhist monks, Mr. Lee's comments reflect dissatisfaction with the way his own brother, the abbot, runs the temple. In addition, he associates his own wife with blind faith and the ritualism of the past, for she too can often be found chanting and beating the *moktak* throughout the temple. In this way he seems to draw a large distinction between his own form of intellectual, lay, and male Buddhism and the premodern Buddhism of his brother and of his wife. Although he is the younger brother of the abbot, he rarely sits through any of the worship services on Sundays except during public celebrations. He claims that he meditates in the morning and sometimes reads texts. Nonetheless, his comments point to an important means that men have found to recover self-esteem living in America—by opting for an ideal view of the male self as intellectual and political as distinguished from a female self that is emotional and dependent.

The desire for a program and worship style that will attract men to the temple also reveals the experiences of dislocation that men might feel in contrast to those of women. The transition from a position of authority in Korean culture to a state of minority status seems to drive men to seek out other areas where status enhancement may occur. As noted in the introduction, scholars of Korean Christianity Ai Ra Kim and Jung Ha Kim suggest that Korean men are attracted to the church because it offers a kind of gender hierarchy similar to what they knew in Korea, where men are in positions of authority as elders and deacons.[13] That men in the Buddhist temple complain about a lack of programs suited to their intellectual interests indicates a similar desire for status enhancement among co-ethnics. Thus, as another member of Sa Chal, Andrew Park, complains:

> There are really no [male] activities at the temple and that's why it's mostly women who go to temple. Monks don't have any leadership, that's why. If you go to a place that has a lot of male worshippers, it means that the system is going well. . . . Your mind and the monk's mind have to match. If they don't, then the men and the younger generations won't come out. The meaning of religion for men is that once a week they want to be peaceful and have their minds made comfortable. Men have to always worry about money, working, and making payments; they worry so much about things. They want to listen to the Buddha's beautiful teachings and want to meet the monks and talk comfortably. If the system was like that it would be good, but they haven't made it that way. So that's why there are more female worshippers than men. Men don't want to go to temple and talk about work and the office and money. If you talk about that stuff, they are sick and tired of working every day.

Andrew advocates that the temples should coordinate programs that would provide men with opportunities to take on more lay leadership roles in ways similar to Christian churches. Without this appeal to men's desires to be in charge, a temple will be filled with women only.

The association of men's intellectual and scholarly pursuits with philosophical Zen-like practices has also led to the belief that men can take their practices anywhere they want without having to be in a temple, because Buddhism is about "finding one's mind," an association that connotes self-reliance and a state of mind rather than physical presence. Here in these descriptions of different typologies of practice, we find the reproduction of gender ideology and Confucian culture in the temple where men are associated with the mind and woman associated with the body, which is disciplined through ritual worship and devotion. In this case, men elevate their own positions vis-à-vis women because they understand that Buddhism is "most importantly about finding one's mind" and not falling prey to begging and praying to the Buddha for good fortune. This type of "fortune-praying" practice is considered simplistic if not superstitious and, interestingly, is associated with many male Buddhist critiques of Christianity. The "fortune-praying" Buddhist practices of women are equated with Korean Christianity, by men who believe that all that Korean Christians have to do is put their faith in God, who will take care of the needs of the faithful. Just as women are said to blindly pray to the Buddha to take care of their needs, Korean Christians are said to attach themselves to God in relationships of weakness and dependence. Yet, as I have shown, women do not adhere to the belief that their practices are geared merely toward fortune-praying, but rather toward self-transformation.

Because worship in the Buddha halls and bowing are conventionally coded as women's religious work, men have sought to find a place for themselves in the social setting of the temple through activities that provide them with a positive sense of self following the transition of immigration. That men attempt to create new roles for themselves as missionaries, support reunification projects, make associations between Buddhism and Korean nationalism, and seek to establish programs aimed at the male intellect indicates that the ethnic religious institution continues to play a pivotal role in the psychological, emotional, social, and economic adjustment of immigrants in a new land. While women are still perceived as the primary caretakers of religion for the family, a factor men attribute to their larger presence in worship services, men still aim to establish meaningful positions for themselves in the temple separate from women's work. Whether or not such projects and positions will continue in the long run depends on the desire of men to generate enough enthusiasm among themselves to actually participate, a difficult task since Buddhism is seen as an open-minded religion that does not coerce members into practicing.

7

Being Buddhist in a Christian World

The Christians think that Buddhists are devils and that you only have to believe in God to be saved! In Korea, Buddhism was the original teaching but now they [Christians] think of it as the devil. I used to follow my younger sisters to church when I first got here because I wanted to learn something about Christian beliefs. But now, even though I don't go to church anymore, my sisters still think I believe in Christianity. They don't know that I go to temple because I don't tell them. If they knew they would keep asking me why I didn't believe in God and they would keep on bothering me. But belief is my own choice, so I don't want to hear any protests. I don't say a word: I just go alone to temple diligently and think of the Buddha inside my heart. [Mrs. Oh, a fifty-one-year-old Buddhist woman living on her own in Los Angeles]

That a woman should find it necessary to hide her Buddhist identity from her own sisters (themselves previously Buddhist) illustrates what many Korean Buddhists encounter on a daily basis: the ubiquity of church affiliation among Koreans living in America. Since it is widely assumed that Koreans are Christian, many Buddhists like Mrs. Oh choose not to divulge their Buddhist identity. In this chapter, I examine Buddhist responses to the increasing Christianization of the Korean American community to reveal (1) how a Buddhist identity shapes an individual's response to religious marginalization within his or her own ethnic community, (2) how a Buddhist identity can lead to the development of high self-esteem despite this religious minority status, and (3) how the Buddhist injunction of "finding and knowing one's mind" has been interpreted by women and men at Sa Chal as a strategy of self-elevation in relation to their Korean American Christian counterparts.

Because Buddhist teachings are believed to foster open-mindedness, self-knowledge, and independence, many members of Sa Chal believe that, despite the apparent success of Korean American Christianity in providing for the needs of its worshippers, it is Buddhists like themselves who are better able to adjust to life in America. For Buddhists in this study, the psychological virtues cultivated through Buddhist practices and the ability to "find and know one's mind" are equated with what are esteemed as the highest virtues of American culture—self-reliance, the ability to make it on one's own, open-mindedness, and democratic values. The capacity to acculturate and become "American" serves as the terrain and the arena for competition with Korean American Christians, whose teachings are held to foster narrow-mindedness, dependence, and weak-mindedness—the very opposite of what they believe "Americanness" connotes. In this way, Buddhists at Sa Chal maintain that rather than the higher numbers of worshippers, better economic resources, and facility in the English language that the churches possess, it is the psychological strengths found in Buddhism that lead to success in the United States.

Yet views on what it means to be American and successfully adjust to life in this country are not uniform but highly contradictory. On the one hand, being American signifies an erosion of the traditional Korean values that hold families together. This negative evaluation leads to equating Buddhism with an authentic Korean identity in contrast to the position of Korean Christians, who are criticized for being duped by Western culture. In this instance, we find that conversion to Christianity both in Korea and the United States is a central concern among Buddhists at Sa Chal, for many Buddhists disparage the conversion of Koreans to Christianity as taking an easy route to Americanization. Yet ironically this situation has the unexpected result of Buddhists competing with Christians over what it means psychologically to be an American. Thus, the positive attributes of American culture that motivated many members of Sa Chal to immigrate in the first place—better opportunities, greater freedom, self-reliance—are then equated with what it means to be a Buddhist. In this instance we find

BEING BUDDHIST IN A CHRISTIAN WORLD

that "to be Buddhist is to be a better American than the Korean American Christians." The oppositional rhetoric of identity espoused by men and women at Sa Chal signifies here that what it means to be Buddhist is utilized in different contexts to develop self-esteem in response to a perceived double psychological burden—being an ethnic minority in the larger United States and being a religious minority in the smaller Korean American community.

THE GROWTH OF THE CHURCH IN THE KOREAN AMERICAN COMMUNITY

The rapid multiplication of Korean American Christian churches comes as no surprise to Buddhists at Sa Chal. Many Buddhists in fact complain that they are often urged to convert to Christianity while they shop at the Korean markets, do business with fellow Koreans, and meet with friends. Even their children are pressured to convert at their high schools and colleges, where Korean Christian church groups are becoming an increasingly powerful presence. One Sunday afternoon at Sa Chal, Michael, a fourteen-year-old member of the temple's youth group, complained to his friends about how "an old woman kept following [me] in a car and tried to give [me] flyers to come to her church." Kristine, a college student, sympathized and added, "Once I was in the Korean market and some grandmother tried to get me to go to her church but I told her I was Buddhist. She then got really upset and told me that it was wrong for young people to believe in Buddhism!" Both students then rolled their eyes in exasperation and sighed, "Christians just don't understand about free choice!" Lisa, a high school senior, concurred: "Yeah, my friends are always trying to get me to come to church. They tell me that I am going to go to hell because I don't believe in God." As an indication of the growing presence of Christian student groups on campuses, fewer and fewer Korean American students have been attending Sa Chal services over the years.[1]

Well aware of the decreasing numbers of Buddhist youth attending temples, the abbot of Sa Chal has been working feverishly to attract more members through a recruitment campaign in Korean language newspapers, radio, and local televisions spots. As recently as January 1999, Abbot Lee opened an art gallery on the first floor of the temple to feature shows dedicated to contemporary and traditional Korean art from Korea and the United States. That Christianity looms large in the minds of Buddhists was noted even in the abbot's sermon following the gallery's opening reception, in which he informed worshippers how excited he was that even Korean Christians attended the event and "were so surprised that we Buddhists could do something as big as this!" The abbot also converted one of the first-floor spaces of the temple into a Buddhist bookstore in the hope of attracting more Korean Buddhists from the local Koreatown district.

While these programs have the specific goal of *pogyo*, or the dissemination of Buddhism to the Korean and, recently, the non-Korean community, they also reflect the struggles Buddhists encounter as they move from a historical position of relative religious majority in the homeland (28 percent of the entire population in Korea) to a marginal position in Los Angeles.[2] Yet, in the contemporary Korean context, Christianity has experienced phenomenal growth. According to one study, there were 2,050 Christian churches in Seoul in 1979, and by 1981 the number had doubled to 4,700. By 1990, of the 49 percent of Koreans who reported being religious, 54 percent reported that they were either Catholic or Christian, while 42 percent claimed to be Buddhist.[3] The figures for Korean Americans are significantly higher: an estimated 70 to 80 percent of all Korean Americans are affiliated with the Korean Christian church, yet 40 percent of that population is said to have converted to Christianity after immigration.[4]

The everyday reality of Korean Buddhists living in the Korean American communities of Los Angeles can be characterized as increasingly Christianized. This situation becomes readily apparent in a cursory drive down the busy Wilshire Center district of Koreatown, where churches dot both the commercial and residential streets that make up this urban sector catering to Korean immigrants. South of Beverly Boulevard, north of Olympic Boulevard (the prime sections of Los Angeles's Koreatown), Korean Christian churches dominate the religious landscape. Some churches are part of large-scale mainline American Protestant churches and have their services after the English services of the churches that they rent. Others are located in small residences, and on Sunday mornings cars are crammed onto the driveways and in the streets nearby. Some Korean churches are even located in commercial buildings with signs out front welcoming visitors and members in the Korean language.

No wonder that people have said, "When two Japanese meet, they set up a business firm; when two Chinese meet, they open up a Chinese restaurant; and when two Koreans meet, they establish a church."[5] There are many factors that explain the rise of Christianity among Korean Americans—factors that make Korean Americans the largest Christian group among all Asian Americans, second only to the Filipinos.[6] Briefly these reasons can be attributed to the predominantly Christian immigrant population composed of urban middle-class individuals who first came to the United States in 1903–05, when newly converted Christians comprised 40 percent of the nearly 8,000 Korean immigrants to first land in Hawaii. For these immigrants, "to become a Christian in Korea meant to become Westernized or Americanized," which accounts for the larger number of Christians than non-Christians who first arrived.[7] In addition to the historically Christian background of many of the early immigrants who associated Christianity with modernity, there are a number of other factors leading to their phenomenal growth—the social services, psychological comfort, opportunities to worship and socialize with fellow ethnics, and the pluralistic nature of American society in which religious distinctiveness has played an important role in the preservation of cultural and ethnic identities.[8]

Anthropologist Kyeyoung Park further attributes the growth of Korean Christianity to the dual role of promoting economic success and attainment of the American dream and the preservation of ethnic identity. According to Park, "Korean devotion to small business success is ideologically intensified at the church," where rotating credit clubs *(kye)* are established among church members to finance businesses and where labor pools and business networks abound.[9] Yet, despite the increasingly large percentage of Korean Americans who identify themselves as Christian (70 percent for those living in Los Angeles and 77 percent for Chicago), most adult Buddhists that I encountered at Sa Chal express no interest in converting to Christianity.

THE BUDDHIST RESPONSE

In response to their smaller population in the United States, temple members claim that the only way to effectively reach out to the younger generation of Buddhists is by educating the parents, who would then bring their children to temple with them. Some parents maintain that the temple should be held responsible for passing the tradition on to students and providing English-speaking dharma instructors who could then teach the children about Buddhism. Others at Sa Chal advocate that the only way to spread Buddhism throughout the Korean American community is to offer programs that appeal to men, for if more men were interested in Buddhist temples, then membership would double. Yet a significant portion of the remaining members have come to terms with their newfound minority status within the Korean community by invoking Buddhist discourses on karma and Buddha Nature where individuals are held to be their own agents in determining their religious identities. Many parents thus argue that their children must make up their own minds about which religion to follow, for Buddhism "is about karma" and "awakening the Buddha Nature." Children must not be "forced to become Buddhists."

Implicit in these statements is a strong distinction between Christians who are viewed as "too aggressive" in their proselytizing and Buddhists who are praised for being more liberal and independent. Ironically, however, this emphasis on Buddhist karma and self-agency has had the unintended consequence of an increasing Christianization of many second-generation Buddhist children, who simply choose to socialize with their Korean American peers, most of whom are involved in the church. Similarly, although threatened by the rise of Christianity, many Buddhists envy the style of proselytization of the churches and the ministers' efforts to attend to the social, economic, and psychological needs of their congregants. In many ways, Buddhists at Sa Chal long for a monastic clergy that could provide the type of personal contact they perceive to exist between minister and churchgoer. Furthermore, they lament the fact that the majority of Korean Buddhist monks in Los Angeles cannot speak English—a major deterrent to reaching out to the offspring of current worshippers at the temple.

Yet, given the slight percentage of Buddhists in the Korean immigrant community and the large percentage of former Buddhists who convert and seem to enjoy a more successful life economically (according to my participants), what is it that makes individuals maintain their religious identities? In other words, why have Buddhists at Sa Chal remained Buddhists even when their children and siblings are turning to the Christian church?

Furthermore, what does being a Buddhist in a Christian world mean for the person who consciously chooses not to convert? Does he or she equate being Buddhist with a stronger sense of self, open-mindedness, independence, and, by extension, "Americanness" despite or in reaction to his or her minority status? It is to these questions that I have sought answers and interpretations among members of Sa Chal. For these are some of the primary concerns and the "stakes" involved in the religious practices of contemporary lay Korean Buddhists in the United States. Not one of my participants at the temple is unaware or unconcerned about these issues, since all of them have had a family member convert and have also felt the pressure to convert. In fact, most Buddhists at Sa Chal have had the experience of attending church either by going to a missionary school in Korea or by going to church in the United States with a friend or family member.

Of the fifty Buddhists interviewed in this study, most participants appeared rather flexible about passing down their religious traditions to their children. Although most parents preferred to see their children attend temple as devout Buddhists, members' responses have centered on two main reasons for their flexible views. First, since karma *(innyon)* plays so important a role in Buddhism, most participants believe that their children will become Buddhist if and only if they have had a certain past relationship based on karma. In other words, since Buddhism is about self-awakening, a Buddhist identity cannot be arbitrarily forced upon a person. The second reason is that since Christian churches have become a hot spot for young adult socialization, most Buddhist mothers and fathers would rather see their children co-mingling with fellow Koreans who share similar values outside of religion than spending time with non-Koreans. Parents ease the anxiety they feel about their children's informal conversion by maintaining that they themselves have a more profound understanding of Buddhist doctrines and therefore must act in a more liberal fashion. For these Buddhist parents, children must be allowed to act according to their own karma. Thus, when comparing themselves with Christians, Buddhists at Sa Chal take pride in their more democratic natures.

Conspicuously absent from regular Sunday worship services, the second generation has become a main concern among parents at Sa Chal who nonetheless wish that their children would be more inclined to attend temple. In fact, throughout my research and interviews, I noticed that only one of my participants had a child above the age of twelve who attended Sa Chal on a weekly basis. Most of the children in the temple youth groups are younger than twelve and therefore unable to take care of themselves while their mothers attend temple. Hence, most can be found in the basement playing with other children while their parents worship upstairs in the main dharma hall. At the same time, while most parents I spoke with would prefer to have their children become Buddhist and attend on a regular basis, most also felt that the idea of forcing them to become Buddhist was highly unsavory and particularly un-Buddhist, for self-knowing Buddhists know they cannot determine the karma of another individual.

WOMEN'S RESPONSES

Mrs. Jin, a fifty-year-old mother of two sons in their early twenties, vehemently believes that her children should choose their own religion. Even though she herself lived as a Buddhist nun for ten years in Korea before marrying at the age of twenty-eight, she still believes that it is more important for her sons to choose for themselves what religion they want to practice. This choice, according to Mrs. Jin, is the measure of what being a Buddhist is all about; in fact, she even encouraged her two sons to go to church so that when they chose a religion, they would make an informed decision:

> I even sent my kids to church. Why did I send them to church? I told them that they should try going to church and try to compare the merits of each faith. Since I have taken them to temple with me since they were young, they were not influenced by [Christianity]. Rather than telling them not to go to church, I told them that they should try to understand the Christian faith in God so that later on, if they chose to believe in Buddhism, their beliefs would be deep and strong because they have chosen for themselves. For us [parents], since we have had such a strong and deep faith in Buddhism, we can't just convert to Christianity so easily, but my kids didn't have that experience. So I told them to go to church.

When asked if she though it was strange that her children would go to church even though she and her husband are Buddhists, she replied quickly:

Oh no! I want to teach them the Buddha dharma, but as the kids grow up they will eventually outgrow their mother's influence and will have so many things they want to do on their own. Also, more so than their mother, they actually think their friends are better to listen to. Because of that, I told them that if they went to temple or to church, no matter where they placed their faith, it was their choice.

Although she and her husband are deeply involved in Buddhism, the notion of individual choice, interpreted as the central aspect of Buddhist practice and ideology, necessitates giving their children the freedom to do as they wish.

Mrs. Jin's comments also indirectly draw a comparison between Buddhism and Christianity in which the latter is interpreted as a religion demanding strict adherence to a specific set of beliefs. However, since Buddhism "is about having to control oneself so that nobody is going to tell you to come and go [to temple], for Buddhism is not about evangelization [like the Christian churches are], it's not like that" at all. Citing Buddhism's more liberal attitude, Mrs. Jin says that she goes to temple because the desire rises out of her own heart. In other words, religion for her is self-motivated, and one controls one's own fate.

Although she does want her own children to attend the temple, she is well aware that the church offers many services appealing to immigrants. This outreach to immigrants and their children is something that she believes Korean monks at Sa Chal have failed to achieve:

Right now if you have ten Korean Buddhist temples, they will have ten different youth groups, but the monks won't invest in them. If you go to church, even from nursery school age, kids listen to teachings about Jesus and they remember this forever and they won't convert. But that doesn't work at the temple because the monks haven't really . . . invested in the youth's education. So that's why even in Korea, Buddhists keep leaving to Christianity. About eighty percent switch to Christianity or maybe even more than that. Why? At church, they do a lot of things to help immigrants. But Buddhism [is not like that]. When I first came to the U.S. and went to Sa Chal, we didn't know where anything was! Even though we went to the temple, the monks didn't ask us when we came to America, where we lived, what we did and what we needed etc. If we didn't have a place to stay, they were supposed to help arrange it for us; if we didn't have a ride, they could have given us a ride! That's what they [monks] have to do, but they think they are too good for that! I heard that at the church, when the minister sees people coming and going, he will greet them and tell them to have a good week. At the temple here, it is just about giving money and leaving!

Mrs. Jin's critique of the temples and comparisons with Christianity reveal her disapproval of Buddhist monks for not taking an active role in helping immigrants adjust to life in the United States. She herself has yet to make this transition even after living in the United States for almost five years. Because the monks do not have much in terms of financial resources to offer social services, Mrs. Jin claims that many Korean immigrants convert to Christianity because it provides an easier path to adjustment. Yet she herself still chooses to struggle on her own and, in so doing, believes that she maintains her integrity as a Korean Buddhist. Her own experiences of dislocation in a new world where she still cannot speak the language have led to an isolation that she had hoped the Buddhist temple would help combat. This, however, has not been the case and she now spends most of her days either assisting her husband in his acupuncture and Eastern medicine clinic on the first floor of their home in Koreatown or socializing with her neighbor, a fellow Buddhist member of Sa Chal.

While Mrs. Jin maintains that her own children should choose which religious path to follow, she abdicates any responsibility for making Buddhists out of her sons. For this former nun, Buddhist doctrines of karma work in conjunction with free choice. At the same time, however, she continues to criticize the Buddhist temples for not providing her sons with the proper education and incentives to become Buddhist by utilizing the techniques of the Christian churches she so admires. Thus she sighs and muses, "if the monks just worked on *pogyo* (dissemination), Buddhism would increase so much. But they have to make programs to bring young people out every day." The responsibility for making her children Buddhists rests on the temple and the resident monks rather than herself despite her conviction that Buddhism is about self-choice. When she speaks of her own responsibility, she claims that karma will decide her son's fate in much the same way that her own fate as a nun was chosen during her teenage years. Mrs. Jin lived as a nun for ten years in Korea, a situation she attributes to her karma being "so deep." However, at the age of twenty-seven, she was forced by her parents to leave the nunnery, because "basically my relatives demanded that I get married. Besides, the time had come."

In both of these situations, Mrs. Jin leaves the responsibility of religious identity to karma, yet when karma does not work in her favor, she holds the monks responsible for not getting her sons to become Buddhist and her parents responsible for making her leave the monastic life. That she is still bothered that her sons are not Buddhist comes through in her disappointment over the scarcity of young Buddhist women in the Korean American community with whom she can match her sons for marriage. When asked if she preferred her sons to eventually marry a Buddhist or a Christian she responds:

> If they have chosen to believe in Buddhism then a Buddhist will be good. If they chose Christianity then a Christian would be good. Whatever they want to be is fine. But Buddhist girls that go to temple don't exist! So there are no people for Buddhists kids to marry. Right now, at Sa Chal too, there are only older bachelors and old maids! Young people who go to temple don't exist! So, even if you want to find them, you can't! Our family has gone to a matchmaker and asked them to find a Buddhist spouse for our sons, but they said that we had to go to church to find a daughter-in-law! But if our sons marry a Christian. . . . well people who go to church don't do *chaesa* [ancestor memorial rites]. So, then people without ancestors won't even have descendants come to look after them. . . . [and still] the Christians will not do *chaesa*. The Buddhists hate that! They agonize over that! But there are no Buddhists available! If we don't do anything about that then Buddhism will not survive! The temples will survive for those monks who are here now but after them, they will disappear. If you have a monk, you have to have worshippers! If you only have a monk and no worshippers, how is Buddhism going to survive?

Mrs. Jin's comments illustrate the anxiety she feels over her sons' disinterest in Buddhism, an anxiety that emerges only in her comments about monks and Christians. For here she views Christianity as a direct repudiation of an authentic Korean past. Although she is extremely concerned about the future of her family, she will not take responsibility for changing her circumstances. Instead, she appropriates Buddhist teachings of self-reliance, choice, and karma to explain her own lack of success at making Buddhists out of her kids, yet holds the monks responsible for what she perceives to be a similar response. On the one hand, she wants to tout self-reliance and coming to one's own decisions without outside help. Yet, she is highly critical of monks who do not offer help like the churches do in practical matters such as caring for new immigrants. Her comments also show an awareness that Christianity is succeeding in gathering the support of younger generations of Korean Americans, a situation that is both threatening and, at times, enviable.

Throughout my interviews at Sa Chal, comparisons were constantly drawn between Buddhist and Christian doctrines, with Buddhism usually described by women as a more independent practice that relies on the self as the arbiter of experience. Included in these descriptions is the characterization of Buddhism as free and unintrusive. For Dr. Lim, a forty-six year-old woman who recently converted to Buddhism following her second marriage, Buddhism seems to produce less stress in her life, for it has far fewer rules and regulations.

Through the influence of her grandmother, Dr. Lim was raised a Buddhist as a young girl growing up in Korea. Yet like many Korean women, she converted to Christianity for her first marriage because her first husband's family "was a Christian family and they told [her they] had to go to church together." Dr. Lim admits that she had no problem switching religions since she had attended a Christian junior high, high school, and the Christian affiliated Ewha Women's University in Seoul.

When she married a second time a little over six months ago (her first husband died years ago), she renounced her membership at a local Korean Presbyterian church and began to attend Sa Chal's Buddhist services. The transition back to Buddhism was quite smooth for her and she claims that since the temple's service had a choir, sermon, and songs, it does not seem that different from Christian services. When asked if going to the temple was difficult, she quickly replied:

> Well, this temple, Sa Chal, is different from regular temples because it is modernized. It's very similar to the church, so there aren't any problems for me.

> Frankly speaking, Buddhism just teaches that a person should try to live with high principles and do good things, so it is fairly simple.

Based on her experiences at both a Korean Christian church and a Buddhist temple, Dr. Lim indicates that she prefers Buddhism because it offers her much more flexibility to do as she wishes:

> It seems like the dharma is a little more liberal, it's not exclusive, and Buddhists don't believe that "only my way is the right way." There really are some easier things about [the temple]. At church, first of all, you always have to attend services; there are so many meetings and they always tell you to go to them. If you don't go, then a phone call comes . . . and also they say that you *have* to proselytize. If you don't do it very well, then they sort of publicly recognize it. But if you go to the temple and say that you couldn't proselytize other people, it's just not a big deal; but in church it's sort of a sin.

In her comments we clearly see that the independence of Buddhism is believed to foster the democratic value of freedom of religion. Furthermore, the Buddha dharma is held to be a liberal doctrine that does not intrude into one's personal life. Given that Dr. Lim is a rather soft-spoken and shy woman, it comes as no surprise that she prefers not being pressured to bring in new members to the temple. When she goes to Sa Chal, she need only sit in the pew with her husband, listen to the sermons and choir, pray, and then join in eating a fellowship luncheon. Following the service she is free to do as she pleases. Since she runs her own medical clinic, she tends to have only Sundays off and prefers to take care of personal errands after the service rather than focus on bringing in potential members. In this respect, religious affiliation among Buddhists suits her busy schedule, for Buddhists do not expect too much of a commitment from her.

She nonetheless acknowledges that for some people the Korean Christian church offers opportunities for socializing and making business connections that might in fact be more beneficial for her own clinic:

> There are too many churches, aren't there? Korean people believe too much in blessings [from God]. The reason why there are so many churches here . . . is that people are lonely and think that they should go to church so

they can meet with other Koreans. Another reason is because of business. We have heard . . . if you do a business like I do, when you know a lot of people through church you get closer to them and can find more potential clients, so that's why a lot of people go as well. . . . Some traditional people will preserve their [Buddhist identities], but if a person doesn't believe in Christianity [in America] then there will be very few people around like that person and so that person can't really do much.

Dr. Lim thus maintains that Christians are too afraid to rely on themselves to "make it" in America like the Buddhists. At the same time, she also believes that a spiritual connection through Christianity creates a bond of mutual trust and generosity that can be useful for economic success in America. Despite this allure, she feels that Buddhist worship on Sundays suits her just fine, for "Christians seem to want to fight a lot among each other and the Buddhists seem a lot more relaxed." Like many Koreans, she believes that Christianity has spread among Koreans because it provides an opportunity to worship in Korean as well as a place for good business contacts, especially for someone like her who runs an ethnic-specific business.

To Dr. Lim, the main difference between Buddhism and Christianity is a question of agency. She says that Christianity teaches that one has only to believe in God and all will be taken care of, if one is faithful. Buddhism, on the other hand, teaches about self-reliance, an aspect that all my participants cited as very important. This characteristic self-reliance leads to agency and, by extension, the instantiation of the American values of independence, which a Christian dependence on God and the church is believed to prohibit. Because Buddhism does not interfere with her personal life, Dr. Lim maintains that she will continue practicing it with her husband. Although she does have a sixteen-year-old son, she continues to allow him to attend her old church and believes that it is up to him to "choose for himself what religion he will follow."

Aware of the discrimination that many Buddhists feel in the Korean American community, Chin Mi Young, a divorced fifty-two-year-old mother of one, responds by drawing a strong distinction between the self-knowledge and reliance derived from Buddhist practice and the dependence on an outside agent in Christianity. Mrs. Chin arrived in the United States

BEING BUDDHIST IN A CHRISTIAN WORLD

in the spring of 1992 and has since been divorced from her husband, a Christian. A member of the Buddhist choir, she attends Sa Chal weekly and devotes much of her time socializing with her Buddhist friends when she is not working as a babysitter for two Korean children. As a child, Mrs. Chin attended church a number of times and also had a friend who was a minister in the United States. Yet after attending this friend's church several times, she found:

> In Christianity, you ask for your well-being. In Buddhism, though, you are the subject and therefore you have to come to a realization of yourself and discover your well-being through the teachings. I find this to be more practical in daily living. In Christianity, you are not the subject, you leave everything up to the spirit [of God to decide]. This does not make sense to me because if you need to go somewhere, you have to know the directions for getting to that destination. When I go to the health spa and there are some Christians there who ask me why I attend the temple, I turn and ask them the same question about why they go to church. Their only response is because "God is the creator of all things." I tell them, however, that coincidences have gathered and formed everything. And besides, how could a man and a woman form a family if there was a creator God? If there was a creator God, then the creator should be forming all humans and then there would be no need for humans to involve themselves in reproduction. Really, before the development of technology, the Christian religion might have made sense to people but as technology developed, the people have awakened.

In her comments, Buddhism is held to be the more practical and modern religion that creates a strong will. Mrs. Chin further equates those who have converted from Buddhism to Christianity with loneliness and weak-mindedness and believes that because Christians help people find jobs and visit them at home, the weak-minded are more likely to switch religions. As she puts it, "I think that most people convert because they are lonely but the ones that stay Buddhist are strong-minded and will always stick with Buddhism."

Mrs. Chin also finds Christianity to be rather coercive, for Christians "believe one should believe in one god, only their God and if you don't believe then you can't go to heaven. Christianity tells people that if you don't follow the ways of God, then you will not go to the right path." She then contrasts this with Buddhism, "a philosophy which shows a way of living that people can experience and choose for themselves." For Mrs. Chin, "people should experience and decide for themselves" which religion they want to follow, again a very American value.

While most temple members believe that the monks should be responsible for spreading Buddhism among the second generation, Mrs. Chin feels that the American public is ready for the teachings that Korean Buddhism has to offer. Thus, as a side endeavor, she has been introducing members of her health spa to Korean Buddhist books written in English which she picks up at local temples. In many ways she finds that the temple lacks the foresight to expand and spread Buddhism to the American public through lectures—a task she has taken up herself. She also believes that the monks at Sa Chal should spend more time studying the sutras and explaining them to the worshippers, thus giving them a stronger connection to their faith— a comment also made by many men at the temple. At the same time, however, she maintains that she prefers the noncommital aspect of Buddhist practice. Describing her own practice, she comments:

> I don't have a set practice. I practice whenever I am in need of it. It's like an alarm clock. I don't set a specific time in order to get up in time. If I need to wake up at a certain time then I tell myself to wake up and my eyes open automatically at the right moment. Ever since I became aware of Buddhism, I no longer needed the alarm clock to tell me what to do.

For Mrs. Chin, Buddhism consists of self-regulation and agency, a practice she believes far surpasses that of Christianity, which demands faith and dependence on someone other than oneself.

In addition to associating Christianity with a nonintellectual grasp of religion, there are many women at Sa Chal who believe that Christianity fosters an overly dependent relationship on a force outside oneself—that is, God. For these women, Buddhism is viewed as a more sophisticated teaching that encourages individuals to develop strength and courage through self-knowledge and self-reliance. Thus even though Christianity might attract more Korean immigrants, it is the Buddhists who are said to be more successful at withstanding life's ups and downs, particularly the psychological struggles of immigrant life. Kwak Soo Young, a nursery school teacher in her early fifties who attends Sa Chal every few weeks, was raised a Buddhist in Korea and eventually married a fellow Buddhist. She has lived in the United States since 1982 and has three children, ages twenty-seven, twenty-nine, and thirty. Although she used to bring her kids to temple with her, she no longer attempts to bring her adult children to worship services because temples do not seem to offer much personal support:

> When you go to temple, the monks don't say things to you like "Welcome!" to make you feel comfortable. The monks just look at people and say, "Oh you're here." That's a problem for Korean Buddhism, but for the monks, they have these rules regarding their existence and so it is sort of hard to get close to them. But once people immigrate, if you go to the airport there will be a lot of ministers there for the sake of preaching. Ministers that you don't even know will come up to you and ask people, "Oh did you just immigrate here? What church do you belong to?" They ask them all these things and if they don't have a car, they [recent immigrants] are given a ride somewhere. But really, what monk exists who would do that sort of thing?

Mrs. Kwak's comments indicate that Christian ministers provide support systems that reach out and comfort people in ways that Buddhists monks are not accustomed to doing. For these reasons, she believes that the temple has not been successful in attracting new members, in particular the second generation.

Although she originally raised her children as Buddhists, she claims that "it is not so much that you really teach your kids about religion but that you show them what you are doing and they eventually will follow on their own," if they choose. This flexible attitude toward her family's religion is also reflected in her early experiences of allowing her children to attend church so that they could spend time with their Korean friends, a point of great concern for Mrs. Kwak. Although her children followed her freely to temples in Korea where a certain monk "taught them how people are supposed to live and not be wasteful," the situation changed when she arrived in America. She recalls:

After we came here, the temples didn't have enough of a system for the students. My kids wanted to go to church since their friends were going to church. So I said to them, "don't feel bad, just go." But when I sent them to church, they wouldn't come home right away or follow the schedules that I wanted them to. And after we sent them to church, when they would meet new people they would just say, "Oh hi," and they didn't know how to respect their elders anymore. But if they came to temple, they would just sit here straight through and it was difficult for them because Buddhism is difficult for children. It's also difficult for adults because to really understand the religion is very difficult. But after they went to church, they got around to comparing the two different religions and after some comparison they began to realize that the church teaches you that everything is taken care of by God and so you really had to be dependent on him. But in Buddhism, you really have to do everything on your own, no matter what happens, it depends on you. . . . It's not that I told them not to go to church but since they checked it out for themselves they chose for themselves and decided not to continue going. That is the Buddhist style; Buddhists are like that.

Here, Mrs. Kwak criticizes Korean Christians whom she believes do not know how to raise proper Confucian children and who are also too dependent on others. To her, Buddhism is a far more liberal and self-regulated religion in contrast to the coercion of Christianity. Mrs. Kwak's belief that Buddhists advocate free choice, a position that eventually attracted her own kids back to Buddhism, resonates with many of the women interviewed in this study. Because she knew how to give her children free choice, she believes that they have learned to value free choice as the most important aspect of religion (and by extension, being American). Even though she is well aware that Buddhists are often ostracized by Christians, she believes nonetheless that being a Buddhist is a better option because it promotes self-reliance. She comments:

> Churchgoers will never come to the temple if there is a big dharma talk or if there is a famous monk giving a lecture. The way I see it, that means that the Christians are really looking down on the Buddhists. Really now, why won't they come? We Buddhists go and listen and compare the two religions

and then decide for ourselves. You have to compare and choose, but Christians don't go anywhere else. They just think that Christianity is supreme and that they don't need to make any comparisons. But I think that thinking that just your own religion, even if it is God's teachings, is the most supreme is self-conceit. We should all see things together and decide and follow what is right.... I am not the type of person that is going to tell other people what to do. I come to temple if I want to and I am not coming to the temple just to tell others to come. That's not what being a Buddhist is about.

Although Mrs. Kwak herself will never become a Christian, in many ways she wishes that Sa Chal's monks were as successful at missionization as ministers are:

> Sometimes I tell the monks that we have to have a Buddhism for our lifestyle. Such difficult things like the Thousand Hand Sutra and the Heart Sutra are not going to help people. If you only focus on those things, you will remain inside the temple. Right now though, there are more difficult problems facing new immigrants, like where to go to get a license, and they need someone who has already been here for a while who can give advice. But it's not like that, so people who come here to the temple don't even know the streets well and how to start things up in a new world. It's not like they are just moving around Seoul, they are moving to a new country and the first thing monks have to do is go out to the airport to meet people. I always say to the monks that they have to make an appearance and really help people with their living conditions if they can. If they help those people, those people, if they are Buddhists, will end up coming here. But all people who are here at the temple now came on their own. It's not like the monks said anything to them. Since the Buddhist method is about knowing things on your own, a lot of Buddhists end up going to church. About eighty percent are going over there you know.

Mrs. Kwak's comments reflect an unintended consequence of Buddhism at Sa Chal: since Buddhists do not consider themselves demanding people, they are unable to garner the support among the monks to actively bring people to the temple. Since Buddhism is about karma and self-reliance, the general belief is that people should be individually motivated to practice.

Many Buddhists take pride in the flexibility such an orientation provides although they are aware that such a hands-off policy has a detrimental effect on the survival of the religion. Even though she criticizes the monks for not offering practical services to possible members, Mrs. Kwak still finds that Christians are too concerned with prayer:

> You pray if you have a lot of problems. When you pray, it's all about having things done for you and getting help with things. Maybe it's because people don't really understand Buddhism. Within my mind, if I have a lot of selfishness, my prayers increase and I think "oh please do this for me, do that for me, let my kids be successful etc." But because I don't have that sort of greed in my heart, I don't have any prayers.

Despite the success of Christianity, Mrs. Kwak upholds Buddhist doctrines that indicate for her a stronger sense of self than Christianity can provide. In many ways, she prefers being a Buddhist, for Buddhism represents self-agency and free will, something that the Christian submission she experienced with her friends can never accomplish.

Although she claims that Buddhism is about free choice, she limits this association to religious practices. She has no problem allowing her children to choose their own religion, but when it comes to choosing an appropriate spouse, she practically shouts, "Marry an American? No, never!" Despite this seemingly contradictory interpretation of Buddhist doctrines of karma and self-reliance, she explains, "Ever since my children were young, I told them that getting married isn't just about two people, it's about the whole families as well." Fearing a language and culture gap between the families, she explains, "to the mother and father, it would be so hard because there will no longer be that tie with parents and you will be further apart." So she often warned her children: "You have to think of how many other people are going to be uncomfortable about the decision that you make and not just think about yourself!" Buddhist doctrines of karma and free choice, then, have their proper application in choosing religious affiliation but not in choosing a mate. Here we find that Korean cultural traditions run counter to the individualism and independence she values in being American, yet there are some aspects of American culture she chooses to ignore.

While many women respond to the rise of Christianity with both admiration and disdain, others have had direct experiences of proselytizing from friends and family, often leading them to subvert or hide their Buddhist identity among Christians. Such is the case with In Soon Song, a woman born to Korean parents. During college she moved to Japan and married a Japanese Buddhist. Mrs. Song arrived in Los Angeles in September 1999 to live with her two sons, currently attending high school. She is a woman who has lived in three cultures—Korean, Japanese, and American—though she is most connected to Japanese culture. She does not readily acknowledge this fact to people at Sa Chal out of concern that there are some who might judge her for marrying a non-Korean, especially a Japanese man. Although she grew up in a Buddhist household in Korea, she is the only one of her siblings who has remained Buddhist. Her older brothers converted to Christianity and her children in the United States do not attend temple. While living in Japan, In Soon felt very comfortable practicing Buddhism: "There are so many temples and small shrines wherever you go walking along that you can stop and bow at." In the United States, however, churches seem to dominate, especially in the Korean community.

Although she states that she is a devout Buddhist who attends temple services on Sundays and prays on her own daily in her apartment, she admits that she has no plans to force her children to practice Buddhism:

> I do not have any intention of making my kids practice one religion. I believe that their minds are their own and it is unreasonable to talk to them about coming to temple if they don't want to. I really don't care about whether they marry a Buddhist or not because . . . the meaning of people's religious aim, [whether it is] toward the Buddha or to God or to the Catholic's Mary, is the same. So I don't talk about an individual's beliefs and believe that you should believe in what you desire and believe wholeheartedly. Also, if I go to temple and they end up following me, then I am even more thankful and happy.

Mrs. Song feels that since she has not demanded temple attendance from her sons but has provided a good model as a self-motivated Buddhist, her sons have at least chosen not to go to church and they admire her for her Buddhist devotion. Her friends, however, have not adopted the same "live and let live" American attitude that this woman seeks to maintain. Instead, since coming to the United States her religious choices have been much scrutinized within her circle of Korean female friends, all of whom are heavily involved in the church. She expresses her frustration with her Christian friends, who insist on converting her and not respecting her decision to remain a Buddhist:

> A month ago, I met a classmate who is now a very close friend. But this friend goes to church, and in my English class all my friends want to take me to church and they are after me about it all the time. But this is what I have to say to them, "In my life, I look for religion, but religion should not be the most important thing between us because you are my close friend. Since you are a deep Christian you go to church diligently and I go to temple diligently because I am a Buddhist. Our religions are different. But when we meet outside the church, don't talk to me about going to church." I have another friend who is a *chondo sa* [evangelizing woman]. She prays every day at the church and always wants me to come to church. Since this *chondo sa* kept asking me to just come to church with her, I finally said that I would think about it. Then she says, "Well first go to temple and then plan to go to church afterwards." So, I came to Sa Chal early one morning and finished my prayers in the *bopdang*, I didn't even get to eat because there were two church people waiting right outside for me at Sa Chal in their car! So, I did my bowing to the Buddha and since I made a promise, I went to church.

Mrs. Song maintains that she relented to her friend's request out of friendship and continues:

> That day I listened to the minister's sermon and to everything that was said. I ate at the church and quietly kept my promise to my friend. But the very next Sunday morning before I went to temple, the phone rang and she says, "Let's go church!" My friend said that she was going to pick me up at my house and so I finally said to her, "Look I can't do it today," and she kept saying that the minister and everyone else really wanted me to come. I finally said to her, "I kept my promise before, but I am going to go to temple and during that whole time I am going to pray to the Buddha and Kwan Um Posal only."

Because of the constant pressure from her friend, Mrs. Song eventually told her that she could not get together on Sundays because she was too busy and she realized that many of her friendships were dependent on sharing the same religious affiliation. In many ways, In Soon Song has been extremely disappointed. She is living alone with her two sons away from her friends in Japan. Meeting friends through her English classes seemed to be an ideal situation, but these friendships began to change once it became apparent to her friends that she did not wish to attend church.

Nowadays, she explains that in her English classes, when her classmates and instructors discuss weekend plans, she keeps silent about her temple attendance. She admits, "I just say that I am going to do some sports or go to the health club. Since I play golf, I just say that I am going golfing." In this way she is able to avoid the gaze of Korean women who might criticize or proselytize her into going to church. In many ways, she keeps her Buddhist identity hidden among Christians for she fears being singled out as different. She related to me a story of one of her Buddhist girlfriends whose livelihood in America depends on the suppression of her religious identity:

> If you want to do business anywhere around here, Korean Christians will always ask you what your religion is. So the owner of the business will say things like if your household is not Christian, then you can't do business here. Since they said that to my friend, she said that she couldn't say a thing about being Buddhist and so she replied, "I am non-religious," when they asked her what religion she was. She couldn't say that she believed in Buddhism! She wanted to come here to America and look for a job but each time she went looking, [employers] would ask what religion she was and if she was a Christian. Since there are so many difficulties for my fellow Koreans who live in America, I think that half of them change their religions for the sake of making a living and finding jobs. So, when I heard that from my friend, my heart hurt so much! When you come here [to the United States] you come for the sake of business and making a living. If you go to the Christian religion, it seems that your life is easier, it is good for finding jobs and so there are some people who will go to church. I have seen a lot of people doing that, for the sake of living standards. And when I see that my heart really hurts. Even now, when I go to school on Fridays, our American teacher

BEING BUDDHIST IN A CHRISTIAN WORLD

always asks us students, what are you going to do this weekend? As soon as he asks that, then if there are ten people they will all say "church."

For Mrs. Song, Christianity symbolizes an easier lifestyle but also a marked betrayal of Korean tradition. Despite these constant challenges to her religious identity, she is an unwavering Buddhist who continues to pray alone both in the morning and the evening, when she reads the *Chunsoogyung* (Thousand Hand Sutra) and does not get interrupted by her children "because it is her quiet time." She sees herself as a good model of Buddhism for her kids although she will not force them to come to temple, because "Buddhism is about doing things yourself." Similarly, as a Buddhist who understands self-reliance, she is not afraid to be alone in America, and in fact takes pride in being independent.

MEN'S RESPONSES

The topic of Christianity and business success emerged as one of the most common distinctions drawn between Christians and Buddhists by men at Sa Chal. Most men insisted that Koreans frequented churches because one could bring along business cards and expect to find both jobs and potential customers. The Buddhist men criticized the churches for functioning as places of business run by ministers held to be social brokers. These comments often reflected a sense of envy at the perceived ease with which Christian men could pursue economic success supported by the religious community. Nonetheless, not one male respondent indicated that he wished the Buddhist temple and the monks would perform similar functions or that the temple ought to provide business opportunities between members. Rather, most men indicated that the monks should spend less time involved in worldly affairs and more in studying the sutras and Buddhist philosophy.

In fact, unlike the women, most male respondents believed that the monks should offer sermons with less everyday advice on how to survive as immigrants and spend more time on Buddhist teachings. Implicit to this criticism of monks at Sa Chal is a belief that laymen should have more responsibility in the general and administrative affairs of the temple, thus encouraging male participation. Such responsibilities were also thought by some to undermine the monks' respectability. Some participants even said that such activities carried out by the monks were done out of a desire to become well known throughout the Korean community. In other words, many male members of the temple want the monks to remain "traditional" and withdrawn from involving themselves in American culture.

As noted in the previous chapter, this critique of monks reflects the male desire for self-edification through high status positions in an ethnic group—positions largely unavailable outside the Korean American community. This yearning for status leads many of them to compare the temple with the Christian churches that offer more ritual and administrative positions. Furthermore, since Buddhist men are highly conscious and sometimes envious of the economic and social benefits of belonging to the church, many have responded by highlighting what Buddhism has to offer that Christianity cannot—independence, self-reliance, and freedom (also noted by the women). These three benefits are considered more important than business success and social prestige, for they are not contingent upon what Buddhists deem a submission to an outside agent—authority figures like God, Jesus, or ministers. Furthermore, these attributes are held to be compatible with American democracy and values of independence. In fact, it is the benefits accrued from practicing Buddhism that are said to keep a man from becoming a Christian in spite of the obvious financial attractions and prestige among peers. Aware of their marginal status within the Korean American religious community, Buddhist men respond by placing a higher value on self-knowledge over submitting to an authority figure.

Jae Woo Shin, a twenty-eight-year-old Eastern medicine student, maintains that Buddhist meditation and worship focus on self-awakening as opposed to relying on an outside force to attain religious salvation. It is this difference of agency that appeals to him, for Buddhism teaches him to depend on and awaken himself. Having visited a number of Protestant churches in Korea during his sojourn in the army and while living as a college student in Iowa, he explains, "I believe in Buddhism because I don't believe in any God or other person. If I go to heaven when I awaken, then I go by my own self-effort. But the church believes in many things like that God will actually pick you up and save you." Mr. Shin prefers to rely on himself, a desire consistent with his motivations for remaining in the United States—to develop independence and live free from the social constraints he still finds in Korea's Confucian culture. Based on his early experiences as a foreign student in Iowa during his undergraduate years, he strongly sympathizes with new immigrants and even admits that he originally started attending a Christian church in Iowa although he was raised a Buddhist because he wanted to learn English. In the early nineties, there were no Buddhist temples for him to attend in Iowa so he began to go to a church where he could take free English classes and be with other Koreans:

> Because people can't find Buddhist temples, they usually go to church and they often go for business reasons and not really for a belief in the church in my opinion. Maybe forty percent really believe in the church and forty percent are not even native speakers of English and so they come to the church so that they can speak in Korean. If you have no company, you just go to church on Sunday and many Korean people gather together and he [sic] can have an easy time getting some business items and ideas. Or he can sell things because he can meet many people... because usually they can't speak English well. Their English is really poor and so they go to church and learn business, [but] they don't believe in the church.

As this Buddhist sees it, the church is the "easier way," but for those "who *really* believe in Buddhism, they will come to the temple." That there are fewer Korean Buddhist temples for people to attend indicates to Jae Woo that those who do manage to worship as Buddhists in America are more faithful and more independent. Furthermore, since he posits that independence and self-reliance are the hallmarks of American culture, he believes that in the future Buddhists will have an easier time adjusting to American culture since they share the same values. Mr. Shin enjoys the fact that the Buddhist attitude of free will enables him to attend different temples. But for the moment he usually just attends Sa Chal services because: "I don't want to talk to a lot of people at temple. If I go to Sa Chal, there are so many people and I don't have to meet them all, so I just feel more comfortable on my own."

For this Korean student, being a Buddhist is a more difficult challenge in the United States, yet it ultimately symbolizes stronger character and independence by not taking the "easy way out" of joining a church. For him, being a Buddhist means having the freedom to come to temple or to stay at home in meditation: "[W]hether one is in the house, in the office, in the bathroom, or in the ocean, if you just think for one moment that you are a Buddha, then that is [Buddhism]." Thus, when asked about the future of Korean Buddhism in America, he maintains that people should not be forced to practice religion but that an interest will gradually grow. He also believes that since Americans are becoming more interested in Buddhism, the percentage of Buddhists in the United States will increase as more Americans begin to convert. Although he does not believe Buddhism will spread among second-generation Korean Americans, he hopes to eventually spread Buddhism through his Eastern medicine practice among English-speaking clients who are already predisposed to "Asian customs and Asian religions" by seeking out alternative medicine. By establishing rapport with his future American clients, Jae Woo Shin believes he will be engaged in a noncoercive form of missionization.

Mr. Koh, a volunteer accountant for Sa Chal, has attended Sa Chal since retiring from his job as a liquor store owner in 1993. According to him, the rise of Christianity in the Korean American community can be attributed to the inability of many Koreans to comprehend the subtle complexities of Buddhist doctrines. Born in 1935, Mr. Koh is a retired Buddhist who moved to the United States to provide his four children with better educational opportunities. A university graduate, he took a job with a liquor store owner in Glendora and worked almost seven days a week with his wife for ten years. During this period he was so busy that he "never really had time for religion." Although raised as a Buddhist by his parents, two of his sisters ended up converting to Christianity—one before marriage and one after. He himself has never set foot in a church and did not attend any temples in the United States for the first ten years because of his busy work schedule. He admits that he thought about Buddhism but didn't bother to pray: "It wasn't until after I closed the liquor store that I started thinking that it was time to start going to a temple." He found Sa Chal "while reading through a Korean newspaper one afternoon" and for the past six years has come to the temple weekly to see friends and be in a Buddhist environment, though he rarely goes into the worship hall. He sits at the desk above the stairwell entrance where he collects and records donations and prayer fees from temple members and stores them in a small lockbox.

Even though Mr. Koh and his wife are practicing Buddhists, his four children attend no religious services at all, a situation that concerns him very little since he believes that "Buddhism is something you believe in yourself and choose to believe in and not about forcing someone [else to] believe in religion." Mr. Koh thinks that many Koreans convert to Christianity because the Christians settled in America earlier than the Buddhist and have a longer history of networking, and also Christian ministers are more inclined to seek additional members by offering more social services than the Buddhists monks can provide:

> The churches were established here long before Buddhism so that's why it turned out this way [with more Korean Christians]. The churches help old people get welfare and since lots of people organize there and you need to really know a lot of people if you want your business to do well, you go to church. It's not just out of faith or a belief in Jesus exactly that makes people go. Here at the temple, if you want to come you come, if you want to go you go, that's the way the temple is. At the church, it is more intimate and so if you don't go to church, people will call you and ask you why you didn't come and then they will come to your house to find you. A lot of young Buddhists go to Christian churches and yes that's a bit of a problem but religion is really of one's own accord. I myself come here to cleanse my mind and my troubles.... Christians say that we believe in idols because we believe in Buddhism so strongly. [But] I also believe that Buddhism will probably grow in the next ten years or so because it is truthful and Christianity is a naive type of teaching.

It is the "live and let live" attitude of Buddhism that appeals to this gentleman, an attitude that he attributes to the confidence that comes from "finding/knowing oneself." Like Mrs. Min, Mr. Koh is less concerned with the future of Buddhism, believing that eventually people will realize that Buddhism is the "more truthful" religion.

For Mr. Hong, a seventy-year-old gentleman who reads the Diamond Sutra, Heart Sutra, and Thousand Hand Sutra every morning from five to seven, religion is a matter of personal choice. The father of four children who don't attend temple, he explains that Buddhists believe "that it is up to yourself [to choose] your own religion, so I would tell them that if they were going to be Christian, they would have to decide that for themselves."

Like Mr. Kim, Mr. Hong says that he comes to temple to cleanse his mind although he has attended church from time to time to be with his children. Citing the differences between the two religions, he states: "Buddhism does not believe in any kind of god like the Christians do. We Buddhists think that you have to awaken your own mind by yourself. [Christians] completely cling to God for everything, but Buddhism is about awakening one's own mind and then enabling your morality to rise. If you increase your morality, then you are practicing Buddhism." For Mr. Hong, to be Buddhist is to be responsible for your own religious salvation and not dependent on an agent outside yourself.

According to Mr. Hwang, although many people convert to Christianity from Buddhism upon arriving in America, they "don't convert because they really want to believe but because they are isolated in the U.S. and so if they go to church, they meet other immigrants and people they know." Unlike Buddhists who "rely on themselves to get through their difficulties in America," Mr. Hong maintains that Christians are less capable of taking care of themselves and therefore more dependent on God. Furthermore, since he believes that Buddhism is a better and more truthful religion, he exhibits little anxiety over its future:

> If you look at it, Christians are coming back to the temple. A lot of old people are doing the same because there's a lot of lies in their beliefs [in the church] and so they come back to Buddhism because they are of a true nature. Ministers say to live and believe in them and believe in God, but the monks say that you have to awaken your own mind. Ignorant people think that if I believe in God then I will live well and be well off. So ignorant people tend to follow that way. But a smaller number [of people], if they have knowledge and know how, then they decide to come back over this way [to Buddhism].

For Mr. Hong, Buddhism symbolizes wisdom and a natural ability to "make it" in the new world whereas Christianity symbolizes a blind faith in ministers and God to make life more fruitful. Despite the large presence of Christians in the Korean American communities, he has no fear or concern for the future of Korean Buddhism and firmly believes that to be Buddhist is the better and more intelligent option. The strength of character he associates with Buddhism leaves him confident of both his own future and that of his fellow Buddhists in the larger Korean American community.

Dr. Jin, a member of Sa Chal, contends that missionization of the second generation will be a very difficult task since Buddhism in Korea has historically concerned itself less with the day-to-day task of bringing in more adherents and more with "lofty philosophical concerns." Dressed in a blue and maroon traditional Korean style suit that he wears every day, Dr. Jin sits behind his desk looking very much like a Confucian scholar. In his Eastern medicine office, an old Confucian Korean style hat and pipe hang on the wall and bookshelves are stacked with volumes of Chinese medicine books. The only time I have seen Dr. Jin at Sa Chal is at the twenty-fifth anniversary even though he has spent much time in Korea as a Buddhist youth leader working to teach Buddhism in Seoul. In fact, he has known Abbot Lee since that time in Korea and the two of them have a long-established friendship. Yet in America he Jin feels very little need or inclination to attend temple regularly. A fifty-three-year-old man born in Seoul who has lived and studied in Korea and China, Dr. Jin arrived in Los Angeles in 1997 to open his Eastern medicine clinic in Koreatown.

Having gained a positive impression of American culture through his stint in the army in Korea, Dr. Jin decided to move to the United States with his wife and two sons (now twenty-three and nineteen). He claims he will be a Korean until the day he dies even though he has no intention of leaving the United States any time soon. Like many Koreans, he came to the United States for better educational opportunities for his sons and financial success for his family. The son of a civil servant, he was raised in a Buddhist household and spent much time shuttling back and forth between temples in Seoul with his mother and grandmother a few times a month. After marriage, he began attending temple with his wife, whom he met twenty-five years ago through a matchmaker, and his children. In America, his temple attendance and Buddhist practice have been curtailed for lack of time because of his busy work schedule and no feeling of necessity. As he puts it, Buddhism "is about awakening" and one need not rely on a temple to achieve that goal.

When asked about the current state of religion in the Korean American community, Dr. Jin agreed that Christianity has been more successful in attaining converts for reasons he attributes to the different roles of the minister and the monk. Throughout our conversation, he mentions that traditionally monks have not fulfilled the task of offering services to the laity, yet upon arrival in America it is precisely these services that immigrants seek out. Because monks are considered religious virtuosos by temple members, they historically have not provided for the economic and social needs of worshippers. The minister of a church, however, has traditionally played more of a role in offering advice and counsel to church members; because of this relationship, Dr. Jin maintains that immigrants feel more comfortable seeking out the support of a church.

Dr. Jin also believes that it was the rise of Confucianism in Korea that brought about the distinction between gender roles which discouraged men from attending temples in Korea. Hence even today, women are the majority in temples in both the United States and Korea. This gender distinction also serves as one of the main reasons behind the rise of Christianity and the departure of men from Buddhist temples. Dr. Jin also maintains that women traditionally have gone to temples to pray for the well-being of their families but that "men are probably still too embarrassed to publicly worship at temples since Buddhism had been so denigrated as low class during the Yi dynasty." Furthermore, he adds:

> Men think that if they go to temple, they will seem like they are somewhat backward because people tend to think that those who believe in Christianity are more modern. If you believe in Buddhism you will be considered old-fashioned and so that's why it seems that there are less men in the temple. . . . In Korea there were a lot of Buddhists who did not admit that they were Buddhists. Because they were worried about looking somewhat ignorant, they didn't tell people that they were Buddhists.

As a result of being considered old-fashioned and ignorant, men did not and still do not mention their Buddhist affiliations publicly nor do they worship in the presence of women. Dr. Jin's comments illustrate why some Buddhists choose to hide their religious identity or seek out the social comforts and benefits offered through the churches. But these Buddhists are "not real Buddhists, for real Buddhists who have a knowledge of the philosophical tenets of Buddhism, an understanding of the sutras, and a desire to attain enlightenment could never convert!"

Although Dr. Jin is well aware of the success of the church for business purposes and the association of Buddhism with an outdated form of practice, he remains both unconcerned and quite proud that he has remained a Buddhist, for being a Buddhist is much more difficult:

> Christianity has the Ten Commandments which are really easy—don't steal, don't kill, etc. But Buddhism does not have any commandments; instead it talks about purifying the mind. When I look at the church's Bible and the Buddhist sutras, I think that the Buddhist sutras are better, but if someone doesn't understand them, they might decide not to go to temple anymore. The church, however, talks about things very simply and the most important thing is just that you shouldn't consider anyone higher than [God, Jesus] or the minister. . . . Buddhism is a religion based on awakening for the sake of enlightenment, so one devotes oneself to worshipping and reading the sutras. The aim . . . is enlightenment, it's all about enlightenment. So it is harder to understand Buddhism and read the sutras.

Although Christians may think that Buddhism is a more traditional and therefore less modern and less sophisticated religion, Dr. Jin maintains that being a Buddhist is intellectually more challenging. Relying on oneself to purify the mind and understand the sutras is not something everyone can do. Those who lack the mental apparatus tend to go to church where one need only follow the Ten Commandments, which are already laid out for the individual. Although he may not attend temple regularly, he does take pride in his ability to comprehend the sutras and devotes himself on his own time to attaining enlightenment, but he certainly will not attend a church.

The Jin family's two sons also do not attend temple and in fact have attended Korean Christian churches, a situation faced by many members of Sa Chal. Yet, instead of insisting that his sons carry on the family's religion, Dr. Jin maintains that religion is something that must be decided by the individual, a position that coincides with what being a Buddhist is all about—free choice. Instead of worrying about the rise of Christianity and the possible rift between parents and children based on religion, he responds to this situation by drawing a distinction between how Buddhist parents and Christian parents raise their kids: "perhaps because Buddhists minds are more lofty, they are not too worried or too concerned about their children doing other things [like going to church]." He continues:

> My kids went to Sa Chal a few times but there weren't any other students for them [to spend time with]. Also, this is another thing—for Christian homes, the parents say that the kids *have* to go to church. But people at the temple follow their minds and so they aren't going to force their kids to temple because more so than the Christian teachings, the Buddhist teachings teach about future lives and that people will always be reborn, so if you don't have Buddhist karma, then you won't really believe yet.

In other words, for many Buddhists like Dr. Jin, proselytizing and forcing one's religion onto one's children seem to go against Buddha Nature, karma, and self-knowledge, which constitute, for Dr. Jin at least, the most important aspects of Buddhist teachings. Even though many Buddhist children go to church, Dr. Jin maintains that as a Buddhist he will not force his kids to follow his decision. They must choose for themselves what religion to profess. This act of free choice is held in higher esteem than the Christian method of "forcing one's kids to go to church." Furthermore, since Buddhists also believe in karma, Dr. Jin can remain worryfree since one does not become a Buddhist without having that karmic connection.

Perhaps the individuals most affected by the rise of Christianity within the Korean American community are those students who encounter Christianity on a daily basis. For many Buddhist youths at Sa Chal, Christianity plays an important role in their everyday interactions with their co-ethnic friends. Encouraged by their parents and comforted by the familiarity afforded in such friendships, Korean Buddhist kids are often challenged by their Christian friends to attend churches. For many of these students, such challenges and invitations to come to church serve as a source of pressure because if they do attend church, they will participate in a religious practice counter to their parents'. Yet if they do not attend churches and Christians activities, they may risk losing the friendships they have with fellow Koreans. It is a difficult social position when not only are they a minority in the larger context of American culture but they also have to defend their religious identity as well. Based on my interactions with Buddhist students, it appears that religion is very much at the forefront of these students' relations with Korean Christians. The questions of the validity of Buddhism and the issues of conversion seem to emerge quite frequently in everyday life. Yet, there are also those students who pride themselves on being Buddhist despite acknowledging that Korean Christian churches often provide services and company that temples do not.

James Jang, a twenty-one-year-old college student, maintains that being Buddhist is synonymous with being independent, a characteristic far more important than being a dependent, albeit comfortable, Christian. James says that he was "practically born in a Buddhist temple since [his] grandmother was the head of her own temple." "Since she was a nun," James fondly recalls, "me and my mom used to go there almost every day. So, I literally grew up in temple." Even when he arrived in Los Angeles in 1991, his family moved into the top floor of another temple, for his grandmother had immigrated before his family and had established a small temple inside a residential home in Koreatown. Since that time, James has been a devout Buddhist who "still love[s] coming to sit in the *hopdang* [dharma hall] all night." For James, being a Buddhist has never been a source of stress or embarrassment, for despite having numerous Korean Christian friends, his religious practice is something he is drawn to for personal and not social reasons.

Nonetheless, James does envy the Korean Christian churches for providing what the temple does not—a strong sense of community. Based on the few times he attended churches with his Korean friends he comments:

> I don't know why but the Christians have a really good sense of community building. I think it sort of goes back to the question of whether or not a religion can provide some sort of social activities. As Buddhists, we are used to sitting in a room, meditating and praying. But Christians are used to praying, singing, and going out to reach for other people. They go to a particular house weekly and practice a service there and that provides an opportunity for other people to meet one another. For those people who [immigrated] to the United States who are really unfamiliar with the culture, tradition, and language, they kind of long to [keep] being Korean even before they decide to make themselves United States citizens. So they go out looking for people who can understand them and who speak the same language, know the same culture and traditions. I think that's what created a whole different

BEING BUDDHIST IN A CHRISTIAN WORLD

community of Christians. But as far as the Buddhists are concerned, I see a lot of individualism among Buddhists in Los Angeles.

The churches better fulfill an immigrant's need for comfort among fellow ethnics and opportunities to socialize as a group to escape the challenges of adjusting to life in a new country.

James also notes that churches provide "hookups" or networks for people to meet and develop business relationships based on a sense of trust fostered through similar religious beliefs. He adds, "If I run a business, I have to know all these people who are important for the business to run and survive." If one goes to church, then one will find fellow Christians and potential workers and business partners. In the matter of business affairs and social support, James admits that being a Buddhist "is really hard." Speaking of his own parents' retail clothing business and their relative social isolation within the larger Korean community, he admits:

> I am pretty sure that if my dad were a Christian, he would do a much better job running his business. That's what I feel but knowing my dad and how [my parents] act in front of other people, I think that they are doing a great job of making other people feel more comfortable looking at Buddhists. My parents tell other people they are Buddhists all the time; they don't hide it. I tell all these people that I am a Buddhist and I am really proud of it. My family has a social life involving all these Buddhists activities like going to temple every week and meeting all these people that are involved in the temple. But I guess in a sense we limit ourselves within a boundary because if you are a Buddhist and want to meet all these Buddhists who live in Los Angeles then you are bound to end at a certain point. There are only a limited number of Buddhists living in Los Angeles. There are so many people who are Christian or Catholic, so we don't have as large of a connection between Buddhists like Christians or Catholics. My parent's don't have that social life created by being involved with other Christians. So, in that way, it's really hard being a Buddhist in Los Angeles.

Yet as noted from his comments above, James remains extremely proud of his parents and himself for not hiding their religious identities no matter what the social and economic consequences may be. Here we find that Buddhism is held to be the tougher yet ultimately more rewarding path. Furthermore, he believes that while the Christians may have better community-building tactics, a stronger network of social support, and economic success, Christianity cannot provide the one critical element that makes being a Buddhist the better option—self-reliance. Speaking of the freedom of choice and the need to depend on oneself that he finds so attractive in Buddhist teachings, James adds:

> I think that being a Buddhist, you have to know actually who you are and about your innermost feelings. For example, Christians do what Jesus tells them to do—do this, do that, follow this way then I will lead you to [salvation] and you will get a better life. But I think we Buddhists have to create our own way and find our own path. We have to create our own future and our own pathway that's going to lead us to our main goals. I guess it's really hard for any individual to create a pathway that's going to lead them straight to the nirvana stage. But that's what I really love about being a Buddhist, sitting in a really big dharma hall and sort of meditating and breathing in and out. While you sit there you think about what you did in the past and what you want to do in the future. And in that spot, you sort of create your own path.

Choosing one's own path then becomes the most important aspect of religion as opposed to following the tenets set out for an individual.

James's belief that the Korean Christian church has a stronger sense of community building was echoed throughout my interviews with members of Sa Chal. As noted earlier in this chapter, many men and women express envy at the church's commitment to meeting and greeting new immigrants at the airport and offering more opportunities for becoming involved in social activities and receiving support. Yet, despite the obvious benefits of such activities as perceived by the Buddhists, they also see them as unnecessary to being a Buddhist. As many members put it, "being a Buddhist is about doing things on your own." This belief, according to Sa Chal members, rests in the philosophical belief in self-reliance and self-awakening. Some members assume that the monks should take up responsibilities similar to a minister's by doing things such as going out to meet new immigrants and offering more social services. Yet other members believe that monks should not be overly involved in mundane affairs; thus they advocate that the Sa Chal monks remain in the temple providing guidance in Buddhist teachings and officiating over ritual and worship services. I have found that those who espouse this view tend to be the men at Sa Chal who want to take on more responsibility in the administrative affairs of the temple. Thus, while Christians in the Korean churches may feel more bound to their community theologically, thus increasing their commitment to catering to the needs of the congregation, Buddhists at Sa Chal may in fact be less inclined to take part in such activities, since service activities and fellowship carry less religious significance in their interpretation of the Buddhist tradition.

When asked about his views on the conversion of Korean Buddhists to Christianity, James equated conversion with self-weakness and an inability to make one's own decisions:

> I see myself as really unique person. I don't like to do stuff that other people are doing. I don't like following other people. I see all these people who don't have much pride in themselves so when other people lead them into doing certain things, they actually commit themselves to doing that. But I am not like that. So, it's not likely that other people are going to pursue me to convert to change from Buddhism to Christian. I . . . am pretty sure that being a Christian is going to help you out in your career, because you have better connections and that Christian community where you can bond. But I never thought about converting.

Like many Buddhist men I met at Sa Chal, James finds utmost importance in being responsible for his own actions and making decisions based on deliberation rather than responding to a set of rules laid down for him. Thus, even though the churches may have more members and greater success, he believes that Christians are incapable of thinking for themselves.

Nonetheless, being a self-reliant Buddhist does have disadvantages, for there is little opportunity for growth if most Buddhists are more interested in relying on themselves in their religious practice. Because of this tendency, James believes that Buddhism among the second generation may die out. At the same time, this hands-off approach of Buddhism, and its independence, are the very things that attract James to the religion. As he puts it,

"I really love being Buddhist because you get to find out about yourself. I see all these people who think [they know] who they are . . . but I think they don't know [anything] about themselves!" Buddhists, he contends, do know something about themselves and how to depend on themselves. As such, James remains confident about the long-term success of Buddhism, for he believes that eventually more and more people will be come disillusioned with Christianity:

> I think at a certain point . . . the Christian community is going to get smaller. As science and technology develops even higher and higher, then Christians are going to lose interest. There are a lot of unbelievable things stated in the Bible by Christians. There are always those things that cannot be backed up by science. As science grows even further and further and the sense of philosophy embedded in individuals grows deeper and deeper, they are going to start looking for other religions that do not revolve around following direct orders. They will look for a religion that revolves around finding yourself, finding your innermost feelings, and finding what you should do instead of listening to what you should do.

Thus, for this Korean American student, "being a true Buddhist, you create your own life," which James considers a much better option than relying on others to tell you how to live your life.

In this chapter, I have shown how religious affiliation represents more than different spiritual orientations and practice. For example, as noted previously, "to be Buddhist is to be Korean," implying that religion and ethnicity are intricately bound together. This association of Buddhism with an "authentic" Korean identity enables some Buddhists to distinguish themselves from Korean Christians, whose faith is then interpreted as an adoption of Western ideals. In many ways, the large-scale conversion of Koreans to Christianity both in Korea and in the United States is a central concern and perceived threat to Buddhists at Sa Chal who disparagingly attribute those conversions to an easy form of "Americanization" and "weak-mindedness." The perception of Christian churches dominating Korean immigrants through their powerful resources can also be found in the rhetoric of Buddhist re-missionization and re-education of Korean Americans espoused by many temple members. Throughout this chapter,

I have shown how views of "the other" (Christians) play a crucial role in negotiating identities and developing self-esteem for temple members, and I drew specific attention to the tension and irony in the association of Buddhism's injunctions of self-reliance and independence with the cardinal virtues of American culture itself—independence, self-rule, and democratic values. By contrasting their own beliefs and practices with those of Christians, who are defined as "weak willed," "overly dependent," and "coercive," Buddhists indirectly claim that despite the greater economic success enjoyed by Christians in churches, such Christians are not as "American" as the Buddhists because their practices are too dependent on others for support. A Buddhist identity and the rhetoric of self-reliance are thus strongly tied to improving one's self-esteem both as an immigrant and as a Korean American living in a Christian world. Buddhists are seen as better Americans while Korean Christians are seen as too Westernized for having adopted Christianity. This paradox reflects tensions between the pros and cons of American values. Yet "to be Buddhist" is to be independent from the majority, and for many participants in this study that quality enhances self-esteem. Buddhists thus perceive themselves simultaneously as more authentic Koreans *and* better Americans.

8

Epilogue

    In the spring of 2002, I returned to Los Angeles to visit with several friends I had met during my two years of research at Sa Chal. Reacquainting myself with Los Angeles's intricate system of freeways, I found my way off the 101 freeway by taking the Vermont exit that would lead me straight into the heart of Koreatown. Much has changed in three years: a new subway line and station replace what was once just a run-down street corner, and new signs in Spanish are seen here and there where Korean shops had once been. Yet the ethnic diversity and vibrance of this section of Los Angeles remain. As I drove down the main strip where Sa Chal stands, I could not help but note the many changes to the temple itself. Gone are the old guitar shop and women's boutique that had rented part of the first floor of the temple. Replacing them are new stores owned most likely by first-generation Korean immigrants. But what clearly struck my eye was the nearly completed multicolored mural gracing the walls of the building adjacent to the rear of the temple. It used to be an acupuncture center and now it seemed to have been rebuilt as a school. When I pulled my rental car into the temple's parking lot, I stopped to take a closer look and saw that the mural was actually a giant lotus flower, a common Buddhist symbol.

    As I got out of my car and walked toward this new building, I found that its brand new sign in Korean reads "The Lotus Preschool." Suddenly I began to smile as I realized that Abbot Lee must have accomplished his latest goal of introducing Buddhism to the larger Korean American community of Los Angeles—offering a school for young children that would educate them

EPILOGUE

in the ways of Buddhism. As the school had not yet opened officially, I peeked in the windows and discovered a state-of-the-art facility with pristine pictures on the walls, books lined up that had never been opened, and neatly stacked rows and rows of toys. I admired the brand new wooden tables and chairs set low at just the right height for little bodies and the stacks of little beds for naptime. "Abbot Lee has done it," I thought with pride and admiration.

When I left Los Angeles in the summer of 1999, I remember having lunch with Abbott Lee and friends from Sa Chal at a nearby Korean restaurant as the abbot talked about plans for teaching kids how to be Buddhist and maintain the family's religious traditions. He had talked longingly about finding the right teachers and establishing the first Buddhist preschool in the United States. Now a mere three years later, the school existed.

Shaking my head in wonder at his accomplishments, I quickly entered the temple where I found Abbot Lee and my friends from Sa Chal waiting for me. It did not seem as though I had been away for more than a few months. We quickly picked up our usual forms of conversation and finally I got the full tour of the Lotus Preschool. Abbot Lee smiled as he explained how the temple had purchased the building, received proper building permits, and reconstructed the entire building to suit the needs of little children. He then spoke of the previous week's open house and said that as of March 2002 ten Korean American children were enrolled in this first ever Buddhist preschool. A cursory look at the daily schedule suggested a day like any other preschool day, except that the Lotus Preschool set aside a morning session of meditation for ten to fifteen minutes each day for children who are probably not used to sitting still for more than two minutes at a time. The only other distinctively Buddhist feature of this school is that its doors are open on major Christian holidays and closed for the celebration of the Buddha's birthday. As we soon departed for our usual lunch in Koreatown, I looked back at the preschool and hoped that it would be filled with all the little children the abbot had envisioned learning Buddhist teachings and spreading the Buddha dharma in the United States.

I have found during my two years at Sa Chal that the impact of religious worship and belief on the daily lives of Korean American men and women is quite profound. The development of self-esteem is integral to the process of renewing the self, for to "find and know one's mind" requires the indi-

EPILOGUE

vidual to rely on his or her own agency to make change. In other words, self-reliance has the direct effect of increasing self-esteem, for problems are not only experienced but also acknowledged, worked on, and ultimately vanquished.

Buddhism was an obvious choice of comfort for many women and men who were raised as Buddhists and were familiar with temples even though they had no recollection of any strict Buddhist training or regular temple attendance when they were children. In addition, the change from once-a-month to weekly attendance for many individuals shows their increased desire for aid and comfort while living in the United States. Most participants in my study maintained that they found religion at critical junctures in their lives such as immigration, midlife crises, marital distress, and financial or social decline. Furthermore, many participants tended to reinterpret troubling and traumatic events as object lessons—positive learning experiences in their life trajectories to make sense of their struggles and imbue them with spiritual and emotional significance.

The significance of religion for the individual often lies in the realm of private meaning, where public and textual discourses like "finding and knowing one's mind" are articulated. In choosing to present a series of abbreviated ethnographic religious biographies centered on themes of self-renewal, I have deliberately aimed at individualizing and personalizing the stories of the men and women at Sa Chal. In so doing, I focus on religion as lived "on the ground" to capture the patterns of everyday experience. I have also chosen to focus on individual stories of religious flourishing at Sa Chal to reflect the personalities and desires of the participants, a number of whom have become lifelong friends who still call to "check up on me" after I left Koreatown. Without paying attention to their particular lives, personalities, and idiosyncrasies, this book never would have gotten off the ground, for it was through their efforts and willingness to share their personal lives that I learned to see how Buddhism references and solves problems of a quotidian nature and not just a future-oriented soteriological framework.

An individual's religious faith is what enables him or her to endure multiple struggles, yet at the same time it is the flexibility of the interpretation of doctrines that allows members of Sa Chal to deploy religious meaning in their daily lives. By casting negative and harmful experiences in a religious light as lessons in impermanence, the individual alters the perception of events from painful to self-actualizing and healing. Thus, for example, a particularly painful divorce may signify that either a woman is and has always been better off being alone or that a relationship was not meant to be; rather it was the unawakened self that made it appear that it was meant to be. In this instance, I have found that the Buddhist injunction of finding and knowing one's mind also includes a measure of self-protection.

The complexity of gender relationships and practices in the temple illustrates the tension between Buddhist constructions of gender largely inherited by Confucianism, which are generally perceived as limiting to women and liberating for men. At the same time, as Jung Ha Kim notes, most women would not want a complete departure from traditional norms, for that is also where they find their strength as immigrants, and what grounds them in something familiar. Thus, in her own study of Korean American "churched women," Kim argues against the separability of gender struggles from racial struggles. She notes:

> Korean American women often share in the church setting their reluctance to identify with feminism, for they perceive it as "someone else's movement." Feminist goals and methods do not address struggles of Korean American women in their racial-ethnic communities where in order to survive racism, capitalism, and imperialism, *both* women and men have had to be interdependent.[1]

Similarly, most women at Sa Chal do not have an active interest in completely separating themselves from their co-ethnic male counterparts and do not operate in the Western feminist mode of actual equality between the sexes. At the same time, women and men have to improvise in America, choosing to uphold some traits of Korean culture because to repudiate them leaves too much at stake (e.g., the possible loss of family ties). In this respect, their predicament is very similar to that of fundamentalist women studied by Brenda Brasher who, despite biblical proscriptions of gender, are able to create spaces of importance and independence for themselves in the church without explicitly resisting biblical gender norms.[2] In this way, they construct new roles for themselves outside the jurisdiction of men yet do not raise the suspicion of the men. Thus, like fundamentalist Christian women, female members of Sa Chal can be said to be accommodating, improvisational, and resistant.

Being a Buddhist woman holds a particular appeal for many women because, on the doctrinal level, the attainment of Buddhahood is said to be genderless and therefore liberating in the long term. Similarly, in the short term, Buddhist worship and teachings are liberating on the practical level of everyday engagement because they provide women with self-reliance to change problems in their lives either in response to men or in spite of men. Most men at Sa Chal distinguish between their own intellectually oriented practices and the emotional devotions of women whose practices are deemed less authentic and less conducive to enlightenment in the future. Although I rarely heard any man discuss women's bodies as spiritual hindrances, I did hear equally gendered rhetoric in their associations of women's religion with fortune-praying and beseeching the Buddha for support. In so doing, the men in this study draw similar (albeit inaccurate) conclusions about women's Buddhism as they do about Korean Christianity—that both are for the weaker minded. As such, they elevate their status vis-à-vis women and Korean Christian men. Hence, men at Sa Chal did not feel that they needed to worship and discipline the body through prayer and bowing since, for them, as an intellectual and philosophical tradition, Buddhism could not dictate when and where a man would practice his religion. This perspective, in turn, reproduced Korean gender hierarchies in the United States as a way of grounding men in the familiar.

"Finding and knowing one's mind" becomes a particularly salient source of empowerment for men and women at Sa Chal, for by coming to America many were forced to pick up the pieces and start over again. I found that through finding and knowing one's mind, members of Sa Chal come to reorder their lives and recreate new identities as either Koreans living in America, Korean Americans, or Americans. For many participants in this study, the struggle for self-esteem and subjectivity occurs in direct opposition to the attitude of Korean Christians living in the United States, from whom Buddhists in this study experience discrimination. In this case, critiques of Buddhism as devil worship and backwardness, and the exclusion

EPILOGUE

from potential business and social interaction experienced by Sa Chal members, could potentially detract from Buddhists' positive view of themselves and their religion. It is in direct opposition and response to the Korean Christians that many members of Sa Chal chose to articulate their identities. In this context, we find that Buddhist virtues of knowing one's mind and self-reliance become associated with the widely held American values of independence and democracy in opposition to Korean Christian doctrines of relying on God (an external agent) for support and comfort. That is, for Buddhists at Sa Chal, to be Buddhist is to be an independent party with the psychological endurance to make it on one's own and to allow others to do as they wish.

The religious ideology of finding and knowing one's mind is directly related to increased self-esteem, for one relies on the self to take responsibility over his or her life which, in turn, is the condition that promotes the agentive self who chooses what he or she wants to do in life. Sa Chal members thus envision Buddhism's ideals to be the same as American values and demonstrate to themselves that despite hard times in America, Buddhists have the psychological wherewithal and strength of mind to achieve success.

As I conclude this study, I am left to ponder how the men and women's views of the main goals of Buddhist worship as self-reliance and the pride derived from independence can sustain the future of the Sa Chal community in America. While the men and women encountered in this study have displayed a remarkable strength of character and resilience in renegotiating their identities in the United States through their religion, it remains to be seen how the temple itself will fare in the next few decades. The lack of desire to force others to bend to one's will may in fact have the unintended and undesired result of diminishing the temple's impact on the lives of future generations of Korean American Buddhists.

I have already noticed the population of second-generation Buddhists at Sa Chal diminishing from Sunday worship services at a remarkable rate. There are also many members of Sa Chal who believe that once the senior citizens and middle-aged Buddhists pass away, there will be scant resources to pass down this distinct form of lay worship and scant recipients to hand down the "torch of Buddhism." In response to this threat, Abbot Lee works ceaselessly to train Buddhist parents as missionaries to their own families

EPILOGUE

and to expand the temple's influence in the non-Korean communities of Los Angeles. As a further indication of the uncertainty regarding the temple's future, I found that when I completed my field research at Sa Chal, I was continually requested to take on more and more responsibility for teaching the second-generation students about Buddhism. Thus my role at the temple was not just one of an outside researcher, but in the eyes of the abbot and other members of Sa Chal, I had become an integral part of their vision for the future of Chogye order Buddhism in America. This situation indicates both the strength of personal relationships that I developed in the temple and the rather difficult situation currently witnessed by this religious community, whose members do not feel that they have adequate resources and English-speaking leadership to succeed in passing down their own tradition to their children. It remains to be seen, however, who will be filling the temple's crushed velvet pews and worshipping in front of the Kwan Um Bodhisattva statues in the future.

NOTES

1 / INTRODUCTION

1. Won Moo Hurh and Kwang Chung Kim, "Religious Participation of Korean Immigrants in the U.S.," *Journal for the Scientific Study of Religion* 29 (March 1990): 19–34.

2. Harvey Cox, *Fire From Heaven: The Rise of Pentacostal Spirituality and the Reshaping of Religion in the Twenty-first Century* (New York: Addison-Wesley, 1995), pp. 213–41.

3. Won Moo Hurh, *The Korean Americans* (Westport Conn., and London: Greenwood Press, 1998), p. 106.

4. Hurh (ibid., p. 114) maintains that, Korean Americans who affiliate themselves with the Buddhist religion comprise only 1.5 percent of the population of Korean Americans living in America. However, according to the abbot of one of the largest Korean American Buddhist temples in the United States, Buddhists comprise approximately 10 to 15 percent of the Korean American population (based on an interview with the abbot of Sa Chal Temple, Los Angeles, 1999).

5. See, for example, Karen J. Chai, "Intra-Ethnic Religious Diversity: Korean Buddhists and Protestants in Greater Boston," in *Korean Americans and Their Religions: Pilgrims and Missionaries from a Different Shore*, ed. Ho-Youn Kwon, Kwang Chung Kim, and R. Stephen Warner (University Park: Pennsylvania State University Press, 2001), pp. 273–94; Karen Chai, "Protestant-Catholic-Buddhist: Korean Americans and Religious Adaptation in Greater Boston," Harvard University Ph.D. dissertation, 2000; and Okyun Kwon, "Religious Beliefs and Socioeconomic Aspects of Life of Buddhist and Protestant Immigrants," City University of New

NOTES

York Ph.D. dissertation, 2000. Samu Sunim's article, "Turning the Wheel of the Dharma in the West: Korean Son Buddhism in North America," in *Korean Americans and Their Religions*, pp. 227–58, examines Korean Son Buddhism in the United States, a form of religion that tends to have more Euro-American practitioners than ethnic Koreans.

6. The pseudonym Sa Chal is a Korean word for "temple."

7. Timothy Smith, "Religion and Ethnicity in America," *American Historical Review* 83 (December 1978): 1175.

8. Recent studies of gender relations in Korean American Christian churches by Ai Ra Kim and Jung Ha Kim also indicate that women find ways to resist some of the challenges of sexism within a primarily Confucian context. However, as both authors note, the overall structure of the Korean American Christian churches is highly patriarchal, with few opportunities for women to take on leadership roles. See Ai Ra Kim's *Women Struggling for a New Life: The Role of Religion in the Cultural Passage from Korea to America* (Albany: SUNY Press, 1996) and Jung Ha Kim, *Bridge-Makers and Cross-Bearers: Korean American Women and the Church* (Atlanta: Scholars Press, 1997).

9. The population of first-generation immigrants active at Sa Chal heavily outweighs the number of 1.5 generation and second-generation members. While the 1.5 generation and second-generation members of Korean American Christian churches has been quite substantial, at Sa Chal, combined active membership of 1.5 generation and second-generation members never exceeded twenty-five persons. For a look at the rising phenomenon of 1.5 generation and second-generation Korean American Christian churches, see Kwon, Kim, and Warner, eds., *Korean Americans and Their Religion*.

10. Yen Le Espiritu, *Asian American Women and Men: Labor, Laws and Love* (Thousand Oaks, Calif.: Sage Publications, 1997).

11. Young In Song, "Critical Feminist View of Patriarchal Structure of the Korean American Christian Church" in *Korean American Women Living in Two Cultures*, ed. Young In Song and Ailee Moon (Los Angeles: Keimyung-Baylo University Press, 1997); Kim, *Women Struggling for a New Life*.

12. Open-ended interview techniques place control of the dialogue in the hands of the participant, thus enabling access to the participant's ideas, experiences, and memories in her own narrative.

13. David Dunaway and Willa K. Baum, *Oral History: An Interdisciplinary Anthology*, 2d ed. (Walnut Creek, Calif.: Alta Mira Press, 1996).

NOTES

14. Ibid., p. 17.

15. I refer here to Shulamit Reinharz's definition of feminist methodology based on themes found in her work *Feminist Methods in Social Research* (New York and Oxford: Oxford University Press, 1992), p. 241. Reinharz's feminist methodology rests on the following assumption: women as individuals are worth examining through the use of a multiplicity of research methods. This approach involves a critique of nonfeminist scholarship and it may be transdisciplinary, guided by feminist theory, and aimed at creating social change and representing human diversity. It also involves the researcher as a person, develops special relations with people studied through interactive research, and defines a special relationship with the reader.

16. Quoted in Barbara Babcock, "Not in the Absolute Singular: Re-reading Ruth Benedict," in *Women Writing Culture*, ed. Ruth Behar and Deborah Gordon (Berkeley: University of California Press, 1995), p. 115.

2 / FINDING AND KNOWING ONE'S MIND

1. To "find one's mind" and "know one's mind" are direct translations from Korean phrases that participants in this study used extensively when describing their motivations for religious worship.

2. Sung Bae Park, *Buddhist Faith and Sudden Enlightenment* (Albany: State University of New York Press, 1983), pp. 18, 20.

3. Here, I draw upon Maureen Mahoney and Barbara Yngvesson's definition of subjectivity as "the experience of self as a subject who acts, who wants, and who must sometimes act 'against the grain' in the face of contradictory desires." Mahoney and Yngvesson, "The Construction of Subjectivity and the Paradox of Resistance: Reintegrating Feminist Anthropology and Psychology," *Signs: Journal of Women in Culture and Society* 18:1 (1992): 246.

4. Morwenna Griffiths, *Feminisms and the Self: The Web of Identity* (London and New York: Routledge Press, 1995), p. 85.

5. See Jung Ha Kim, *Bridge-Makers and Cross-Bearers*, and Ai Ra Kim, *Women Struggling for a New Life*.

6. Kim, *Bridge-Makers and Cross-Bearers*.

7. Dorinne Kondo, *Crafting Selves: Power, Gender and Discourses of Identity in a Japanese Workplace* (Chicago: University of Chicago Press, 1990), pp. 43, 33–34.

8. Feminist scholar Chilla Bulbeck notes that "western notions of the self . . . must be interrogated, both because they do not readily apply to people in other

cultures and ... [they] suggest some of the limitations of our often unquestioned assumptions of individual agency." Chilla Bulbeck, *Re-Orienting Western Feminisms* (Cambridge, U.K.: Cambridge University Press, 1998), p. 63. That is to say, the notion of a self *in relation* to others and *in community* may have more resonance for the women in my study who do not always put their struggles as women ahead of their struggles as an ethnic minority living in the United States.

9. Wikan, *Managing Turbulent Hearts: A Balinese Formula for Living* (Chicago and London: University of Chicago Press, 1990).

10. As Wikan succinctly puts it, "the main battle of crafting one's self is composed of the multiple successes and defeats of action: narrative can best serve to embellish the successes and obscure the defeats." Wikan, "The Self in a World of Urgency and Necessity," *Ethos* 23 (1995): 269.

11. Ibid., p. 277.

12. Steven Collins, *Selfless Persons: Imagery and Thought in Theravada Buddhism* (Cambridge: Cambridge University Press, 1982).

13. Melford Spiro, "Is the Western Conception of the Self 'Peculiar' within the Context of World Cultures?" *Ethos* 21:2 (1993): 108, 117.

14. Kenneth Pargament and Chrystal Park, "In Times of Stress: The Religion-Coping Connection," in *The Psychology of Religion: Theoretical Approaches*, ed. Bernard Spilka and Daniel N. McIntosh (Boulder: Westview Press, 1997), p. 49.

15. Anthropologist Sherry Ortner refers to this view of the self as one of embedded agency and involved in the "serious game," where "social life is culturally organized and constructed, in terms of defining categories of actors, rules and goals of the games and so forth; that social life is precisely social, consisting of webs of relationship and interaction between multiple, shiftingly interrelated positions, none of which can be extracted as autonomous 'agents'; and yet at the same time there is 'agency,' that is, actors play with skill, intention, wit, knowledge and intelligence." Ortner, *Making Gender: The Politics and Erotics of Culture* (Boston: Beacon Press, 1996), p. 12.

16. Griffiths, *Feminisms and the Self*, p. 93.

3 / SA CHAL CONTEXT, PROGRAMS, AND DEMOGRAPHICS

1. Eun Sik Yang, "Koreans in America, 1903–1945," in *Koreans in LA: Promises and Prospects*, ed. Eui Young Yu, Earl Phillips, and Eun Sik Yang (Los Angeles: Koryo Research Institute, Center for Korean and Korean American Studies, 1982).

NOTES

2. Ronald Takaki, *Strangers from a Different Shore* (Boston: Little, Brown, 1989), pp. 53–56.

3. Yang, "Koreans in America, 1903–1945."

4. Marion Dearman, "The Structure and Function of Religion in the Los Angeles Korean Community," in *Koreans in LA: Promises and Prospects*.

5. Yang, "Koreans in America, 1903–1945."

6. Eun Sik Yang, "Korean Women of America: From Subordination to Partnership, 1903–1930," *Amerasia* 11:2 (1984): 1–28.

7. Included within this group of Korean nationalists fighting the Japanese occupation of Korea were such famed leaders of the Korean provisional government later established in Shanghai in 1918, Ahn Chang Ho and Syngman Rhee.

8. Won Moo Hurh, *The Korean Americans* (Westport, Conn., and London: Greenwood Press, 1998), p. 35.

9. Eui-Young Yu, "Korean Communities in America: Past, Present and Future," *Amerasia* 102 (1983): 23–51.

10. Ibid., pp. 28–29.

11. Hurh, *The Korean Americans*, p. 33.

12. Won Moo Hurh and Kwang Chung Kim, "Religious Participation of Korean Immigrants in the U.S.," *Journal for the Scientific Study of Religion* 29 (March 1990): 19–34.

13. Bill Hong Hing, *Making and Remaking Asian America Through Immigration Policy, 1850–1990* (Stanford: Stanford University Press, 1993); Roger Waldiger and Mehdi Bozorgmehr, eds., *Ethnic Los Angeles* (New York: Russell Sage Foundation, 1996).

14. For a history of the early Korean American church, see Yang's "Koreans in America, 1903–1945," and Hyung-Chan Kim, ed., *The Korean Diaspora: Historical and Sociological Studies of Korean Immigration and Assimilation to North America* (Santa Barbara: ABC-Clio, Inc, 1977).

15. Eui-Young Yu, "The Growth of Korean Buddhism in the United States, with Special Reference to Southern California," *Pacific World: Journal of the Institute of Buddhist Studies*, new ser. 4 (1988):83.

16. Ibid., p. 89.

17. Information on the temple's history has been translated and excerpted from Sa Chal's *Twentieth Anniversary Almanac (1974–1993)*, published by the Korean Buddhist Chogye Order of America Inc., 1994.

18. The Chogye Buddhist order refers to the Zen Buddhist sect that emerged

NOTES

from the unification of nine earlier sects of Zen Buddhism in Korea during the fourteenth century.

19. James Paul Allen and Eugene Turner, *The Ethnic Quilt: Population Diversity in Southern California* (Northridge: Center for Geographical Studies, California State University, 1997).

20. Ibid., p. 150.

21. Following the Japanese Occupation of Korea (1919–45), Korean Buddhism was divided into eighteen sects, the largest of which is the Chogye order. Historically, Chogye-jong (order) has been associated with celibate monks in contrast to the married clergy associated with the newer Taego order, which had split from Chogye-jong. The Taego and Chogye orders are the largest of the eighteen sects. The other sixteen sects in Korea include the Maitreya sect, the Lotus sect, and the Tantric sects. For more information, see Chong-bae Mok, "Korean Buddhist Sects and Temple Operations," in *Korea Journal* 23:9 (September 1983): 19–27.

22. Abbot Lee's title in Korean is *Chuji sunim*. The term *chuji* has been translated by Robert Buswell as abbot and refers to the "spiritual and temporal head of the temple, combining teaching and administrative roles in one office." As such, the abbot's duties are largely managerial. Buswell, *The Zen Monastic Experience* (Princeton: Princeton University Press, 1992), p. 110.

23. The term *pogyo* has been translated by Sa Chal authorities variously as "dissemination" and "missionization." In this study, I use the term "dissemination" because it refers not only to the desire of the Buddhists at Sa Chal to spread the dharma but also to the process of conversion. The targeted audience for conversion is specifically the younger generations of Korean Americans as well as those Korean immigrants who have converted from Buddhism to Christianity. A third targeted audience of dissemination is the non-Korean English-speaking population of Los Angeles.

24. Interview with the abbot, October 1998.

25. I myself taught classes in Tibetan Buddhism for one semester at the request of the abbot.

26. See chapters six and seven for discussions of male attitudes toward the monks at Sa Chal.

27. Hong Yoon Sik, "Kongyang: Offerings and Commensulism in Korean Buddhism," *Korean Journal* (Spring 1991):53.

28. The forty-nine day ceremony facilities the deceased's entry into the Pureland.

29. According to Kyeyong Park, the shift for many Koreans to Christianity appears to have had a positive effect on daughters of the family who also adopt roles traditionally held by the first son, a situation that contributes to the elevated status of the daughter within the family. Kyeyoung Park, *The Korean American Dream* (Ithaca, N.Y.: Cornell University Press, 1997), p. 96.

4 / BUDDHIST PRACTICE AND SELF-TRANSFORMATION

1. James L. Peacock and Dorothy C. Holland, "The Narrated Self: Life Stories in Process," *Ethos* 21 (1993): 371.

2. Unni Wikan, "The Self in a World of Urgency and Necessity," *Ethos* 23 (1995): 276.

3. Ai Ra Kim, *Women Struggling for a New Life*, p. 74.

4. Luke Kim, "The Mental Health of Korean American Women," in *Korean American Women: From Tradition to Modern Feminism*, ed. Young I. Song and Ailee Moon (Westport, Conn.: Praeger Publishers, 1998), p. 216.

5. Here I borrow a phrase used by Wikan to refer to the experience of dislocation and a lack of coherence to a positive view of the self resulting from natural yet difficult life experiences. See Wikan, "The Nun's Story: Reflections on an Age-Old, Postmodern Dilemma," *American Anthropologist* 98: 2 (1996): 279–89.

6. R. Marie Griffith, "Submissive Wives, Wounded Daughters and Female Soldiers: Prayer and Christian Womanhood in Women's Aglow Fellowship," in *Lived Religion in America: Toward a History of Practice*, ed. David D. Hall (Princeton: Princeton University Press, 1997), p. 171.

7. Kondo, *Crafting Selves*, p. 304.

8. Sherry Ortner, *Making Gender: The Politics and Erotics of Culture* (Boston: Beacon Press, 1996), p. 20.

9. Helen Hardacre, *Lay Buddhism in Contemporary Japan: Reiyukai Kyodan* (Princeton: Princeton University Press, 1984).

10. Jae Woong Kim, *Polishing the Diamond, Enlightening the Mind: Reflections of a Buddhist Master* (Boston: Wisdom Publishing, 1999).

11. Peter Stromberg, *Language and Self-Transformation: A Study of the Christian Conversion Narrative* (Cambridge: Cambridge University Press, 1993), p. 6.

12. Dorinne Kondo, "Dissolution and Reconstitution of the Self: Implications for Anthropological Epistemology," *Cultural Anthropology* 1:1 (1986): 74–88.

NOTES

5 / BUDDHISM—AN ANCHOR IN AN UNCERTAIN WORLD AND A SOURCE OF INDEPENDENCE

1. Robert A. Orsi, "Everyday Miracles: The Study of Lived Religion," in *Lived Religion: Toward a History of Practice,* ed. David D. Hall (Princeton: Princeton University Press, 1997), pp. 1–21; quotations, 8, 16.

2. Pargament and Park, "In Times of Stress," p. 45.

3. Ai Ra Kim, *Women Struggling for a New Life.*

4. Beverley Skeggs, "Situating the Production of Feminist Ethnography," in *Researching Women's Lives from a Feminist Perspective,* ed. Mary Maynard and June Purvis (London and Bristol, Penn.: Taylor and Francis, Inc., 1994), pp. 72–92.

5. For a further discussion of women's silence as strategy of resistance, narratives as self-fashioning and refusals to 'tell' in ethnographic projects, see Kamala Visweswaran's "Betrayal: An Analysis of Three Acts," in *Scattered Hegemonies: Postmodernity and Transnational Feminist Practices,* ed. Inderpal Grewal and Caren Kaplan (Minneapolis and London: Minnesota University Press, 1994), pp. 90–109.

6. Sherna Gluck, "What's So Special About Women? Women's Oral History," in *Oral History: An Interdisciplinary Anthology,* ed. David Dunaway and Willa K. Baum (Walnut Creek, Calif.: Alta Mira Press, 1996), p. 219.

7. For a study of reflexive ethnography and constructions of identity in "the field," see Ruth Behar's *Translated Woman* (Boston: Beacon Press, 1993), and Ruth Behar and Deborah A. Gordon, eds., *Women Writing Culture* (Berkeley: University of California Press, 1995).

8. Kondo, *Crafting Selves,* p. 10.

9. Alejandro Portes and Ruben Rumbaut articulate the similarities among new immigrant groups and the coming of age of their children in their chapter "Growing up American," in *Immigrant America: A Portrait* (Berkeley: University of California Press, 1996).

10. Young In Song, "Korean American Women in Midlife: Patterns of Response to Change," in *Korean American Women Living in Two Cultures,* ed. Young In Song and Ailee Moon (Los Angeles: Academia Koreana, 1997), p. 161.

11. Ibid.

12. Kwang Chung Kim and Won Moo Hurh, "The Burden of Double Roles: Korean Wives in the U.S.A.," *Ethnic and Racial Studies* 11:2 (April 1988): 163.

13. Christians were said to comprise only 18 to 21 percent of the entire popula-

NOTES

tion in 1986 according to Jung Ha Kim. "Labor of Compassion: An Ethnographic Study of Churched Korean American Women," in *Korean American Women Living in Two Cultures*, ed. Young In Song and Ailee Moon, p. 124.

14. Park, *The Korean American Dream*, pp. 127–28.

15. Studies of immigrant religions by Raymond Brady Williams, *Religion of Immigrants from India and Pakistan: New Threads in the American Tapestry* (New York: Cambridge University Press, 1988); Stephen R. Warner and Judith Wittner, eds., *Gatherings in Diaspora: Religious Communities and the New Immigration* (Philadelphia: Temple University Press, 1998); Robert A. Orsi, *The Madonna of 115th Street: Faith and Community in Italian Harlem* (New Haven: Yale University Press, 1985). and Kim, *Women Struggling for a New Life*. All authors maintain that migrants seek out organizations, churches, and temples to worship for reasons centering on ethnic identification.

16. Kim, *Women Struggling for a New Life*, p. 81.

17. Ibid., p. 86.

18. Young In Song, "Critical Feminist View of Patriarchal Structure of the Korean American Christian Church," in *Korean American Women Living in Two Cultures* (Los Angeles: Keimyung-Baylo University Press, 1997), p. 71. To Song's analysis, I would add that competition between immigrant women in the same congregation may also be pronounced and enacted in terms of wealth, their children's academic success, and their marital prospects.

19. Song and Moon, eds., *Korean American Women Living in Two Cultures*, p. 177.

20. Throughout my interactions with Helen, I noted the contrast between her view of an ideal self-reliant Buddhist and her own dependence on me as the researcher to help her feel comfortable in the social setting of the temple. Her desire to have me call her "Mom" and to act as my mother reveals her extreme discomfort in the temple and the irony in her interpretation of "finding and knowing one's mind" yet dependence on others to help her fit in.

21. Kondo, *Crafting Selves*, p. 17.

22. Song, "Life satisfaction of the Korean American Elderly," *Korean American Women, from Tradition to Modern Feminism*, p. 203.

23. Kyeyoung Park, for example, has noted that for Korean Christians in New York, religious identity invokes an association with the "American dream," for by "adopting the religious language that they believe their American hosts use, Koreans dream that they will have success." Park, *The Korean American Dream*, p. 187.

NOTES

24. Pierrette Hondagneu-Sotelo, *Gendered Transitions: Mexican Experiences of Immigration* (Berkeley: University of California Press, 1994).

25. Kim, *Women Struggling for a New Life*, and Jung Ha Kim, *Bridge-Makers and Cross-Bearers*. Ai Ra Kim argues that women are further encouraged to emulate the model of Christ through self-sacrifice for spouses and children.

26. Ok-yun Lee, "Sociolinguistic Study of Mutual Address Terms Among Spouses," in *Korean Women and Culture* (Seoul: Research Institute of Asian Women, 1998), pp. 253–72. The terms *jip saram* and *an saram* are still used today to refer to a housewife. These terms date back to the Yi dynasty in Korea, during which New Confucian legislators sought to confine women to the domestic sphere. According to Martina Deuschler's study of Confucianism in Korea, Confucian legislators marked the public as male and private as female. She writes, "In practical terms, the separation of 'in' and 'out' had a number of implications for the new bride who took up residence as primary wife in the inner quarters of the house *(anch'ae)*. Her freedom of movement was completely curtailed so that she virtually lost contact with the outside world." Martina Deuschler, *The Confucian Transformation of Korea: A Study of Society and Ideology* (Cambridge: Harvard University Press, 1992), p. 261.

27. Hondagneu-Sotelo, *Gendered Transition*, p. 192.

28. Silvia Pedraza, "Women and Migration: The Social Consequences of Gender," *Annual Review of Sociology* 17 (1991): 309.

29. See Park's *The Korean American Dream*, chapter 9, "The Comforts of Christianity for Korean Immigrants: Religion and Reproduction of Small Business Activity," pp. 183–97.

30. Lawrence C. Watson and Maria-Barbara Watson-Franke, *Interpreting Life Histories: An Anthropological Inquiry* (New Brunswick, N.J.: Rutgers University Press, 1985), p. 3.

31. Jean Lipman-Blumen, *Gender Roles and Power* (Englewood Cliffs, N.J.: Prentice-Hall, 1984).

32. According to K. K. Lee, ancestor worship "devolves upon the family head. From early childhood a first-born male learns that he is responsible for taking care of his parents while they are alive and later, for performing ritual services for them when they die. These acts serve as repayment for parental love and affection." Lee, "Family and Religion in Korea," in *Religion and the Family in East Asia*, ed. George A. DeVos and Takao Sofue (Berkeley: University of California Press, 1986), p. 193.

33. As Ai Ra Kim notes of Korean Christian women, "Women continue to be

recognized and treated as persons mainly according to their marital status. To many devout *ilse* [first-generation] women, divorce is now viewed not only as a violation of Korean customs and a failure to fulfill one's womanhood, but also as a violation of God's order and betrayal of one's commitment to the Almighty Father." Kim, *Korean Women Struggling for a New Life,* p. 103.

34. Siyon Rhee, "Separation and Divorce Among Korean Immigrant Families," in *Korean American Women: From Tradition to Modern Feminism,* ed. Young I. Song and Ailee Moon (Westport, Conn.: Praeger, 1998), pp. 151–59; quotations, 151, 152.

35. Kim, *Women Struggling for a New Life,* p 103.

6 / FINDING MALE SELVES: MEN'S RELIGIOUS PRACTICES

1. Eui Hang Shin and Hyung Park, "An Analysis of the Causes of Schisms in Ethnic Churches: The Case of Korean-American Churches," in *Korean in North America: New Perspectives,* ed. Seong Hyong Lee and Tae-Hwan Kwak (Seoul: Kyungnam University Press, 1988), pp. 235–36.

2. Sheba George points to a similar phenomenon among Keralite men in a Christian immigrant church who seek to negotiate and expand their roles in the church by taking over the activity of caroling and cooking at public events. George maintains that men's activities are in direct relation to gendered patterns of immigration from India, where women and wives tended to immigrate first and earn higher incomes than their spouses who followed. See George, "Caroling with the Keralites: The Negotiation of Gendered Space in an Indian Immigrant Church," in Warner and Wittner, eds., *Gatherings in Diaspora,* pp. 265–94.

3. Transnationalism is a useful category of analysis, for it provides a way of viewing immigrants within an ethnic group as compelled by multiple allegiances across national borders. Transnationalism enables us to view people within larger social networks that extend beyond one particular society, group, or country and entails the flow of capital, investments, remittances, culture, bodies, and ideas to and from the country of origin to the host country. Thus immigration does not evoke a permanent sense of separation from the homeland. For further inquiry, see Linda Basch, Nina Glick Shiller, and Christina Szanton-Blanc, *Nations Unbound: Transnational Projects, Postcolonial Predicaments and Deterritorialized Nation-States* (Langhorne, Penn.: Gordon and Breach, 1994).

NOTES

4. Unlike earlier immigrants of European descent, the new post-1965 Immigration Act Koreans are better able to transport themselves back to the homeland through the advent of telecommunications, computers, and numerous flights back and forth from Asia. Furthermore, as John Lie claims, "it is no longer assumed that immigrants make a sharp break from their homelands. Rather, pre-immigration networks, cultures and capital remain salient. The sojourn itself is neither unidirectional nor final. Multiple, circular and return migrations rather than a singular great journey from one sedentary space to another, occur across transnational spaces. People's movements, in other words, follow multifarious trajectories and sustain diverse networks." Lie, "From International Migration to Transnational Diaspora," *Contemporary Sociology* 24:4 (July 1995): 304.

5. Won Moo Hurh, *The Korean Americans*, p. 143.

6. The Kwangju Uprisings took place in 1980 as a demonstration calling for the end of military rule in South Korea. The uprisings led to the violent death of approximately 2,000 civilians.

7. Basch, Shiller, and Szanton-Blanc, *Nations Unbound*.

8. I did note, however, that the men in higher paying professional jobs tended to speak of themselves as Korean Americans.

9. Luin Goldring, "The Power of Status in Transnational Social Fields," in *Transnationalism from Below*, ed. Michael Peter Smith and Luis Eduardo Guarnizo (New Brunswick. N.J.: Transaction Press, 1998).

10. Kim, *Women Struggling for a New Life*, p. 67.

11. Orsi, *The Madonna of 115th Street: Faith and Community in Italian Harlem* (New Haven: Yale University Press, 1985).

12. Young-Ja Lee, "Current State of Buddhism Among Women in Korea," *Korea Journal* 23:9 (September 1993): 18–32. *Chima Bulgyo* (Skirt Buddhism) is another term used to refer to lay women's practices.

13. Ai Ra Kim, *Women Struggling for a New Life*, and Jung Ha Kim, *Bridge-Makers and Cross-Bearers*.

7 / BEING BUDDHIST IN A CHRISTIAN WORLD

1. From my own observations, I noted that during the period between June 1997 and June 1999, the Buddhist youth group attendance dropped over 50 percent, from twenty-five students to just under fourteen. According to the remaining students, those who left went to church either because they felt it offered

better opportunities to meet with friends or because English was the primary language of communication.

2. Only 1.5 percent according to Won Moo Hurh, *The Korean Americans*, p. 114, although the abbot of Sa Chal places the number around 10 to 15 percent.

3. See Harvey Cox, *Fire From Heaven: The Rise of Pentacostal Spirituality and the Reshaping of Religion in the Twenty-first Century* (New York: Addision-Wesley, 1995), pp. 213–41.

4. Ai Ra Kim, *Women Struggling for a New Life*, p. 66.

5. Hurh, *The Korean Americans*, p. 107.

6. Ibid.

7. Ibid., p. 109.

8. Shin and Park, "An Analysis of Causes of Schisms in Ethnic Churches," pp. 231–54.

9. Kyeyoung Park, *The Korean American Dream*, pp. 186–87.

8 / EPILOGUE

1. Jung Ha Kim, *Bridge-Makers and Cross-Bearers*, p. 24.

2. Brenda E. Brasher, *Godly Women: Fundamentalism and Female Power* (New Brunswick, N.J.: Rutgers University Press, 1998).

BIBLIOGRAPHY

Abelmann, Nancy and John Lie. *Blue Dreams: Korean Americans and the Los Angeles Riots.* Cambridge: Harvard University Press, 1997.

Abu-Lughod, Lila. "The Romance of Resistance: Tracing Transformations of Power Through Bedouin Women." American Ethnologist 17:1 (1990): 41–51.

Albanese, Catherine. *American: Religion and Religions.* Belmont, Calif.: Wadsworth Publishing Company, 1981.

Allen, James Paul and Eugene Turner. *The Ethnic Quilt: Population Diversity in Southern California.* Northridge: Center for Geographical Studies, California State University, 1997.

Babcock, Barbara. "Not in the Absolute Singular: Re-reading Ruth Benedict." In *Women Writing Culture.* Edited by Ruth Behar and Deborah A. Gordon. Berkeley: University of California Press, 1995.

Bahri, Deepika, and Mary Vasudeva, eds. *Between the Lines: South Asians and Postcoloniality.* Philadelphia: Temple University Press, 1996.

Basch, Linda, Nina Glick Shiller, and Christina Szanton-Blanc. *Nations Unbound: Transnational Projects, Postcolonial Predicaments and Deterritorialized Nation-States.* Langhorne, Penn.: Gordon and Breach, 1994.

Bateson, Gregory and Margaret Mead. *Balinese Character: A Photographic Analysis.* New York: New York Academy of Sciences, 1942.

Behar, Ruth. *Translated Woman.* Boston: Beacon Press, 1993.

——— and Deborah A. Gordon, eds. *Women Writing Culture.* Berkeley: University of California Press, 1995.

Berger, Peter. *The Sacred Canopy: Elements of a Sociological Theory of Religion.* New York: Doubleday, 1967.

BIBLIOGRAPHY

Brasher, Brenda E. *Godly Women: Fundamentalism and Female Power.* New Brunswick, N.J.: Rutgers University Press, 1998.

Brown, Karen McCarthy. *Mama Lola: A Vodou Priestess in Brooklyn.* Berkeley: University of California Press, 1991.

Bulbeck, Chilla. *Re-Orienting Western Feminisms.* Cambridge, UK: Cambridge University Press, 1998.

Buswell, Robert. *The Zen Monastic Experience.* Princeton: Princeton University Press, 1992.

Bynum, Carolyn Walker, Steven Harrell, and Paula Richman, eds. *Gender and Religion: On the Complexity of Symbols.* Boston: Beacon Press, 1986.

Cabezon, Jose Ignacio, ed. *Buddhism, Sexuality and Gender.* Albany: SUNY Press, 1992.

Canda, E. R. and T. Phaobtong. "Buddhism as a Support System for Southeast Asian Refugees." *Social Work* 37:1 (January 1992): 61–67.

Chai, Karen J. "Intra-Ethnic Religious Diversity: Korean Buddhists and Protestants in Greater Boston." In *Korean Americans and Their Religions: Pilgrims and Missionaries from a Different Shore.* Edited by Ho-Youn Kwon, Kwang Chung Kim, and R. Stephen Warner. University Park: Pennsylvania State University Press, 2001.

———. "Protestant-Catholic-Buddhist: Korean Americans and Religious Adaptation in Greater Boston." Harvard University Ph.D dissertation, 2000.

Chan, Sucheng. *Asian Americans: An Interpretive History.* Boston: Twayne Publishers, 1991.

Choy, Bong-Youn. *Koreans in America.* Chicago: Nelson-Hall, 1979.

———. "The History of Early Koreans in America, 1883–1941." *Koreans in North America: New Perspectives.* Edited by Seong Hyong Lee and Tae-Hwan Kwak. Seoul: Kyungnam University Press, 1988.

Chung, Sei-wha. *Challenges for Korean Women: Women's Studies in Korea.* Translated by Shin Chang-hyun. Seoul: Ewha Women's University Press, 1986.

Collins, Patricia Hill. "Learning from the Outsider Within: The Sociological Significance of Black Feminist Thought." *Social Problems* 33(6) (1986): 14–32.

Comaroff, John and Jean Comaroff. *Ethnography and the Historical Imagination.* Boulder, San Francisco, and Oxford: Westview Press, 1992.

Cook, Judith and Mary Margaret Fonow. *Beyond Methodology: Feminist Scholarship as Lived Research.* Bloomington: Indiana University Press, 1991.

Cox, Harvey. *Fire From Heaven: The Rise of Pentecostal Spirituality and the Reshap-*

ing of Religion in the Twenty-first Century. New York: Addison-Wesley Publishing Co., 1995.

Dearman, Marion. "The Structure and Function of Religion in the Los Angeles Korean Community." In *Koreans in LA: Promises and Prospects*. Edited by Eui Young Yu, Earl Phillips, and Eun Sik Yang. Los Angeles: Koryo Research Institute, Center for Korean and Korean American Studies, 1982.

Deuschler, Martina. *The Confucian Transformation of Korea: A Study of Society and Ideology*. Cambridge: Harvard University Press, 1992.

DeVault, Marjorie. "Talking and Listening from Women's Standpoint: Feminist Strategies for Interviewing and Analysis." *Social Problems* 37:1 (February 1990): 96–116.

DeVos, George and Takao Sofue, eds. *Religion and the Family in East Asia*. Berkeley: University of California Press, 1986.

Dunaway, David and Willa K. Baum. *Oral History: An Interdisciplinary Anthology*. Second Edition. Walnut Creek, Calif.: Alta Mira Press, 1996.

Espiritu, Yen Le. *Asian American Women and Men: Labor, Laws and Love*. Thousand Oaks, Calif.: Sage Publications, 1997.

Gans, Herbert J. "Symbolic Ethnicity and Symbolic Religiosity: Towards a Comparison of Ethnic and Religious Acculturation." *Ethnic and Racial Studies* 17:4 (October 1994): 577–92.

Geertz, Clifford. *The Interpretation of Cultures*. New York: Basic Books, 1973

George, Sheba. "Caroling with the Keralites: The Negotiation of Gendered Space in an Indian Immigrant Church." In *Gatherings in Diaspora: Religious Communities and the New Immigration*. Edited by R. Stephen Warner and Judith Wittner. Philadelphia: Temple University Press, 1998.

Gilligan, Carol. *In a Different Voice: Psychological Theory and Women's Development*. Cambridge: Harvard University Press, 1993.

Gluck, Sherna. "What's So Special About Women? Women's Oral History." In *Oral History: An Interdisciplinary Anthology*. Edited by David Dunaway and Willa K. Baum. Walnut Creek, Calif.: Alta Mira Press, 1996.

Goldring, Luin. "The Power of Status in Transnational Social Fields." In *Transnationalism from Below*. Edited by Michael Peter Smith and Luis Eduardo Guarnizo. New Brunswick, N.J.: Transaction Press, 1998.

Grayson, James H. *Korea: A Religious History*. Oxford: Clarendon Press, 1989.

Grewal, Inderpal and Caren Kaplan, eds. *Scattered Hegemonies: Postmodernity and Transnational Feminist Practices*. Minneapolis: Minnesota University Press, 1994.

BIBLIOGRAPHY

Griffith, R. Marie. "Submissive Wives, Wounded Daughters and Female Soldiers: Prayer and Christian Womanhood in Women's Aglow Fellowship." In *Lived Religion in America: Toward a History of Practice*. Edited by David D. Hall. Princeton: Princeton University Press, 1997.

Griffiths, Morwenna. *Feminisms and the Self: The Web of Identity*. London and New York: Routhledge Press, 1995.

Hall, David D., ed. *Lived Religion in America: Toward A History of Practice*. Princeton: Princeton University Press, 1997.

Hardacre, Helen. *Lay Buddhism in Contemporary Japan: Reiyukai Kyodan*. Princeton: Princeton University Press, 1984.

Hing, Bill Hong. *Making and Remaking Asian America Through Immigration Policy, 1850–1990*. Stanford: Standford University Press, 1993.

Hondagneu-Sotelo, Pierrette. *Gendered Transitions: Mexican Experiences of Immigration*. Berkeley: University of California Press, 1994.

Horner, I. B. *Women Under Buddhism: Laywomen and Almswomen*. New York: E. P. Dutton, 1930.

Hurh, Won Moo. *The Korean Americans*. Westport, Conn.: Greenwood Press, 1998.

——— and Kwang Chung Kim. *Korean Immigrants in America: A Structural Analysis of Ethnic Confinement and Adhesive Adaptation*. Teaneck, N.J.: Farleigh Dickenson University Press, 1981.

——— and Kwang Chung Kim. "Religious Participation of Korean Immigrants in the U.S." *Journal for the Scientific Study of Religion* 29 (March 1990): 19–34.

Kashima, Tetsuden. *Buddhism in America: The Social Organization of an Ethnic Religious Institution*. Westport, Conn.: Greenwood Press, 1977.

Kendall, Laurel and Griffin Dix. *Religion and Ritual in Korean Society*. Korea Research Institute Monograph, no. 12. Berkeley: Institute of East Asian Studies, 1987.

Kikumura, Akemi. *Through Harsh Winters: The Life of a Japanese Immigrant Woman*. Novato, Calif.: Chandler and Sharp Publishers, Inc., 1981.

Kim, Ahn-Soo. *Almanac: Korean Buddhist Chogye Order of America Inc: Kwan Um Temple 20th Anniversary*. Los Angeles: The Buddhist Times and Society, 1994.

Kim, Ai Ra. *Women Struggling for a New Life: The Role of Religion in the Cultural Passage from Korea to America*. Albany: SUNY Press, 1996.

Kim, Elaine H. and Eui Young Yu. *East to America: Korean American Life Stories*. New York: The New Press, 1996.

——— and Chungmoo Choi, eds. *Dangerous Women: Gender and Korean Nationalism*. New York and London: Routledge, 1998.

BIBLIOGRAPHY

Kim, Jae Woong. *Polishing the Diamond, Enlightening the Mind: Reflections of a Buddhist Master.* Boston: Wisdom Publishing, 1999.

Kim, Jung Ha. *Bridge-Makers and Cross-Bearers: Korean American Women and the Church.* Atlanta: Scholars Press, 1997.

———. "Labor of Compassion: An Ethnographic Study of Churched Korean American Women." In *Korean American Women Living in Two Cultures.* Edited by Young In Song and Ailee Moon. Los Angeles: Academia Koreana, Keimyung-Baylo University, 1997.

Kim, Hyung-Chan, ed. *The Korean Diaspora: Historical and Sociological Studies of Korean Immigration and Assimilation to North America.* Santa Barbara: ABC-Clio, Inc., 1997.

——— and Wayne Patterson. *The Koreans in America: 1882–1974, A Chronology and Fact Book.* Dobbs Ferry, N.Y.: Oceana Publications, Inc., 1974.

Kim, Ilsoo. *New Urban Immigrants: The Korean Community in New York:* Princeton: Princeton Univesity Press, 1981.

Kim, Kwang Chung. "The Burden of Double Roles: Korean Wives in the USA." *Ethnic and Racial Studies* 11:2 (April 1988): 151–67.

———. "Beyond Assimilation and Pluralism: Syncretic Sociocultural Adaptation of Korean Immigrants in the U.S." *Ethnic and Racial Studies* 16:696–713.

Kim, Luke. "The Mental Health of Korean American Women." In *Korean American Women: From Tradition to Modern Feminism.* Edited by Young I. Song and Ailee Moon. Westport, Conn.: Praeger Publishers, 1998.

Kivisto, Peter A. "Religion and the New Immigrants." In *A Future for Religion? New Paradigms for Social Analysis.* Edited by William H. Swatos, Jr. Newbury Park, Calif.: Sage, 1992.

Klein, Anne. "Finding a Self: Buddhist and Feminist Perspectives." In *Shaping New Vision: Gender and Values in American Culture.* Edited by Clarissa Atkinson, Constance Buchanan, and Margaret Miles. Ann Arbor: UMI Research Press, 1987.

———. *Meeting the Great Bliss Queen: Buddhists, Feminists and the Art of the Self.* Boston: Beacon Press, 1995.

———. "Primal Purity and Everyday Life: Exalted Female Symbols and the Women of Tibet." In *Immaculate and Powerful: The Female in Sacred Image and Social Reality.* Edited by Clarissa Atkinson, Constance Buchanan, and Margaret Miles. Boston: Beacon Press, 1985.

Koh, Hesung. "Religion and Socialization of Women in Korea." In *Religion and the Family in East Asia*. Edited by George De Vos and Takao Sofue. Berkeley: University of California Press, 1986.

Kondo, Dorinne. *Crafting Selves: Power, Gender and Discourses of Identity in a Japanese Workplace*. Chicago: Chicago University Press, 1990.

———. "Dissolution and Reconstitution of the Self: Implications for Anthropological Epistemology." *Cultural Anthropology* 1:1 (1986): 74–88.

1999 Korean Community Directory. Los Angeles: Korea Times and Korean Central Daily, 1999.

Kurien, Prema. "Becoming American by Becoming Hindu: Indian Americans Take Their Place at the Multi-cultural Table." In *Gatherings in Diaspora: Religious Communities and the New Immigration*. Edited by R. Stephen Warner and Judith Wittner. Philadelphia: Temple University Press, 1998.

Kwon, Okyun. "Religious Beliefs and Socioeconomic Aspects of Life of Buddhist and Protestant Immigrants." City University of New York Ph.D. dissertation, 2000.

Lancaster, Lewis R. "Buddhism and Family in East Asia" In *Religion and the Family in East Asia*. Edited by George DeVos and Takao Sofue. Berkeley: University of California Press, 1986.

———. "Elite and Folk: Comments on the Two-Tiered Theory." In *Religion and the Family in East Asia*. Edited by George DeVos and Takao Sofue. Berkeley: University of California Press, 1986.

Lang, Karen C. "Lord Death's Snare: Gender Related Imagery in the Theragatha and Therigatha." *Journal of Feminist Studies* 2 (1986): 63–79.

Langness, L. L. and Geyla Frank. *Lives: An Anthropological Approach to Biography*. Novato, Calif.: Chandler and Sharp Publishers, Inc., 1991.

Lee, K. K. "Family and Religion in Korea." In *Religion and the Family in East Asia*. Edited by George De Vos and Takao Sofue. Berkeley: University of California Press, 1986.

Lee, Mary Paik. *Quiet Odyssey: A Pioneer Korean Woman in America*. Edited by Sucheng Chan. Seattle and London: University of Washington Press, 1990.

Lee, Ok-yun. "Sociolinguistic Study of Mutual Address Terms Among Spouses." In *Korean Women and Culture*. Seoul: Research Institute of Asian Women, 1998.

Lee, Young-Ja. "Current State of Buddhism Among Women in Korea." *Korea Journal* 23:9 (September 1993): 18–32.

Lefferts, Jr., H. Leedom. *Textiles and the Tai Experience in Southeast Asia*. Washington, D.C.: The Textile Museum, 1992.

Lie, John. "From International Migration to Transnational Diaspora." *Contemporary Sociology* 24:4 (July 1995): 303–6.

Lin, Irene. "Journey to the Far West." *Amerasia Journal* 22:1 (1996): 107–32.

Lipman-Blumen, Jean. *Gender Roles and Power*. Englewood Cliffs, N.J.: Prentice-Hall, 1984.

Lowe, Lisa. *Immigrant Acts*. Durham and London: Duke University Press, 1996.

Mahoney, Maureen and Barbara Yngvesson. "The Construction of Subjectivity and the Paradox of Resistance: Reintegrating Feminist Anthropology and Psychology." *Signs: Journal of Women in Culture and Society* 18:1 (1992): 245–74.

Mauss, Marcel. "A Category of the Human Mind: The Nation of Person; the Notion of Self." Translated by W. D. Halls. In *Category of the Person: Anthropology, Philosophy, and History*. Edited by Michael Carrithers, Steven Collins, and Steven Lukes. Cambridge: Cambridge University Press, 1985.

Min, Pyong Gap. "The Korean American Family." In *Ethnic Families in America: Patterns and Variations*. Edited by Charles Mindel et al. New York: Elsevier, 1983.

Mok, Chong-bae. "Korean Buddhist Sects and Temple Operations." *Korea Journal* 23:9 (September 1983): 19–27.

Nattier, Jan. "Who Is a Buddhist? Charting the Landscape of Buddhist America." In *The Faces of Buddhism in America*. Edited by Charles Prebish, and Kenneth K. Tanaka. Berkeley: University of California Press, 1998.

Numrich, Paul. *Old Wisdom in the New World: Americanization in Two Immigrant Theravada Buddhist Temples*. Knoxville: University of Tennessee Press, 1996.

Omi, Michael and Howard Winant. *Racial Formations in the United States*. New York: Routledge Press, 1986.

Orsi, Robert A. "Everyday Miracles: The Study of Lived Religion." In *Lived Religion: Toward a History of Practice*. Edited by David D. Hall. Princeton: Princeton University Press, 1997.

———. *Thank You, St. Jude: Women's Devotion to the Patron Saint of Hopeless Causes*. New Haven: Yale University Press, 1996.

———. *The Madonna of 115th Street: Faith and Community in Italian Harlem*. New Haven and London: Yale University Press, 1985.

Ortner, Sherry. *Making Gender: The Politics and Erotics of Culture*. Boston: Beacon Press, 1996.

Pargament, Kenneth and Chrystal L. Park. "In Times of Stress: The Religion-Coping Connection." In *The Psychology of Religion: Theoretical Approaches*. Edited by Bernard Spilka and Daniel N. McIntosh. Boulder: Westview Press, 1997.

BIBLIOGRAPHY

Park, Kyeyoung. *The Korean American Dream*. Ithaca, N.Y.: Cornell University Press, 1997.

Park, Sung Bae. *Buddhist Faith and Sudden Enlightenment*. Albany: State University of New York Press, 1983.

Paul, Diana. *Women in Buddhism*. Berkeley University of California Press, 1985.

Peacock, James and Dorothy C. Holland. "The Narrated Self: Life Stories in Process." *Ethos* 21 (1993): 367–83.

Pedraza, Silvia. "Women and Migration: The Social Consequences of Gender." *Annual Review of Sociology* 17 (1991): 303–25.

Personal Narrative Group, eds. *Interpreting Women's Lives: Feminist Theory and Personal Narratives*. Bloomington: Indiana University Press, 1989.

Phillips, Earl and Eui Young Yu, eds. *Religions in Korea: Beliefs and Cultural Values*. Los Angeles: Center for Korean-American and Korean Studies, California State University, Los Angeles, 1982.

Portes, Alejandro and Ruben Rumbaut. *Immigrant America: A Portrait*. Berkeley: University of California Press, 1996.

Prebish, Charles. *American Buddhism*. North Schituate, Mass.: Duxbury Press, 1979.

——— and Kenneth K. Tanaka. *The Faces of Buddhism in America*. Berkeley: University of California Press, 1998.

Reinharz, Shulamit. *Feminist Methods in Social Research*. New York and Oxford: Oxford University Press, 1992.

Ro, Hea-sook. *Korean Women and Culture*. Seoul: Research Institute of Asian Women, Sookmyung Women's University, 1998.

Robert, Helen. *Doing Feminist Research*. London: Routledge and Kegan Paul, 1991.

Scott, James. *Domination and the Arts of Resistance: Hidden Transcripts*. New Haven: Yale University Press, 1990.

Scott, Joan Wallach. *Gender and the Politics of History*. New York: Columbia University Press, 1988.

Shin, Eui Hang and Hyung Park. "An Analysis of the Causes of Schisms in Ethnic Churches: The Case of Korean-American Churches." In *Koreans in North America: New Perspectives*. Edited by Seong Hyong Lee and Tae-Hwan Kwak. Seoul: Kyungnam University Press, 1988.

Sizemore, Russell F. and Donald Swearer. *Ethics, Wealth and Salvation: A Study in Buddhist Social Ethics*. Columbia University of South Carolina Press, 1990.

Skeggs, Beverley. "Situating the Production of Feminist Ethnography." In *Research-*

ing Women's Lives from a Feminist Perspective. Edited by Mary Maynard and June Purvis. London and Bristol, Penn.: Taylor and Francis, Inc., 1994.

Smith, Timothy. "Religion and Ethnicity in America." *American Historical Review* 83 (December 1978): 1155–85.

Smith, Wilfred Cantwell. "Methodology and the Study of Religion: Some Misgivings." In *Methodological Issues in Religious Studies.* Edited by Robert Baird. Chico, Calif.: New Horizons Press, 1975.

———. "Comparative Religion: Whither and Why?" In *The History of Religions: Essays in Methodology.* Edited by Eliade and Kitagawa. Chicago: University of Chicago Press, 1959.

Song, Young In. "Life Satisfaction of the Korean American Elderly." In *Korean American Women: From Tradition to Modern Feminism.* Edited by Young I. Song and Ailee Moon. Westport, Conn.: Praeger, 1998.

——— and Ailee Moon, eds. *Korean American Women: From Tradition to Modern Feminism.* Westport: Praeger, 1998.

——— and Ailee Moon, eds. *Korean American Women Living in Two Cultures.* Los Angeles: Keimyung-Baylo University Press, 1997.

———. "Korean American Women in Midlife: Patterns of Response to Change." In *Korean American Women Living in Two Cultures.* Los Angeles: Academia Koreana, Keimyung-Baylo University Press, 1997.

———. "Critical Feminist View of Patriarchal Structure of the Korean American Christian Church." In *Korean American Women Living in Two Cultures.* Los Angeles: Academia Koreana, Keimyung-Baylo University Press, 1997.

Spilka, Bernard and Daniel N. McIntosh. *The Psychology of Religion: Theoretical Approaches.* Boulder: Westview Press, 1997.

Spiro, Melford. "Is the Western Conception of the Self 'Peculiar' Within the Context of World Cultures?" *Ethos* 21:2 (1993): 107–45.

Stromberg, Peter. *Language and Self-Transformation: A Study of the Christian Conversion Narrative.* Cambridge: Cambridge University Press, 1993.

Sunim, Samu. "Turning the Wheel of the Dharma in the West: Korean Son Buddhism in North America." In *Korean Americans and Their Religions: Pilgrims and Missionaries from a Different Shore.* Edited by Ho-Youn Kwon, Kwang Chung Kim, and R. Stephen Warner. University Park: Pennsylvania State University Press, 2001.

Takaki, Ronald. *Strangers from a Different Shore.* Boston: Little, Brown, 1989.

Tweed, Thomas. *Retelling U.S. Religious History*. Berkeley: University of California Press, 1997.

Visweswaran, Kamala. "Betrayal: An Analysis of Three Acts." In *Scattered Hegemonies: Postmodernity and Transnational Feminist Practices*. Edited by Inderpal Grewal and Caren Kaplan. Minneapolis: Minnesota University Press, 1994.

Waldiger, Roger and Mehdi Bozorgmehr, eds. *Ethnic Los Angeles*. New York: Russell Sage Foundation, 1996.

Warner, Stephen R., and Judith Wittner, eds. *Gatherings in Diaspora: Religious Communities and the New Immigration*. Philadelphia: Temple University Press, 1998.

———. "Work in Progress Toward a New Paradigm for the Sociological Study of Religion in the United States." *American Journal of Sociology* 98 (March 1993): 1044–1193.

Waters, Mary. *Ethnic Options: Choosing Identities in America*. Berkeley: University of California Press, 1990.

Watson, Lawrence C. and Maria-Barbara Watson-Franke. *Interpreting Life Histories: An Anthropological Inquiry*. New Brunswick, N.J.: Rutgers University Press, 1985.

Wikan, Unni. "The Nun's Story: Reflections of an Age-Old, Postmodern Dilemna." *American Anthropologist* 98:2 (1996): 279–89.

———. "The Self in a World of Urgency and Necessity." *Ethos* 23 (1995): 259–85.

———. *Managing Turbulent Hearts: A Balinese Formula for Living*. Chicago: University of Chicago Press, 1990.

———. *Tomorrow God Willing: Lives in the Back Streets of Cairo*. Oslo: The University Press, 1983.

Williams, Raymond Brady. *Religion of Immigrants from India and Pakistan: New Threads in the American Tapestry*. New York: Cambridge University Press, 1988.

Wilson, Liz. *Charming Cadavers: Horrific Figurations of the Feminine in Indian Buddhist Hagiographical Literature*. Chicago: University of Chicago Press, 1996.

Wulff, David M. *Psychology of Religion: Classic and Contemporary*. New York: John Wiley and Sons, 1997.

Yang, Eun Sik. "Korean Women of America: From Subordination to Partnership, 1903–1930." *Amerasia* 11:2 (1984): 1–28.

———. "Koreans in America, 1930–1945." In *Koreans in LA: Promises and Prospects*. Edited by Eui Young Yu, Earl Phillips, and Eun Sik Yang. Los Angeles: Koryo Research Institute, Center for Korean and Korean American Studies, 1982.

Yoo, David, ed. *Amerasia Journal* 22:1 (1997).

Yu, Eui-Young. *Korean Community Profile: Life and Consumer Patterns*. Los Angeles: Korea Times and Hankook Ilbo, 1990.

———. "The Growth of Korean Buddhism in the United States, with Special Reference to Southern California." *Pacific World: Journal of the Institute of Buddhist Studies*, new ser. 4 (1988): 82–93.

———. "Korean Communities in America: Past, Present and Future." *Amerasia* 102 (1983): 23–51.

——— and Phillips, Earl. *Korean Women in Transition: At Home and Abroad*. Los Angeles: Center for Korean-American and Korean Studies, California State University, Los Angeles, 1987.

———, Earl Phillips, and Eun Sik Yang, eds. *Koreans in LA: Promises and Prospects*. Los Angeles: Koryo Research Institute, Center for Korean and Korean American Studies, 1982.

INDEX

Abbot Lee (abbot of Sa Chal), 36, 40–43
Agency, free (or individual), 83, 131, 150, 152, 154, 178, 180; and Buddhist identity, 121; difference between Buddhist and Christian, 189; self-, 184
Amita Buddha, 39, 47, 50
Ancestor worship, 49, 51
Anthropology, 25–26, 30

Banya Shimgyong (Heart Sutra), 47
"Becoming American," 98; Buddhists, Christians, 166; and transnational identity, 138
Bodhisattvas, 61, 63
Bopbok (lay robes), 26, 98
Bopdang (dharma hall), 79, 84
Buddha: birthday celebration, 39, 45
Buddhahood, 208
Buddha Nature, 29, 71, 93, 105, 109; determining religious identity, 170; development of agency, 16, 17, 21, 24, 61, 80, 81; men and, 137; and transformation of self, 94

Buddhism: American culture and, 150, 166, 209; association with Korean identity, 138, 139, 166, 202; free choice in, 182, 196; idioms of, 115; and independence, 119, 131, 170, 177, 198, 209; open-minded, 130, 164, 166, 192; practices of, 57–95 passim, 180; healing in, 64–71; psychological strengths of, 166; and self-knowledge, 30–32, 132, 180, 189; and self-renewal, 71–77
Buddhist identity: hidden, 165, 185, 187; reliance on temple for, 115; and religious marginalization, 165; self-esteem and, 165; and self-reliance, 109, 119, 132, 135, 178, 180, 188, 201; women and, 94, 96, 98
Buddhist Youth Group, 39, 43, 44, 63, 172

Chaesa (ancestor rites), 49–51, 52, 127
Chinul (twelfth-century monk), 17
Chogye order of Buddhism, 27, 36, 41, 43, 159

INDEX

Christianity, 176, 178, 197; and business success, 188; and Confucianism, 22, 182; betrayal of tradition, 188; coercive, 182; dependent relationship, 180; lifestyle, 188; missionizing in Korea, 159

Christianization, of Korean American community, 165, 168, 170, 191

Christians: Buddhist view of, 142, 164, 166, 170, 173, 203; churches of, 189, 190; doctrines of, 176; ministers, 181

Chukpi (meditative aid), 47, 84

Church: Korean, 136, 152; Korean American, 111

Confucian culture, 118, 147, 150, 164; patriarchy, 116; religious identity, 121; ritual, 49; social status, 137; system, 148; tradition, 120

Confucian gender ideology, 93, 120, 131, 135, 137; and men's roles, 5, 8, 12, 24, 25, and women's roles, 5, 20, 21, 22, 57, 61, 118, 195

Confucianism. *See* Confucian culture

Conversion to Christianity, 3, 19, 33, 69, 72, 94, 112, 166–67, 174, 192; Buddhist perceptions of, 198, 202

Dana (giving for merit), 52

Dharma, Buddha, 37, 156, 177

Dharma talk. *See Sulbop*

Diamond Noodle Factory, 37

Diamond Sutra, 68, 83, 84, 86, 97, 90; recitation group, 79, 80, 81

Divorce, 128, 129

Eastern Mountain Buddhist College, 37, 40, 41–42, 67, 68, 84, 134, 135, 158; and male subjectivity, 160

Enlightenment, 21, 81, 83, 109, 128, 156, 157, 196

Ethnicity, 101, 141, 154, 164; Sa Chal and, 153

Famine relief efforts, 135, 140, 141, 150–53

"Finding and knowing one's mind," 6, 16, 17, 19, 20, 94, 131, 135, 206

Four Vows, 48

Gender: in church hierarchy, 163; ideology, religion and, 121; in Korean American churches, 115; relations, 7, 8, 118, 152, 164, 207; reproduction of, 137; sites of, resistance, 83

Gendered space, 82

Hyphenated identities, 25

Identity, hybrid, 25, 154. *See also* Religious identity

Immigrants, 7, 102, 104, 151; adaptation of, 154; experience of dislocation, 25, 46, 102, 108, 143, 144, 163; and role of religion, 44, 136, 149, 195, 199

Immigration, 115; and Confucian values, 116; economic opportunities, 144; historical waves of, 3, 33–35; impact on self-esteem, 115, 137, 151, 164

Immigration Act of 1924, 34

Immigration Act of 1965, 3, 34

Interview-based research, 101

Interview demographics, 54, 55

238

INDEX

Karma, 18, 19, 20, 21, 31, 71; in Buddhism, 171; and children's fate, 171, 174; explanation of, 63; free choice, 174; and proselytizing, 197; religious identity, 170, 175; self-transformation and, 21, 71–77, 94; women's, 22, 45, 57, 58, 93

Keumgang Gyung (Diamond Sutra), 78. *See also* Diamond Sutra

Kibok ("fortune praying"), 156

Korean American Buddhist Community Service Center, 37, 38, 40, 42

Korean American Buddhist Cultural Library, 40

Korean Americans: and Christianity, 3, 4, 9, 69, 139, 166, 168; churches, 4, 60; population, 34; rise of, 169; women, 116

Korean Buddhism in America, 191

Korean Christian Church, 136, 200

Korean Nurses' Association, 64

Korean War: impact on immigration, 34

Koryo Sa Temple, 35, 37

Kusan Sunim (monk), 35

Kwan Um Bodhisattva, 63

Kwan Um Postal, 52

Lay groups, 53

"Lived predicament," 94

The Lotus Preschool, 204, 205

Maitreya Buddha, 78, 84. *See also* Miruk Chon Yorae Bul

McCarran and Walter Act of 1952, 34

Medicine Buddha, 47

Meditation, 47, 48, 49, 62

Men: Buddhist temple programs for, 163; and leadership positions, 8, 108, 152; religious practices of, 23–25, 152, 133–64 passim

Methodology of resonance, 94

Micro-manipulation, 127

Miruk Chon Yorae Bul, 84, 85, 90

Missionaries, 37, 40, 110, 115, 164, 209

Missionizing, 158, 191

Moktak (wooden gong), 43, 45, 47, 99

Narrative and self-construction, 29

Nationalism: Buddhism and, 140, 141, 148, 154, 159, 164; Korean Christians and, 140

Nirvana, 6, 17

Non-self, 30, 31

North Korea, 26, 27

One Korea Buddhist Movement, USA, 37, 139

Oral history, 9

Paek-palbae ("One Hundred Eight"; ritual bowing), 68

Posals (female Bodhisattvas), 61

Pogyo (dissemination), 37, 40, 108, 168, 174. *See also* Missionization

Pogyo-sa (Buddhist disseminator), 71

Polishing the Diamond, Enlightening the Mind, 87

Pophoe (worship service), 36

Preschools, Buddhist, 38

Pureland. *See* Sukhavati

Pureland Association, 52

INDEX

Reiyukai Kyodan (a Nichiren-based Japanese organization), 85–86
Religion, role of, 44, 96, 97, 104, 106, 111, 155
Religious identity, 111, 114, 123, 137, 170; idioms, 96; participation, 116; practice, 133, 134, 135
Research methodology, 9, 10, 11, 96
Reunification: meetings, 134, 135, 143, 150, 151, 152, 153; movement, 71, 73, 140, 141, 146, 148

Sa Chal Temple, 8, 9, 11, 45, 136–38; community rituals at, 45, 49; general membership, 53; historical context, 35–38; neighborhood, 38; Sunday services, 46–49
Sakyamuni Buddha, 47
Sanbo Sa Temple, 35
Second-generation Korean Americans, 19, 170, 171; and Buddhism, 180, 181, 191, 201, 209; missionization, 194; and Sa Chal, 43
Self: construction of, 11, 18; discourses of, 25–29; fragmentation of, 4, 7
Self-esteem, 112, 116, 150, 167, 205; "finding and knowing one's mind," 17; of men at Sa Chal, 135; and religious language, 57; and subjectivity, 17–20; of women, 137, 151
Self-knowledge, 26, 71, 93; and Buddhism, 88, 119; women and, 115
Selflessness, 5

Self-transformation, 135, 137, 156
Shindo (worshippers), 115
Shishik (Buddhist rite), 51
Son Buddhism, 24, 35, 36, 137
Songgwong-sa Temple, 35
Status inversion, 23
Subjectivity, 4, 5, 18, 20, 26, 28, 32, 70; and self-esteem, 17–20, 115, 208; immigrants develop, 154; inward-gazing, 115; male, 137–38; oral histories, 122
Sukhavati (Pureland), 51
Sulbop (dharma talk), 47, 48

Testimonials, 85, 86
Three Refuges, 47
Thousand Hand Sutra, 49
Transnational identification, 135, 138, 139, 141, 142
Transnationalism, 150–55; assimilation, 41; at Sa Chal, 41, 45

Vesak celebration, 45

War Brides Act of 1946, 34
Women: perception of Buddhist, 137; religious participation, 20–22, 119, 149; religious practices of, 22, 164; roles, 61
Women's Aglow Fellowship, 81, 82
Worship attendance, 136

Yi dynasty, 159
Youth groups, 37, 39, 43–44, 63, 172

www.ingramcontent.com/pod-product-compliance
Lightning Source LLC
LaVergne TN
LVHW051739280825
818994LV00021B/5